ACCENTS ON SHAKESPEARE

General editor: TERENCE HAWKES

# Shakespeare and Modernity

...eare has variously been seen as the last great exponent of
...'ern Western culture, a crucial inaugurator of modernity,
...ophet of postmodernity.
...xciting collection of essays traces the changing reception of
...are over the past four hundred years. Along the way it
... fascinating insights into:

...ture of individuality, identity, subjectivity, and the self
...terrelations of the rise of capitalism, nation-states, modern
...r roles, and secular culture
...velopment of art as a secular and critical mode of knowledge
...eginnings of Western colonialism, racism, and anti-
...sm.

...ι look at Shakespeare's plays is an important contribution
...'ival of the idea of 'modernity' and how we periodize our-
...d Shakespeare, at the beginning of a new millennium.

**...Grady** is Professor of English at Beaver College, Pennsylvania,
author of *The Modernist Shakespeare* (1991) and *Shakespeare's
...versal Wolf* (1996).

# ACCENTS ON SHAKESPEARE
## General Editor: TERENCE HAWKES

It is more than twenty years since the New Accents series helped to establish 'theory' as a fundamental and continuing feature of the study of literature at undergraduate level. Since then, the need for short, powerful 'cutting edge' accounts of and comments on new developments has increased sharply. In the case of Shakespeare, books with this sort of focus have not been readily available. **Accents on Shakespeare** aims to supply them.

**Accents on Shakespeare** volumes will either 'apply' theory, or broaden and adapt it in order to connect with concrete teaching concerns. In the process, they will also reflect and engage with the major developments in Shakespeare studies of the last ten years.

The series will lead as well as follow. In pursuit of this goal it will be a two-tiered series. In addition to affordable, 'adoptable' titles aimed at modular undergraduate courses, it will include a number of research-based books. Spirited and committed, these second-tier volumes advocate radical change rather than stolidly reinforcing the status quo.

IN THE SAME SERIES

# Shakespeare and Modernity

## Early modern to millennium

Edited by
HUGH GRADY

London and New York

First published 2000
by Routledge
11 New Fetter Lane,
London EC4P 4EE

Simultaneously published in
the USA and Canada
by Routledge
29 West 35th Street,
New York, NY 10001

Routledge is an imprint of the
Taylor & Francis Group

© 2000 Hugh Grady

Typeset in Baskerville by
BC Typesetting, Bristol
Printed and bound in Great Britain by
Biddles Ltd, Guildford and King's Lynn

British Library Cataloguing in
Publication Data

A catalogue record for this book is available
from the British Library

Library of Congress Cataloging in
Publication Data

Grady, Hugh.
    Shakespeare and modernity: early modern
    to millennium/Hugh Grady.
        p.    cm. – (Accents on Shakespeare)
    Includes bibliographical references (p.    )
    and index.
        1. Shakespeare, William, 1564–1616 –
    Criticism and interpretation – History.
    2. Literature and history – Great Britain –
    History.    I. Title.    II. Series.
    PR2965.G73  2000
    822.3'3–dc21                    00-025453

ISBN 0–415–21201–4 (pbk)
ISBN 0–415–21200–6 (hbk)

# Contents

# Contributors

**Douglas Bruster** is Assistant Professor of English at the University of Texas at Austin and author of *Drama and the Market in the Age of Shakespeare*.

**Linda Charnes** is Associate Professor of English and Cultural Studies at Indiana University, Bloomington and is the author of *Notorious Identity: Materializing the Subject in Shakespeare*.

**Stephen Cohen** is Assistant Professor of English at the University of South Alabama. He has written for the journals *Criticism*, *Mosaic*, and *REAL: Yearbook of Research in English and American Literature*.

**John Drakakis** is Professor of English at the University of Stirling and editor of several works in Shakespeare studies, including *Alternative Shakespeares* and *Shakespearean Tragedy*.

**Lars Engle** is Associate Professor of English and Honors Director at the University of Tulsa and author of *Shakespearean Pragmatism: Market of his Time*.

**Lisa Freinkel** is Assistant Professor of English at the University of Oregon and author of *Reading Shakespeare's Will: The Theology of Figure from Augustine to the Sonnets*.

**Hugh Grady** is Professor of English at Beaver College and author of *The Modernist Shakespeare: Critical Texts in a Material World* and *Shakespeare's Universal Wolf: Studies in Early Modern Reification*.

**John J. Joughin** is Senior Lecturer in English at the University of Central Lancashire and editor of *Shakespeare and National Culture* and of *Philosophical Shakespeares*.

**Eric S. Mallin** is Assistant Professor of English at the University of Texas at Austin and author of *Inscribing the Time: Shakespeare and the End of Elizabethan England*.

**Charles Whitney** is Associate Professor of English at the University of Nevada at Las Vegas and author of *Francis Bacon and Modernity*.

# General editor's preface

In our time, the field of literary studies has rarely been a settled, tranquil place. Indeed, for over two decades, the clash of opposed theories, prejudices and points of view has made it more of a battle-field. Echoing across its most beleaguered terrain, the student's weary complaint 'Why can't I just pick up Shakespeare's plays and read them?' seems to demand a sympathetic response.

Nevertheless, we know that modern spectacles will always impose their own particular characteristics on the vision of those who unthinkingly don them. This must mean, at the very least, that an apparently simple confrontation with, or pious contemplation of, the text of a four-hundred-year-old play can scarcely supply the grounding for an adequate response to its complex demands. For this reason, a transfer of emphasis from 'text' towards 'context' has increasingly been the concern of critics and scholars since the Second World War: a tendency that has perhaps reached its climax in more recent movements such as 'New Historicism' or 'Cultural Materialism'.

A consideration of the conditions, social, political, or economic within which the play came to exist, from which it derives, and to which it speaks will certainly make legitimate demands on the attention of any well-prepared student nowadays. Of course, the serious pursuit of those interests will also inevitably start to undermine ancient and inherited prejudices, such as the supposed distinction between 'foreground' and 'background' in literary studies. And even the slightest awareness of the pressures of gender or of race, or the most cursory glance at the role played by that strange creature 'Shakespeare' in our cultural politics, will reinforce a similar turn towards questions that sometimes appear scandalously 'non-literary'. It seems clear that very different and unsettling notions of the ways in which literature might be addressed can hardly be avoided. The worrying truth is that nobody can just pick up Shakespeare's plays and read them. Perhaps – even more worrying – they never could.

The aim of *Accents on Shakespeare* is to encourage students and teachers to explore the implications of this situation by means of an engagement with the major developments in Shakespeare studies of the 1990s. It will offer a continuing and challenging reflection on those ideas through a series of multi- and single-author books which will also supply the basis for adapting or augmenting them in the light of changing concerns.

*Accents on Shakespeare* also intends to lead as well as follow. In pursuit of this goal, the series will operate on more than one level. In addition to titles aimed at modular undergraduate courses, it will include a number of books embodying polemical, strongly argued cases aimed at expanding the horizons of a specific aspect of the subject and at challenging the preconceptions on which it is based. These volumes will not be learned 'monographs' in any traditional sense. They will, it is hoped, offer a platform for the work of the liveliest younger scholars and teachers at their most outspoken and provocative. Committed and contentious, they will be reporting from the forefront of current critical activity and will have something new to say. The fact that each book in the series promises a Shakespeare inflected in terms of a specific urgency should ensure that, in the present as in the recent past, the accent will be on change.

Terence Hawkes

# Acknowledgements

When ideas are 'in the air' – when they are developing through collective discursive processes that appear at first as individual, but are instead evolving in several separate places at once – collaboration can be complex and many-sided. The present collection grew out of such a process and from ideas from several places. I want to thank especially Terence Hawkes, who encouraged this collection from its earliest gestation as an idea; Gail Paster and Barbara Mowat of *Shakespeare Quarterly*, who encouraged an article from me on Shakespeare and modernity which crystallized my own ideas on the issue; and Stephen Cohen, whose idea for a panel of speakers on the topic 'How modern was early modern?' helped solidify one of the important subtopics of the collection.

This volume would not have been possible without the existence of the Shakespeare Association of America (SAA), whose annual meeting fosters the kind of creative collegiality and encourages the kind of collaboration represented here. At the annual meeting of 1998 I encountered talks by Eric Mallin and Linda Charnes on Shakespeare and the postmodern which were also among the early sparks for this collection. The 1999 annual meeting of the SAA was the site of a seminar co-chaired by myself and Lars Engle called 'Shakespeare and the boundaries of modernity', which saw the production and discussion of early drafts of most of the chapters included here. My thanks to all those who participated and spurred on the development of the contributions you are about to read.

My thanks as well to two Beaver College students, Margaret Stephan and Diane McDonald, who assisted me in much of the editorial detail work required to produce a critical anthology. Thanks also to Beaver English Department secretary Gwen Taylor for her expert assistance on issues of formatting and word processing.

Hugh Grady

## Note

Unless otherwise indicated, all quotations from Shakespeare in the chapters that follow are taken from *The Norton Shakespeare: Based on the Oxford Edition*, general editor Stephen Greenblatt (New York: W. W. Norton, 1997).

# 1

# Introduction

## Shakespeare and modernity

### HUGH GRADY

One of the many remarkable features of the four-hundred-year-old archive of writings about the plays of William Shakespeare is the frequency with which his work is termed 'modern'. The only major exception occurs in the mid-twentieth century when, for a period of a few decades, a devaluation of the concept of modernity made it a feature scarcely to be prized in a figure of international prestige. Yet, as we begin the new millennium, it seems evident that new thinking about the nature of the topic and its implications has caused the question of Shakespeare's modernity to move once more to the forefront of critical attention. This collection of chapters is dedicated to exploring the most important of those new ideas and to probing the issues at stake in Shakespeare's relationship to that particular constellation of cultural events which has come to be known as 'modernity'.

Of course, just what we mean by 'modernity' is itself a crucial issue within several contentious debates of contemporary critical theory. In fact, it has by now become so complex and variegated a matter (especially since the acceleration of technical and social change characteristic of the past century) that words with the stem or root 'modern' have proliferated. We now speak of the modern, modernity, modernism, modernization and the postmodern (with a number of possible variations for this last), sometimes as rough syno-nyms, sometimes to try to designate specific aspects of the cluster of ideas that has developed around the term. The result has been a confusion of terminology and a corresponding confusion of ideas.

The terms 'modernism' and 'modernity' (and consequently their correlates 'postmodernism' and 'postmodernity') can be particularly puzzling. I will try to maintain a consistent distinction between the two. In what follows, modern*ism* will refer to an aesthetic and cultural period of the twentieth century, typified by radical experimentation across all the different art forms: it refers to the age of Picasso, Joyce, Stravinsky, Faulkner, Lawrence, Pirandello, and so on – a period which may or may not have already ended, to be succeeded by one encapsulated in a new aesthetic term: postmodernism. Modern*ity*, in contrast, will refer to a longer historical period typified by capitalist economics, a secular mentality, and a scientifically based technology. Confusingly, aesthetic *modernism* is in many ways a protest against social and technological *modernity*, although celebrations of modernity were never excluded from it.[1] But many of the modernist masterpieces – Eliot's *The Waste Land* and all of D. H. Lawrence's novels, for example – were passionate protests against a modernity which seemed to have spawned societies that were mechanical, soulless, fragmented, and generally injurious to the human spirit.

The term modern*ity* thus denotes a qualitatively new kind of anti-traditional society which arose in the West.[2] Its beginning is difficult to locate, but it has been variously assigned to the late medieval period, the Renaissance, or the Enlightenment. Its dynamic qualities make it hard to pin down: modernity unfolds as a process developing and changing over time. The issue of Shakespeare's connections with it is complicated by the difficulty of determining precisely when modernity began. But most observers would agree that it most clearly emerges in that epoch in which societies began to develop capitalist economies and centralized national governments, while generating a new sense of individualism and new notions of subjectivity. This notion of modernity as a system, not just a shorthand word for the current period, developed from Hegelian philosophy and migrated from Hegel into Marxism where it was accordingly redefined in reference to Marxist theories of capitalism (Habermas 1987: 4). In the theoretical ferment of recent years, however, capitalism has lost some of its centrality for the intellectual inheritors of Marxism, and notions of a modernity not wholly explicable as an outgrowth of capitalism have been revived in an attempt to reinterpret our historical situation. Because of their complexity, ideas of the modern are prisms through which to try to focus and understand important issues about what kind of society we live in, how we have developed historically, and how we can interpret the art, literature, and culture of the past. In the process, a culturally central figure like Shakespeare necessarily becomes a crucial focus of attention. It is no surprise to discover that critics have been arguing about his 'modernity' for a long time.

## A Romantic/modern Shakespeare

To many in the nineteenth century and the decades just before and after it, Shakespeare seemed remarkably 'modern' (in the word's simplest sense), having been transformed by Romantic critic-poets, first in Germany, then in the rest of Europe (including Britain), into a nearly contemporaneous figure. Indeed, for German writers such as Lessing, Goethe, and Schlegel, Shakespeare functioned almost as a model: a figure to contrast with a French neo-classicism which had come to seem stultifying and mechanical. Where seventeenth- and eighteenth-century neo-classical writers had criticized Shakespeare for his ignorance of the so-called 'rules' of drama and for lapses in diction and decorum, Samuel Taylor Coleridge, echoing the Germans and speaking for a new generation, asserted that Shakespeare's judgment was equal to his genius and that his works were unique, almost organic structures of literary art unsurpassed in world literature. The Romantic Shakespeare, famous for his complex characters and poetic transcendence, reigned until the early twentieth century.

The German philosopher Georg F. W. Hegel crystallized for posterity the notion of Shakespeare as an inaugurator of modernity. Hegel's comments on the individual plays were unremarkable; he saw them more or less as coexisting with the contemporary German dramas he occasionally discussed. But his complex, multi-valent systematizing philosophy enshrined the idea of a progression toward modernity and formalized the now widely accepted division of history into three broad epochs – the ancient, the medieval, and the modern. Hegel attempted to show how politics, art, religion, and the human spirit itself all participated in an interconnected historical development, leading to increasing rationality and freedom. For him, Shakespeare, with his strikingly individualized characterizations, stood as a figure representative of an epochal new individualism and subjectivity characteristic of modernity. Hegel's briefly sketched remarks on the Renaissance were fleshed out and developed in one of the most influential studies of the

Renaissance, Jacob Burckhardt's *The Civilization of the Renaissance in Italy* (1860). Burckhardt (1990) took Hegel's generalizations about a new modern individualism and a new subjectivity and used them to open up and explicate the culture and art of Renaissance Italy from Petrarch to Michelangelo, explicitly treating the Renaissance as the beginning of a modernity defined by a new subjectivity. Shakespeare is mentioned only briefly in Burckhardt's book (1990: 204–5), but he is clearly associated with the central topics of individualism and subjectivity in ways that are still influential in our own time, as the chapters by Stephen Cohen and Douglas Bruster in the present collection illustrate. But this Hegelian-Burckhardtian-Marxist view was soon challenged by a number of the mid-twentieth-century proponents of what might be called a pre-modern Shakespeare.

## A modernist/pre-modern Shakespeare

In clear reaction to the Romantic/modern Shakespeare and under the influence of a new modernist aesthetics, some of the most influential of twentieth-century critics set out to produce a Shakespeare who would represent a vanished, idealized past. Irretrievably lost, such a past was nonetheless useful in the twentieth century as a means of measuring how far from grace modernity had fallen. The hope was that through new artistic practices, open to the primitivism of the past, modern society might yet revive itself.

This pre-modern Shakespeare had many facets, and some modernist-influenced critics – one thinks of Wyndham Lewis (1927) early in the period and Jan Kott (1966) late in it – wrote powerful dissenting views which stressed Shakespeare's modernity. But the prevalent tone was set by T. S. Eliot, who in his chapter 'The beating of a drum' (1923) emphasized Shakespeare's kinship with the rituals of 'primitive' or pre-modern peoples given sympathetic attention by the new discipline of anthropology. Arguing against late Victorian defenders of Ibsen's and Shaw's realist theatre, Eliot claimed that Shakespeare spoke to the twentieth century precisely because he was 'primitive', less encumbered by the stultifying legacy of the post-Enlightenment West. A rhetoric of timelessness often coexisted with the treatment of Shakespeare as pre-modern. But, in contrast to the incessant movement and transformation central to modernity, this reinforced an idea of art as that which, in the modern world, resists change. Art became, as French anthropologist Claude Lévi-Strauss (1966: 219) would put it many years later, a kind of national park for the preservation of the primitive in modern societies. Shakespeare was its largest, most glamorous denizen.

One influential school of mid-twentieth-century critics, the formalists or, as they were ultimately called, the New Critics, turned Shakespeare's plays into closely studied sets of poetic images and figures, generating symbolic statements about eternal truths.[3] Other mid-century critics had misgivings about the ahistoricism of the New Critical approach to literature, arguing that to read centuries-old texts like Shakespeare's outside their own historical context was to commit what historians have called the 'presentist' fallacy – to treat human society and culture as if it were unchanging over time and thus to read the texts of the past as if they were part of the present. For example, the influential British critic F. R. Leavis (1952), although a formalist in many ways, historicized Shakespeare to the extent of seeing him and other valued authors as products of an 'organic community' – one now lost in the fully modernized world of the twentieth century. Another influential Shakespearean, E. M. W. Tillyard (1943), wrote that implicit in Shakespeare's works was an integrated 'Elizabethan World Picture', a view of the universe and of history reflecting a divine order absent in a disenchanted, prosaic modernity. The American New Critic most influential in writing about Elizabethan literature, Cleanth Brooks (1947), endorsed Eliot's notion that Shakespeare and Donne wrote as they did because they lived on the 'unified' side of that historical 'dissociation of sensibility' which had occurred in the mid-seventeenth century and which bequeathed to subsequent English poetry a separation of thought and feeling which only modernism was able to address (Brooks 1947). But, in the midst of all these modernist variations, Shakespeare remained an icon of pre-modernity: a figure of unity and plenitude in stark contrast to a modernity of fragmentation and emptiness.

There were of course many problems with this view of a pre-modern Shakespeare, and many critics dissented from its orthodoxies throughout the period of its ascendancy. It tended to reduce Shakespeare's works to the status of antique relics, ignoring their discussion of themes that persisted as living political issues into the twentieth century: power, gender, identity, subjectivity, and the possibility of utopia. However, the pre-modern Shakespeare prevailed for most of the twentieth century for a number of reasons, perhaps the most important being that it allowed for so central a cultural icon as Shakespeare to be renewed and recontextualized. It permitted him to be saved, as it were, from the ageing Romantic associations with which he had been surrounded for much of the nineteenth century.[4]

## An early modern/postmodern Shakespeare

Just as the Romantic Shakespeare began to seem old-fashioned and played out in the changed artistic, social, and political environment that created twentieth-century modernism, the pre-modern Shakespeare who succeeded him began to show signs of wear late in the twentieth century. By 1980, as newer critical methodologies, such as those involving feminism, poststructuralism, Marxism, and psychoanalysis, began to transform literary studies, he had been largely replaced. The leading versions of the newer critical approaches to Shakespeare studies have been resolutely historical: the term 'new historicism' is a popular label for one of them, and a parallel, if less consistently historicist approach developed in Britain, usually called 'cultural materialism'. Both of these approaches were heavily influenced by French poststructuralist theorists like Michel Foucault and Jacques Lacan, by themes selected from Marxist aesthetics, and by feminist and psychoanalytic theory. While their indebtedness to theory gives them a significantly different conceptual basis than that of the older historicism of E. M. W. Tillyard and company, they share with Tillyard the belief that literary texts should be read in historical context. And historicism inevitably requires periodization. The ungainly flow of the events of recorded history demands manageable narrative units for the sake of intelligibility. And so the new historicists, like other historians, have needed to situate Shakespeare in a period. The favoured approach has been to assign his work to an era called 'the early modern', a term used by contemporary historians (see the chapter by Douglas Bruster) such as the influential French scholar Philippe Ariès:

> There were so many changes in material and spiritual life, in relations between the individual and the state, and in the family that we must treat the early modern period as something autonomous and original, even bearing in mind all that it owed to the Middle Ages (seen of course in a new light). Nor was the early modern era merely a precursor of the modern: it was something unique,

neither a continuation of the Middle Ages nor an adumbration of the future.

(Ariès 1989: 2)

The early modern itself has uncertain boundaries. Sometimes it operates as a fashionable substitute for the earlier term Renaissance (conventionally defined for Britain as the era 1500–1642), but sometimes, as in Ariès's work, it takes on the task of encompassing the three centuries from 1500 to 1800.

It is perhaps worth pausing for a moment to consider periodization and chronologization as practices in the human sciences. They are of course basic to all attempts at a systematic reconstruction of the past, and no history can be written without some explicit or implicit commitment to them. Simply choosing a certain time span to write about constitutes the creation of a period. At the same time, of course, 'periods' have no 'objective' status. They are conveniences of writing, ways of thinking that help us see connections, or 'constellations' as Walter Benjamin termed such artificial but enabling clusters of ideas. To 'periodize' a major figure like Shakespeare, then, is clearly both arbitrary and absolutely necessary if we are to try to understand our own relation to him and his texts. But it can never be done once and for all. It is always a provisional exercise, open to contestation and modification. And this is certainly true of today's widespread use of the term 'early modern'.

The notion of the early modern is attractive to many because it seems to split the difference between the modernist and premodernist conceptions of Shakespeare, situating him in a transitional historical period, partly modern, partly not, and perhaps distinct, as Ariès argued, from either the pre-modern medieval or the modern proper. In several of the chapters in this book, the usefulness of this term is clearly apparent. Stephen Cohen, for example, shows how Queen Elizabeth I constructed her identity from what now seem partly pre-modern, partly modern concepts; John Drakakis situates *The Merchant of Venice* and its surrounding culture 'on the cusp of modernity'; and Charles Whitney demonstrates the incompleteness of modernity in this epoch, justifying a qualifying adjective like 'early'.

But the idea of a transitional early modern need not and should not be accepted as an uncontested orthodoxy of contemporary criticism. In the remaining sections of this Introduction, and in the chapters that follow, this periodizing of Shakespeare will variously be asserted, questioned, modified, restated, and rejected in a multidimensional inquiry into the relation of Shakespeare's works to the idea of modernity and its relation to pre- and post-modernity. After all, the idea of 'modernity' is already in a certain sense inherent in the idea of 'early modernity', especially if we keep in mind the provisional quality of all such periodizations. Even Ariès who, in the quotation above, makes a strong case for seeing the early modern as separate from modernity proper, goes on to define three crucial aspects of life there – advances in literacy, the Protestant Reformation and its aftermath, and the development of the nation-state system – which are clearly continuous with a later fully formed modernity (Ariès 1989: 3–4).

The occasional uncertainty of many contemporary critics concerning how much modernity resides within the early modern is not a result of imprecision. The 'new' in the term 'new historicism' has been earned by a commitment to poststructuralist premises, which, in Louis Montrose's much quoted summary, attempt to deal simultaneously both with the historicity of the text and the textuality of history (Montrose 1989: 20). Viewed in this light, history is not a matter of certainties in respect of some objective set of facts that can be faithfully reproduced; it consists of a complex discourse made in and by language and consequently sharing the uncertainties and multiple meanings characteristic of all linguistic forms. In developing these ideas, the newer critics have seemed to many observers (including this one) to share in the practices and concepts of contemporary postmodernism.[5] Such convergences should not be surprising. Links between techniques for reading the works of the past and those of contemporary forms and techniques of artistic practice are omnipresent in literary and cultural history, as the previous brief sketches of the Romantic and Modernist Shakespearean moments illustrate. In his *Shakespeare Among the Moderns*, Richard Halpern turned to both T. S. Eliot and Walter Benjamin for help in understanding this phenomenon, which he called 'historical allegory' (Halpern 1997: 1–14). The crucial point to note is that because historical interpretation always has a creative dimension, and because there is no way simply to reconstruct 'the truth' without interpretation, our histories are always also allegories of the present: they inevitably represent the historian's situation in the present as well as his/her best attempt objectively to reconstruct the past. In that sense some sort of 'presentism' is inevitable and desirable.

Such convergence is at work, for example, when Tillyard and his modernist generation unfailingly posited coherence as a desirable quality of all art works and consequently proceeded to present Shakespeare as a consummate artist of organic unity. In recent decades, however, contemporary artists and theorists have tended to pursue a different aesthetics of disunity and disjunction. Unsurprisingly, there now appears to be a virtual consensus among critics that Shakespearean texts are multi-valent and open to numerous different, often incompatible interpretations. In short, they have begun to seem decidedly postmodern.

## Are we postmodern yet?

Ideas of the postmodern have taken many forms, but they commonly posit the end of an old 'bourgeois' notion of single, fixed identity and its replacement by a postmodernist 'subjectivity effect' in which individuals in the new media-saturated environments of the late twentieth century take on a plurality of 'self' formations. Postmodernist art typically simulates this 'decentred' mode of being to give us fragmented or disjunctive novels, films, poems, paintings, and performances.[6] The fact that the boundaries – if any – which distinguish them from the popular are porous, has called into question the notion of 'art' itself, especially the idea of its privileged distinction from the world of popular culture and mass media. Instead of being situated in a 'primitivist' enclave, free from the corruptions of capitalist commodification and modernizing technology, the postmodernist decentred self has been more often represented as fully enmeshed in the (ambivalently aestheticized) surfaces of a commodified and reified social reality. Postmodernist theorists like Baudrillard (1988: 166–84) have described this world as one of 'simulacra' or 'hyperreality' in which the 'real' itself is no longer accessible.

Postmodernist themes such as these often surface in new historicist/cultural materialist descriptions of the early modern. For example, Stephen Greenblatt (1980) writes of a sixteenth-century 'great "unmooring"' that men were experiencing, their sense that fixed positions had somehow become unstuck, their anxious awareness that the moral landscape was shifting' (Greenblatt 1980: 88). Earlier in his book, attempting to describe the unintended consequences of the mutual polemics between Protestants and Catholics

in the sixteenth century which created a new space unable to legitimate the vying representations of reality, he had written, 'Thus in
such realms, reality, however powerfully felt, can always be shown
to exclude other meanings; one can always construct, at least in
imagination, a counterreality' (Greenblatt 1980: 61). Similarly, cultural materialist Jonathan Dollimore describes a great sixteenth-
century 'decentring' of meaning in the works of Machiavelli,
Galileo, and Montaigne. In addition, he stresses the need to overcome modernist assumptions of aesthetic unity in favor of a recognition of the aesthetic discontinuities of early modern texts
(Dollimore 1989: 63). Such instances could be multiplied. The
connection between the new historicism, early modern and contemporary postmodernism has by now often been noted and described
– frequently, of course, by those who want to question the historicity
of the new historicists. Others in Shakespeare studies have been
extremely reluctant to discuss the convergence between new views
of Shakespeare and a developing postmodernist aesthetic in the late
twentieth century – apparently because to discuss such convergence
would seemingly call into question the historicity of the new views
of the era and of Shakespeare (e.g. Dollimore 1994: 129–34). However, I believe that acknowledging and accommodating this convergence is necessary and in no way disables the truth value of the
methods at stake – which of course never reach an absolute truth,
but which we can posit as having the kind of imperfect 'adequacy'
to a supposed reality described by numerous pragmatists.

A confusion often arises, however, from the fact that there are two
competing definitions of the postmodern, each based on the different
meanings of modernity and modernism I discussed previously. The
idea of postmodern*ity* theorizes a break with the long-term, social
and technical modern period. The other term, postmodern*ism*,
conceives a break with the twentieth-century modernist movement
in art and literature, a break which may or may not signal the end
of long-term modernity. Both terms are linked to theories which
emphasize the huge impact in our time of new technologies per-
mitting new levels of media penetration into daily life and a new
globalization. They disagree on how this new techno-cultural
development relates to the flow of historical periods.

The idea of postmodernity is most commonly associated with
French cultural theorist Jean-François Lyotard, particularly as it is
expounded in his book *The Postmodern Condition* (1984). Modernity,

Lyotard asserts, began with the Enlightenment and was character-ized by a kind of thinking dominated by science. But he believes that science is unable to justify itself and so must create a narrative outside itself to be legitimate. Modernity created a number of such justifying 'metanarratives' – Hegel's and Marx's accounts of history as a process leading toward rationality and freedom are two perfect examples – but there have been many others. For Lyotard, *post-*modernity can be said to begin when science and its allied modern practices (computer technology is his chief case in point) operate with what he calls 'incredulity toward metanarratives' (Lyotard 1984: xxiv). Postmodernity is above all the condition of living with-out any justifying narrative myths, or simply with an indifference to legitimation. Its context includes a capitalist economy proceeding to a new stage in which knowledge itself is the chief commodity and chief instrument of power for nation-states and corporations. In other words, modernity came into existence through the rise of science, capitalism, and nation-states, but it is now transforming the very institutions which created it. The result, in Lyotard's view, is something completely new.

The distance between this theory of postmodernity and the separate discussion of postmodernism in the Anglophone world can be judged from the fact that Lyotard has little to say about post-modern art and culture, which have been the chief topics of the dis-cussions of the postmodern elsewhere. As Fredric Jameson (1984) has pointed out, Lyotard seems to believe that art will maintain its modernist forms and function as a refuge from and critical resource against the value-free operations of modernity, even in the new world of postmodernity (Jameson 1984: xv–xix). Lyotard's theory is thus a theory of knowledge rather than of culture.

Anglo-American theories of postmodernism, on the other hand, focus on questions of literary-aesthetic periodization. In this dis-course, the major question has been whether the new forms of art and literature which came into existence after the Second World War – for example, the French 'nouveau roman', confessional poetry, pop art, new wave cinema, minimalism in music, post-structuralist criticism itself – mark a break with the earlier 'high modernism' of Picasso, Joyce, Eliot, Faulkner, the New Critics, and so on. Proponents of the idea that postmodernism should be seen as a new aesthetic paradigm, separate from modernism proper, have pointed to two new features of postmodernist art: the end of an aesthetics of mandatory organic unity and the end of a definitive separation of high art from popular culture. The fullest and most influential proponent of this view has been Jameson, particularly in his book *Postmodernism; or, The Cultural Logic of Late Capitalism* (1991). However, Jameson is drawing on and synthesizing an earlier discussion which had centered on defining a new postmodernist art movement in the second half of the twentieth century. For him, post-modernism is a new phase of a modernity characterized most centrally by the processes of developing capitalism. It represents, not a break with capitalist modernity, but rather the development of modernity into an even more thoroughly organized, invasive, and self-perpetuating system.[7]

The recent scholarly construction of an early modern Shakespeare has clearly been influenced by these currents of postmodernism, but the influence has been largely in aesthetic terms, involving issues of unity and disunity and the relation of high art to a surrounding popular culture. Nevertheless, since several of the poststructuralist theorists who have been influential in Shakespeare studies share aspects of Lyotard's views on the end of modernity – Michel Foucault is the most important figure here – postmodernity has been a covert issue within Shakespeare studies as well.

Several accounts of the postmodern/early modern Shakespeare described above are based on a neat symmetry, best represented in a series of influential books by British cultural materialists. In this view, Shakespeare stands as pre-modern because he and his age have not yet arrived at the idea of the humanist or bourgeois subject – a fixed, ideological construct of singular identity or individualism which is the sole legitimate source of history, meaning, and value. Of course, in this theory, such subjectivity is illusory, a kind of myth which works to justify the inequalities of an emerging capitalist system of radical class, racial, and gender inequalities. But it is pos-sible to begin to understand the inadequacies and ideological func-tions of this justifying ideology precisely because it is in crisis in the late twentieth century. We have an affinity with Shakespeare and his contemporaries, the argument goes, because our own emerging postmodern subjectivity is a kind of late 'mirror' (at the end of the era of the humanist subject) of the imperfectly formed subjects at the threshold of modernity. In this view, modernity is the era of a unitary bourgeois or humanist subject, with a fixed identity and an ideology of individualism. The age of Shakespeare is therefore pre-modern, and we are (or are beginning to be) postmodern.

The problem with this labelling, as I have pointed out in more detail elsewhere (Grady 2000), is not with the picture of Shakespeare and his contemporaries which it enables. Precisely because Shakespeare and the other transgressive playwrights of the late-sixteenth-, early-seventeenth-century London theater are exempted from the unitary processes and fixed identities of bourgeois humanism, they are free to be complex, multi-layered, contradictory, disjointed, and disunified, subversive of both authority and doctrine. At the other end of the age of modernity, in the early twenty-first century, we are free to share the same blissful postmodernist qualities. But what this periodization unhelpfully promotes is a severely truncated age of modernity, a false binary opposition of freedom and transgression. A review of any number of texts of this period such as *Moll Flanders, Tristram Shandy, Wuthering Heights, The Red and the Black, Ulysses* or any of dozens more novels (or poems or plays) would illustrate that the same subversion and undermining of authority and doctrine, the same decentring and problematizing of the self's bourgeois subjectivity as has been diagnosed in case of the Renaissance theatre, can be found in abundance in much of the subsequent literary tradition. Art in a modern world, as a number of theorists have emphasized, is a site of resistance against the systematizing and technical thrusts of modernity. The subversive, transgressive, early modern/postmodern Shakespeare of recent criticism is very much a representative figure of what literature becomes in modernized societies. Accordingly, I believe, we need to look again at other ways in which Shakespeare participates in modernity.

In doing so, there is no need to give up the postmodernist component of recent critical developments. I would argue rather that we now see a postmodernist Shakespeare just as we now see a postmodernist Defoe, Sterne, Brontë, Stendhal, or Joyce – because our own aesthetic conceptions, the formal 'lenses' through and with which we constitute literary texts in the creative act of reading, have changed in new, postmodernist directions, in yet another shift of the waves of disparate aesthetics which modernity has produced. The postmodernist Shakespeare that emerges represents, not the final truth about Shakespeare, but rather the state of the art of literary/cultural criticism, the Shakespeare that our own peculiar conjunction of history has produced. This development will certainly be surpassed at some time in the future. In the meantime, we should take it as far as we can.

## Shakespeare in modernity

A new emphasis on modernity as a problematic has emerged in several locations within cultural theory as an alternative or complement to the theories of Lyotard and his disciples. A central example of such developments may be seen in cultural theorist Stuart Hall's anthology *Modernity* (Hall *et al.* 1996). This collection of related chapters draws simultaneously from poststructuralist investigations of the dynamics of modernity associated with Foucault and others, from *Annales* School writings on historical periodization, and from Frankfurt School discussions of modernity from the 1930s through the newer, modernity-centered work of Jürgen Habermas. If we add works indebted to contemporary academic philosophers such as Charles Taylor (1989) and Stephen Toulmin (1990), with their development of traditional approaches to the idea of modernity, as well as works exploring in more general terms theories of subjectivity that surface in the converging currents of Lacanian psychoanalysis, feminism, and French poststructuralism, we will have a sense of the range of approaches to modernity most relevant to Shakespeare studies. Of course there are others who could be cited in what is a complex, cross-disciplinary discussion.[8] In recent years critiques of postmodernity have proliferated, and many have concluded that we had better take a new look at the terms, possibilities, and limits of a modernity which, at the dawn of a new millennium, we are apparently unable to transcend.

For Shakespeare studies this means taking a new look at how Shakespeare's plays and poems participate in those processes of modernity developing in his day. My *Shakespeare's Universal Wolf* (Grady 1996) helped inaugurate this discussion by defining how four cardinal, emergent aspects of it – capitalism, instrumental reason, Machiavellian power, and autonomous subjectivity – became major themes in Shakespeare's Jacobean tragedies. The present anthology broadens the scope of the inquiry considerably. The idea of modernity at stake implies a self-reinforcing system of many originally separate components. Several of these have already received wide discussion in the work of new historicists and cultural materialists, but they take on new dimensions here, for example in the interconnections explored between changing gender roles and the development of nationalism.[9] Others include new forms of subjectivity and new forms of power, shifting gender roles and sexuality, and the rise of colonialism with its new definitions of the Other for

Europeans. Chapters in this book by Stephen Cohen, Lisa Freinkel, John Drakakis, and Eric Mallin re-address such issues in a new context by exploring their relation to a problematic of modernity, thus advancing a discussion of them already underway in Shakespeare studies.

But the topic also suggests others which have been neglected in recent Shakespeare studies. John J. Joughin and Charles Whitney for example explore the issue of the status of classical aesthetic ideas in Shakespeare's era and demonstrate the need for further discussion and exploration of this complex aspect of modernity as it applies to his plays. Lars Engle sifts Shakespeare's intertextual relationship with the related category of Montaignean subjectivity, and probes an ethical dimension of emerging modern subjectivity. The three chapters by Douglas Bruster, Eric Mallin, and Linda Charnes show the relation of Shakespearean texts to twentieth-century ideologies, art, and popular culture, reinforcing the aesthetic dimension of the problematic of modernity and emphasizing the need for a certain theoretically self-conscious 'presentism' in literary interpretation. These chapters could be said to explore three interrelated questions. The first is whether or to what extent Shakespeare participated in and commented on emerging modernity. But this issue itself raises the question of whether Shakespeare has been retroactively modernized, as it were, by anachronistic critics. In other words – and this is the second question – did Shakespeare participate in the construction of modernity, or did modernity construct a pre-modern Shakespeare after its own image? This question in turn connects to a third raised by the practice of any number of previous critics (including myself and several authors represented here) of seeing Shakespeare as uncannily participating in late twentieth-century postmodernism, perhaps, as we have seen, because his status at the beginning of an emerging modernity mirrors our own at the end of the same epoch.

Stephen Cohen's chapter '(Post)modern Elizabeth' touches on issues connected to all three questions. He shows how the pre-modern, the modern, and the postmodern are all categories relevant to a discussion of the age of Shakespeare. He argues that Queen Elizabeth, more even than the Shakespearean comic heroines who seem to have been at least partially inspired by her, makes use of surviving discourses from pre-modernity as well as emergent modern discourses to produce a decentred, ambivalent, gender-shifting identity as a female ruler of a profoundly patriarchal society.

The effect, as Cohen argues, is postmodernist for us: the instabilities of Elizabeth's identities in early modernity prefigure the unstable identities of the postmodernist art and culture of our own time. Elizabeth herself, and Shakespeare's plays generally, stand on the cusp of a series of closely connected transformations whose results help define the world we inhabit.

Working with a similar understanding of the age of Shakespeare as a complex crossroads of pre-modern and emergently modern discourses (here also uncannily postmodernist for us), Charles Whitney makes a strong case that the heterogeneous audiences drawn to the public theaters of Renaissance London were a key factor in subsequent appropriations of Shakespeare in a number of different ways, times, and places. Elizabethan audiences had no concept of 'disinterested aesthetics' to shape their responses to the plays. Instead, several of the day's cultural practices – rhetorical training, ideas of literature as improving morality, the production by the educated of personal commonplace books – prompted audiences to seek in the plays 'applications' to their personal lives and experiences. Consequently, Whitney asserts, playwrights responded by producing plays deliberately open to the disparate individual viewpoints of the socially 'mixed' audiences of the day. Shakespeare's theater, in short, created drama 'as you like it' in more ways than one.

John J. Joughin takes a quite different (but not necessarily conflicting) approach, opening new ground with his chapter on the importance of refunctioning and reinvigorating the 'aesthetic' in order to understand Shakespeare's work in both its contemporaneous and subsequent historical contexts. Moving between a discussion of the recent rise in Britain of Adorno-influenced studies of subjectivity and aesthetics and of the status of mimesis in the last scene of *The Winter's Tale*, Joughin defines the aesthetic in terms of its paradoxical truth-claims, which are at once richer than, yet resistant to, an imperializing instrumental reason dominant both in the world of *The Winter's Tale* and in modernity more generally. In this context art is simultaneously a component of modernity and a site of resistance to some of its most characteristic dynamics. Lars Engle investigates the complexity of Shakespeare's relation to modernity from another direction. In a ground-breaking reading of the Jacobean 'dark comedy' *Measure for Measure*, he unravels several of the mysteries traditionally associated with this play's 'Duke of dark corners', Vincentio, by understanding him as a Montaignean sceptic engaged in one of the most characteristic features of emerging modernity, attempting to construct ethics in the absence of a foundational knowledge of right and wrong.

One Shakespearean play often seen as evidence of Shakespeare's pre-modernity is *The Merchant of Venice*, with its representation of an anti-Semitism based on religious rather than modern racial or ethnic identities. However, the chapters included here by John Drakakis, Lisa Freinkel, and Eric Mallin disclose this complex drama's interplay with discourses and practices of an emerging modernity. The long modern period has been at once an era of a growing ideal of religious freedom and of the most horrific and murderous persecutions of Jews in history, and something of this ambivalent record seems to be prefigured in the clashing discourses of this complex play.

John Drakakis focuses on the occurrence in folio and quarto texts of *Merchant* of the speech prefix 'Jew' interchangeably with that of 'Shylock'. While this textual instability had specific materialist causes resulting from a printhouse shortage of certain kinds of type, Drakakis argues, the printshop 'solution' to this shortage discloses the radical overdetermination of the concept of 'the Jew' in the period – as at once a demonic Other of Christianity, an Oedipal father, and a displaced figure for emerging capitalism and emerging unfixed subjectivity.

Lisa Freinkel also highlights the figure of Shylock as a prism of emerging modernity and anti-Semitism. Her chapter probes the commonly accepted notion that there is a well-defined chasm between pre-modern, religious-based disdain for Jews and post-Enlightenment race- or ethnicity-based anti-Semitism of the sort that culminated in Nazism. She argues that the distinction is much more difficult to maintain in practice than may appear at first glance, with the result that the 'pre-modern' anti-Semitism of the play is revealed to have decidedly modern dimensions.

Eric Mallin also turns to *Merchant* and to Shylock, but in the context of contemporary Hollywood science fiction treatments of the alien, arguing that the same paradoxical structure can be discerned both in Elizabethan and in twentieth-century American popular culture. In both eras the 'alien' displays a covert correspondence with the category of the 'human' from which it is ostensibly being distinguished. Shylock is at once the Other of the sympathetic Christian comic characters and a tragic figure who shares their humanity. If Shakespeare's play differs in this regard from recent Hollywood sci-fi, it is only in its greater contradictoriness.

Douglas Bruster adds a unique dimension to the volume's exploration of historical periodization through his study of the emergence of the terms 'English Renaissance' (in the 1920s and 1930s) and 'early modern' (in the 1980s and 1990s) to describe the era that had previously been simply called 'Elizabethan'. Showing, as he puts it, that periodizations themselves seem to have periods, Bruster charts a complex set of cultural exchanges between the scholarly and the popular spheres in the creation of these terms, showing the influence on scholarship of the market dynamics of a capitalist society which produces ever more alluring commodities – including the highly profitable ones of today's 'Shakespeare industry' in both its academic and popular branches.

Finally, Linda Charnes draws attention to the insertion of Shakespeare into the commodified late twentieth century in her exploration of the interconnections between certain themes of *Hamlet* and such postmodernist art/commodity-effects as the 'unnaming' of the artist formerly known as Prince. *Hamlet*, Charnes argues, is a play about a man who refuses to be a Prince, who fails in, or deliberately refuses, the central princely functions of acceding to the throne and producing an heir. This Hamlet-for-us is thus as unmoored and undefined as the flow of multinational capital which dominates the emerging world of the twenty-first century. Hamlet, who came into being as a carrier of the new form of malleable, protean subjectivity identified by Hegel and Burckhardt as the hallmark of modernity, and who served centrally as the emblem and signifier of art and subjectivity throughout the classical bourgeois era, now emerges into a new century re-newed, uncannily ourselves, yet once more challenging our own understandings of our world, its past, and its uncertain future.

## Notes

1  I have discussed this distinction, which can be found across a broad range of literature in many different disciplines and using the term 'modernization' rather than 'modernity', in Grady (1991: 29–32). But 'modernization' should be understood as a word emphasizing process, 'modernity' emphasizing the resulting system suspended in time.

2  It has clearly been extended into East Asia in the twentieth century and is thus shown to be a global, not merely an Occidental phenomenon.

3  The British academic, creative writer, and actor-director G. Wilson Knight is perhaps the most representative figure here; see Knight (1949) and Grady (1991: 86–112).

4 I have drawn in this discussion on a much more detailed account of twentieth-century Shakespeare criticism influenced by modernism in Grady (1991).

5 See, for example, Howard (1986), Goldberg (1986), Grady (1991: 204–11), and Bredbeck (1992: 237).

6 This new disparateness within postmodernism is described by Bürger (1984: 68–82), Lyotard (1984: 81), and Jameson (1991: 25–31).

7 See Anderson (1998) for a very useful review, centering around Jameson's concepts, of the complex discussion of the postmodern.

8 For a more detailed discussion of these sources and related issues, see Grady (1999).

9 See Howard and Rackin (1997) for an outstanding example of a work using a concept of modernity to discuss hitherto unexplored connections between the rise of nationalism and changing gender roles in the Elizabethan period.

# 2

# (Post)modern Elizabeth

## Gender, politics, and the emergence of modern subjectivity

### STEPHEN COHEN

The critical history of the development of the modern subject in the Renaissance traditionally begins with Jacob Burckhardt's much-quoted account of the post-medieval awakening of an interiorized and self-conscious subjectivity:

> In the Middle Ages both sides of human consciousness – that which was turned within as that which was turned without – lay dreaming or half awake beneath a common veil. . . . Man was conscious of himself only as a member of a race, people, party, family, or corporation – only through some general category. In Italy this veil first melted into air; an *objective* treatment and consideration of the State and of all things of this world became possible. The *subjective* side at the same time asserted itself with corresponding emphasis; man became a spiritual *individual*, and recognized himself as such.
>
> (Burkhardt 1965: 81, original italics)

The heroic teleology of Burckhardt's Enlightenment narrative of the subject's emergence and its subsequent domination of the objective world has since been recast in a less positive light, as a falling away from an organic social unity into an alienated, instrumentalized modern world. Traceable to the modernist historical model behind Eliot's 'dissociation of sensibility' and rendered more explicit by the cultural theory of F. R. Leavis and the early New Critics (Eliot

1975; Grady 1991: 113–57), this critical rather than celebratory stance towards the modern subject can also be seen in discussions of the emergence of early modern hierarchical distinctions between subject and object, mind and body, private and public (de Grazia *et al.* 1996; Barker 1984; Belsey 1985b). Objections have also been raised to both the location and the definitiveness of the Burckhardtian *terminus a quo* of modern subjectivity, by those who relocate the moment of transition from fifteenth-century Italy to seventeenth-century England and France (Eliot 1975; Barker 1984) as well as those who argue that elements of 'modern' interiorized subjectivity can also be found in earlier periods (Aers 1992), and that early modern subjectivity is marked not by the 'invention' of interiority *per se*, but by a new attention to and distrust of inwardness (Maus 1995; Hanson 1998).

Behind these modifications to Burckhardt's thesis lies another, which encapsulates a crucial difference between his 'old' and our own 'new' historicism: where Burckhardt sees the liberation of the subject from the twin oppressions of all-encompassing religious and social structures, recent criticism instead describes the exchange of one set of constraints and controls for another – the older more explicit, the newer more insidious because of its liberatory *appearance*. The critical *locus classicus* for this recognition is Stephen Greenblatt's (1980) *Renaissance Self-Fashioning*, conceived as an exploration of 'the role of human autonomy in the construction of identity' but producing instead the recognition that 'fashioning oneself and being fashioned by cultural institutions . . . were inseparably intertwined' (Greenblatt 1980: 256). The literary and cultural theory of the intervening two decades has renarrativized Burckhardt's epic of liberation as a history of (mostly) containment and (limited, often pyrrhic) subversion, describing the ideological construction of the modern subject that takes place behind the self-determinist rhetoric of liberal humanism, and the political, economic, and psychological causes and effects of that construction. The self-contained, interiorized modern subject and its concomitant hierarchical dichotomization of epistemological, metaphysical, and social terrains into subject/object, mind/body, private/public has been implicated in such diverse phenomena as capitalism's commodity fetishism, modernity's reification of social processes, and humanism's alienation of the individual from the political (de Grazia 1996; Grady 1996; Belsey 1985b; Barker 1984).

Among the fields most affected by this account of the development of the modern subject has been early modern gender studies. While the valorization of the private over the public that accompanied the rise of the interiorized subject, taken in conjunction with the early modern construction of the private or domestic as the woman's realm, would seem to open up new avenues of empowerment for women, the feminist history of the 1970s, 1980s and 1990s has provided a more complex account. The same shift to emergent capitalism that allowed the erosion of traditional feudal social and political subject-positions also deprived women of important structural avenues to power (Kelly 1984). At the same time, the movement from dynastic to companionate marriage, connected on a lower economic level with changes in the labor force that helped transform the family from an economic to an affective unit, further distanced women from the political and economic realms (Belsey 1985a: 167–77). These material circumstances were in turn reflected in and reinforced by the emerging ideology of modern subjectivity: if traditional social and economic roles were sloughed off by the interiorization of individuality, gender roles were not; if anything, the de-emphasis of other categorical differentiations made gender distinctions seem all the more innate and 'natural'. Though theoretically universal, humanist subjectivity was implicitly male (Barker 1984: 100–1; Belsey 1985b: 149–50), and was defined in opposition to the traditionally female: mind, not body; reason, not passion; and, taken to its logical extreme, subject, not object. Agency – speaking in or acting upon the objectified public world – was the prerogative of the (male) subject; for a woman to claim it was to usurp masculine authority, to be 'unnatural' (Belsey 1985b: 178–85). Disqualified materially and ideologically from the subject's mastery of the public world and herself the object of male mastery in the private realm, the female subject, if not an oxymoron, was severely circumscribed, and the private became less her domain than her prison. The ideological containment of the individual within an interiorized, privatized modern subjectivity was in many ways made possible by the even stricter confinement of women within an essentialized gender identity that, rooted in biology, could perhaps be concealed but never escaped.

The explanatory power of this neo-Burckhardtian account of the triumph of an interiorized subjectivity as the hallmark of modernity is suggested by its near-hegemonic status in contemporary criticism.

My intent here is not to challenge its accuracy, but merely to suggest that its obvious utility as an account of a large-scale ideological shift taking place over a period stretching arguably from late medieval to post-Enlightenment has often made the process appear to be a teleological inevitability, and in so doing has obscured or effaced anomalous smaller-scale phenomena that could help nuance our understanding of specific historical moments and their relation to the general process of modern subject-formation. One such phenomenon may be found in the England of the late sixteenth and early seventeenth centuries, when medieval ideologies of subjectivity had by no means been forgotten and modern ones had yet to establish their hegemony, and when the resultant ambiguities and insecurities about gender and power were exacerbated by the central presence of a powerful woman, Queen Elizabeth. The revisionist analysis of the gender politics of Elizabeth's iconographic and oratorical self-fashioning has been one of the most fruitful areas of Renaissance historical studies of the 1980s and 1990s, both supplementing and contesting the earlier work of Roy Strong (especially 1977) and Frances Yates (1975) with more recent developments in feminist and historicist critical methods (see King 1990; Cerasano and Wynne-Davies 1992; Teague 1992; C. Levin 1994; Hackett 1995; Doran 1996). In what follows, I will try to contextualize this already potent mix of gender, history, image and rhetoric within the historical framework discussed above, at once locating Elizabeth's practice within the larger cultural problematic of identity and modernity and exploring the effects of her unique situation on the development of that problematic. I will first read Elizabeth's public (de)construction of her own identity not as a symptom of an emergent modern ideology of interiority but as an exploitation of the ideological instability that marked the transition from a public to a private sense of subjectivity. I will then locate the cultural anxiety provoked by this instability – an anxiety about the malleability of identity that is related to but significantly different from the more widely recognized fear of concealment associated with the emergence of an interiorized subjectivity[1] – in two of the period's symptomatic cultural conflicts, the anti-theatricality and anti-crossdressing controversies. Finally, I will trace both anxieties in two of Shakespeare's comedies in order to demonstrate how an awareness of the difference between the two concerns can deepen our understanding of the politics behind the plays' representations of gender and subjectivity, revealing their ambivalent response to Elizabeth's manipulation of gender and locating it within a more general context of cultural anxiety about the instability of identity.

From the earliest days of her reign, Elizabeth grappled with the problem of defining and justifying herself in response to her subjects' fears about a female monarch. In so doing, she faced the double-bind at the heart of the emergent ideology of interiorized subjectivity. On the one hand, as a woman, Elizabeth was feared to be too weak, mentally, physically, and morally, for the role in which she found herself. But if the queen's gender-based inadequacy as a ruler was a matter for concern, her success would on the other hand be equally problematic: for a woman to play a man's part (especially successfully) was 'unnatural' – a threat to the stability of the gender hierarchy, evoking images of the 'woman on top' and the social chaos that accompanied her (Marcus 1988: 61–2; Davis 1975). Elizabeth's response was not to acquiesce to the assumptions of interiorized subjectivity by appearing to 'disguise' herself – literally or figuratively – as something she 'was not', concealing her essential femininity within a masculine facade,[2] but instead to problematize the very concepts of interior and exterior upon which the modern notion of subjectivity rests. Her ability to do so was in large measure due to her historical situation in the abovementioned period of ideological transition.

An integral part of Elizabeth's self-representation was her use of the medieval doctrine of the king's two bodies, which asserted the priority of the monarch's 'body politic' (the self defined by political and metaphysical position) over the 'body natural' (not just the physical body but much of what we would call the individual personality) (Kantorowicz 1957; Marcus 1988: 53–6). As queen, Elizabeth was in a unique position to pit this exteriorized concept of identity against an emergent interiorized gendered subjectivity. As one might expect, she frequently used the medieval insistence on the priority of the traditionally male body politic to counterbalance the innate inadequacies of her body natural: in a 1563 speech to the House of Commons, for example, she explained that

> The weight and greatenes of this matter might cawse in me being a woman wantinge both witt and memory some feare to speake, and bashfulnes besides, a thing appropriat to my sex: But yet the princely seate and kingly throne, wherein God, (though

unworthy) hath constituted me, maketh these two causes to seme litle in myne eyes.

(Heisch 1975: 34–5)

Seen in this light, Elizabeth's notorious rhetoric of masculinity works not to conceal an essentially female identity behind a masculine guise, but rather to challenge the essentialism of gender through the assertion of a more fundamental definition of the self. It is this challenge, rather than the transvestism of her purported appearance in armor, that generates the power and fascination of Elizabeth's 1588 speech to the troops at Tilbury, where she announced that 'I know I have the body but of a weak and feeble woman; but I have the heart and stomach of a king, and of a king of England too' (Rice 1966: 96). Described in the language of visceral interiority, the essential self is not the gendered body, but a political position.

If this privileging of political over personal identity were the extent of Elizabeth's manipulation of the rhetoric of subjectivity, it would be tempting to ignore her play with the language of interiority and describe her practice as an opportunistic retention of a still-potent medieval doctrine in a period in which the new paradigm of interiorized subjectivity was only beginning to establish itself. But in addition to invoking the gendered body natural only to deny its primacy, Elizabeth also *exploited* the supposed essentiality of her feminine self and its privileged private status when the invocation of political power would not suffice. As early as her accession speech, Elizabeth had discovered the utility of pleading the inadequacy of her body natural to secure aid for her body politic (though the role of gender in the debilitation of the body natural is only implicit, it would have been obvious to her parliamentary audience): 'as I am but one Bodye naturallye Considered though by [God's] permission a Bodye Politique to Governe, so I shall desyre you all my Lords . . . euery one in his Degree and Power to be assistant to me' (Heisch 1975: 33). Elizabeth made similar use of her gender to deflect blame for unpopular actions by invoking as 'natural' certain traditionally feminine traits which were only with difficulty overcome by the demands of state. Not surprisingly, Elizabeth was particularly fond of this rhetorical strategy in the context of the two issues of the first half of her reign that best intertwined the personal and the political, the execution of Mary, Queen of Scots, and the twin questions of marriage and the succession. When the debate over the imprisoned Scottish queen's fate reached its

height and parliament demanded her head, Elizabeth located her
hesitation in her private person, making the 'naturally' merciful
gendered self a scapegoat for the queen's delay. In a 1586 speech
she lamented that if

> we were but as two milke maides, w[th] pailes vpon oure armes, or
> that there were no more dependency vpon us, but myne owne
> life were onlie in danger, and not the whole estate of youre
> religion and well doings, I protest . . . I wolde most willinglie
> pardon and remit this offence.
>
> (Heisch 1975: 49–50)

The milkmaid trope plays a similar role at a crucial moment in the
marriage debate, embodying the queen's private self as it grapples
with her public obligations in this 1575 speech:

> if I wear a milke maide with a paile on my arme, whearby my
> private person might be litle sett by, I wolde not forsake that
> poore and single state, to matche with the greatest monarche. . . .
> Yet, for yowr behalfe, there is no waie so difficulte, that maie
> towche my privat person, which I will not well content my selffe
> to take; and, in this case, as willinglie to spoile myselffe of my
> selffe, as if I sholde put of[f] my upper garment when it weryes
> me, if the present state might not therbie be encombred.
>
> (Harington 1804: 125)

The effect is a complex one: Elizabeth invokes the nascent modern
sense of the sanctity of the private self, proof in its desires against
those of 'the greatest monarche'; and by constructing that self as
female, humble, and virginal, she creates a sympathetic scapegoat
for her notorious temporizing on the subject of marriage. At the
same time, the invocation of the private is finally trumped by the
priority of the political; and in this battle of self against self, the
triumph of the political is figured not as a repressive imposition
from without, but as a stripping away of the confining and inessential private, 'as if I sholde put of[f] my upper garment when it
weryes me', to reveal the public self underneath. In a period in
which the development of an interiorized notion of subjectivity was
raising the troubling issue of the ability of clothing to conceal rather
than confirm identity, Elizabeth's simile exploits the distrust of
clothing as signifier not to privilege but to exteriorize and devalue

the private. Elizabeth's private, gendered self becomes in effect a *persona*, exploiting a nascent ideology of interiority to political effect.

As Elizabeth's control of her own iconographic representation became more assured, her use of gendered personae which evoked her private self in order to obscure or otherwise mystify her political authority became both more common and more elaborate. Unlike the milkmaid figure, these later, more developed personae accomplish this mystification not by contrasting their weakness and innocence with an antithetically conceived political self, but rather by disguising political authority as a form of power more compatible with the personae themselves. The powerless milkmaid was superseded by the adored but unyielding shepherdess of pastoral allegory and her courtly counterpart, the unattainable Petrarchan beloved. Numerous critics have shown that the rhetorics of courtly and pastoral love that flourished between Elizabeth and her courtiers and other seekers of favor were not unequivocal tools of royal control but rather contested grounds upon which both the queen and her suitors sought political advantage (Montrose 1980; Bates 1992; Berry 1989). But by recasting political conflict as romantic tribulation, Elizabeth was able to use a self-consciously fictive version of the body natural to relieve direct pressure on the body politic.

The rhetoric of courtly love was, of course, rooted in the medieval chivalric tradition, and its transformation from a complex ethic of martial service and aristocratic honor into a means of personal advancement and romantic intrigue (Howard and Rackin 1997: 143) was both facilitated by and in turn contributed to the emergence of the modern subject. With this newly privatized subjectivity, however, came an increasing emphasis on love not as courtly display but as private sentiment, the affective bond at the heart of the companionate marriage, apart from the world of politics and economics and hence a particular attribute of women (Belsey 1985b: 193–207). Elizabeth took advantage of this gendered conception of love in her decades-long construction of what one might call the Elizabethan 'national romance'. The roots of this construction may be traced back to Elizabeth's claims early in the marriage controversy that she had 'long since made choice of a husband, the kingdom of England' (Rice 1966: 117): while the traditional figuration of monarch as husband and nation as wife relied on the congruence of public and private hierarchical relationships to reinforce political and familial order, Elizabeth's inversion of the conventional analogy exploited the *disjunction* between public and private, personalizing and romanticizing the relation between queen and subjects. Over the course of her reign, particularly in or after moments of political crisis, Elizabeth made increasingly frequent use of the assertion that her relationship with her subjects was based on neither power nor money but on a love rooted in her 'natural' femininity. The apotheosis of this construction was the 1601 'Golden Speech', which followed a heated conflict with parliament over monopolies and the granting of much-needed funds to the crown:

> I do assure you that there is no prince that loveth his subjects better, or whose love can countervail our love. There is no jewel, be it of never so rich a prize, which I prefer before this jewel, I mean your love, for I do more esteem it than any treasure or riches, for that we know how to prize, but love and thanks I count inestimable.
>
> (Rice 1966: 106)

As the speech drew to a close, the queen invoked the inadequacies conventionally associated with the gender of her body natural that purportedly disqualified her from the male realm of governance, only to overbalance those inadequacies with her equally gender-specific strengths, while reminding her audience that beneath those feminine virtues lay a God-given royal – and masculine – valor:

> And though you have had and may have many princes more mighty and wise sitting in this seat, yet you never had or shall have any that will be more careful and loving. Should I ascribe anything to myself and my sexly weakness, I were not worthy to live then, and of all most unworthy of the mercies I have had from God, Who hath ever yet given me a heart which never yet feared foreign or home enemies.
>
> (Rice 1966: 109)

Through a rhetoric of political masculinity deployed throughout her reign, Elizabeth assured her subjects that they were not being ruled by a 'mere' woman. At the same time, her manipulation of the evolving early modern understanding of interiority and exteriority complicated antagonistic constructions of the queen as a woman behaving like or usurping the position of a man; if anything, her presentation of the masculine body politic as more fundamental than and concealed within a conventional femininity whose 'naturalness' was mitigated by its conspicuous externalization, suggested that the queen was – if not quite a man – a *male* disguised as or acting as a woman. Neither a naive reversion to a medieval conception of the socially defined self nor a surrender to the modern interiorization of subjectivity, Elizabeth's rhetorical self-fashioning instead exploited the early modern transitional juxtapositioning of the two ideologies of identity, offering a model not of the successful containment of the individual by ideology, but of opportunistic resistance from a subject-position uniquely situated to understand and manipulate the forces of containment.

But if Elizabeth's 'inside-out' construction of her own gender identity worked to circumvent the twin fears that comprised the double-bind faced by women under an emergent ideology of interiorized, essentialized subjectivity, it also seems to have exacerbated another anxiety rooted in the very ideological flux that enabled her self-representation. By divorcing identity from biology and exteriorizing the supposedly private in an era in which the socially defined self seemed increasingly inessential, Elizabeth in effect evacuated the realm of essential subjectivity, creating the specter of a self with no *a priori* or fixed determinants, and thus susceptible to self-determination or – more disturbing still – external manipulation. Leah Marcus (1988) has noted that Elizabeth's exploitation of the language and conventions of gender left at least some of her subjects uncertain as to what, finally, the queen's gender was (Marcus 1988: 58–9) – an anxiety that produced a growing obsession with Elizabeth's sexuality (including rumors of clandestine sexual activity and illegitimate children), reflecting a desire to fix her identity by tying it to the biological functions and 'private' desires mystified by her status as 'Virgin Queen' (Marcus 1988: 70; C. Levin 1994: 65–90). Moreover, Marcus further demonstrates that anxiety over the queen's indeterminate gender triggered in some of her male subjects a corresponding anxiety about the fixity of their own gender identity: if Elizabeth could be at different times or in different senses male and female, could her willful masculinity in turn effeminize them (Marcus 1988: 66)? If concerns about the sociopolitical ramifications of Elizabeth's ability to *conceal* her 'true' gender identity by *acting* like a man are symptomatic of the modern interiorization of subjectivity, fears about the *inessentiality* and *malleability* of identity are perhaps better characterized as symptomatic of an ideological instability that marked the early modern transition from a pre-modern to a modern subjectivity – an instability the recurrence of which now marks the postmodern collapse of the essentialized, interiorized modern subject.

Given the persistence, indeed the intensification, of an essentialized gender identity even as other categorical markers like class and occupation were rendered exterior and inessential with the interiorization of subjectivity, it is not surprising that while epistemological concerns about the ability of identity to be hidden focus on both class and gender hierarchies, ontological fears about the transformation of the self fixate primarily on gender. This pattern can be discerned in two of the period's most socially conservative discourses, the anti-crossdressing and anti-theatrical movements of the late sixteenth and early seventeenth centuries.[3] As England underwent a period of unprecedented socioeconomic mobility, the possibility of deception, that one could pose as something one was not, was increasingly seen as a threat to the stability of the class and gender hierarchies at the heart of the English social order (Howard 1988: 418–29; Barish 1981: 166–7). One response to this concern was the intensification of sumptuary regulation under Elizabeth; another was the Jacobean backlash against crossdressing.[4] Perhaps the period's best-known anti-crossdressing tract, the anonymous *Hic Mulier* (1620), makes clear the threat of crossdressing to the maintenance of hierarchical relations in general. Sympathetically considering the possibility that aristocratic women adopt masculine attire to humiliate the citizens' wives who ape upper-class fashions, the tract finally rejects the argument by giving precedence to the need to preserve the integrity of gender distinctions: 'to offend themselves to grieve others is a revenge dissonant to Reason . . . and most pernicious to the Commonwealth' (Anon. 1620: 274). But if aristocratic women are guilty, the lower ranks are more so; the pamphlet locates the origins of the problem in the 'rags of gentry', or worse still, those who aspire to gentility but will instead be dispatched back 'to the place from whence they came, and there rot and consume unpitied and unremembered' (Anon. 1620: 268). The practice decried here is one of imposture, the misrepresentation, whether by clothing or conduct, of the 'true' self; masculine attire and behavior are repeatedly decried as 'disguise', and women who eschew them are praised as 'signs deceitless' (Anon. 1620: 266).

A similar concern underlies much of the period's anti-theatrical sentiment. Jonas Barish (1981: 96) notes two senses of theatricality relevant to Renaissance anti-theatricalists, mimicry and ostentation;

they are linked by their role in presenting an exterior appearance at odds with one's natural, God-given self. This sort of argument is grounded in what Barish calls 'the concept of an absolute identity', citing William Prynne's *Histrio-Mastix*:

> For God . . . hath given a uniforme distinct and proper being to every creature, *the bounds of which may not be exceeded: so he requires that the actions of every creature should be honest and sincere, devoyde of all hypocrisie.* . . . Hence he enjoy[n]es all men at all times, *to be such in shew, as they are in truth: to seeme that outwardly which they are inwardly*; to act themselves, not others.
>
> (Prynne 1633: X4, original italics; quoted in Barish 1981: 92)

It was this logic that underlay the anti-theatricalists' obsessive citation of the Deuteronomic prohibition of crossdressing: 'The woman shal not weare that which perteineth unto the man, nether shal a man put on womans raiment: for all that do so, *are* abominacion unto the Lord thy God' (Geneva Bible, Deut. 22: 5). This theological essentialism, Barish (1981: 167) notes, 'went hand in hand with a powerful social conservatism', defending 'natural' hierarchical boundaries against transgressive dissimulation.

Alongside this fear of epistemological and social disorder and its language of disguise and deceit, however, there coexists – often in the same tracts – a fear of ontological disorder, expressed in a rhetoric of transformation, and most often associated with gender rather than class identity. The anxiety here is not about an essential identity that can be concealed, but about an identity that is inessential and therefore mutable. Anti-theatrical and anti-crossdressing concerns intersected in the figure of the boy actor who by adopting women's clothes and manners would, it was feared, not only seem but actually *become* feminine:

> May *we not daily see our Players metamorphosed into women on the Stage, not only by putting on the female robes, but likewise the effeminate gestures, speeches, pace, behaviour, attire, delicacy, passions, manners, arts and wiles of the female sex.* . . . Is this a light, a despicable effeminacie, for men, for Christians, thus to adulterate, emasculate, metamorphose, and debase their noble sexe? thus purposely, yea, affectedly, to unman, unchristian, uncreate themselves . . .?
>
> (Prynne 1633, original italics: Z2–Z2$^v$)[5]

Worse still, if by playing a woman one could change one's own gender, the anti-theatricalists feared that by witnessing such a transformation one could unwittingly be subject to a similar transformation – that is to say, effeminized. When Prynne inveighs against 'the invirillity of Play-acting' (Z2), he refers not only to the actors themselves but to their audience, 'a confluence of unchaste, effeminate, vaine companions' (Z2$^v$; see also Orgel 1996: 27–30; Levine 1994: 10–25). The ontological anxiety rooted in the inessentiality and malleability of the self is thus twofold: at once the fear of a monstrous, self-mutating subject, and the fear of a self that can be transformed from without – the same fears aroused by Elizabeth's manipulation of her own gender identity. Their persistence some thirty years after her death suggests that while her practice may have made her a focal point for the culture's latent anxieties, the problem itself was larger than a single figure, rooted instead in an ideological instability surrounding the early modern subject that would not be resolved until the modern construction of an interiorized, essentialized subject had fully taken hold, its hegemony obscuring the traces of alternative concepts of identity.

Much of the recent critical attention paid to early modern English anti-theatricality and crossdressing has been in the service of historicist or materialist readings of the drama of the period, especially – though by no means exclusively – Shakespeare's transvestite comedies. The historical material is generally used to evaluate the gender politics of the plays: are their disguised heroines progressive or conservative, subverting or solidifying the boundaries between genders and the constraints placed on female subjectivity? Distinguishing between the epistemological and ontological threats to those boundaries, however – between the fear of concealment and the fear of transformation – complicates the plays' responses, forcing us to separate a qualified social progressivism from a more fundamental metaphysical conservatism at odds with Elizabeth's more radical contemporaneous practice. Given the theater's professional reliance on costume, its financial implication in the new economy, and the social mobility of many of its practitioners, it is not surprising that the comedies' position on the disguising of identity differed significantly from that of the anti-theatricalists. Both sides shared an understanding of the power of disguise in an era of interiorized subjectivity, but while the anti-theatricalists feared it, Shakespeare embraced it: disguise in the comedies is not a destabilizing threat to social hierarchy, but instead a means to reinvigorate and expand a complacent or constrictive social order. This valorization of a malleable exterior as socially efficacious is, however, predicated on an assumption of – and insistence on – interior stability. The dramatic irony that characterizes Shakespeare's transvestite comedies – we, unlike most of the characters, are always aware of the imposture, and much of the plays' humor derives from pointed reminders of both the female body and the feminine subjectivity beneath the male costume – buffers their vision of a flexible social order with the assurance of a fixed, essentialized interiority that at once underpins and transcends the social. In other words, the plays' treatment of identity is *modern*, and in their embrace of the social implications of that modernity, they are progressive – particularly when contrasted with the at-times hysterical conservatism of the anti-theatrical and anti-crossdressing tracts.[6] At the same time, however, in their insistence on an essential, gendered identity, the plays present a conservative reaction to Elizabeth's radical destabilization of identity, both in their general treatment of interiorized subjectivity and in their specific reflections of Elizabeth's tactics.

More than any of the other comedies, *The Merchant of Venice* embodies the progressive aspect of Shakespeare's modern attitude towards disguise and the concealment of interiority. The series of suitors in the casket plot makes clear that the incommensurability of interior and exterior, essence and appearance, is a given, and that success in the play's socioeconomically transitional world requires that the discrepancy be neither denied nor deplored, but instead understood and exploited. Morocco's confident assertion that so rich a prize as Portia could be housed only in the most valuable container (2.7.48–60)[7] is answered with a humiliating gloss on the old saw, 'All that glisters is not gold' (2.7.65ff), as is Aragon's defiant assumption of his own aristocratic desert, which follows his lament on the 'corrupt' separation of the trappings of nobility from their rightful owners, 'the true seed of honour' (2.9.35–50). Whether or not we believe that Bassanio is aided by Portia's song about the superficiality of 'fancy' based on appearance, the conclusion he draws – 'So may the outward shows be least themselves' (3.2.73) – and the consequent choice he makes are precisely the right ones, reflecting the practical wisdom at the heart of the casket test: 'You that choose not by the view/Chance as fair and choose as true' (3.2.131–2). Though rooted in the exploitation of the difference between interior and exterior, Bassanio's victory is neither a vision of social chaos nor a triumph of cynicism and deceit, but rather an endorsement of the value of an interiority protected but untainted by dissimulation.

This modern conception of an essential interior hidden but ultimately unaffected by a manipulable exterior also seems to underlie Portia's use of disguise. Her description of the imposture to Nerissa – their husbands shall see them in Venice 'in such a habit / That they shall think we are accomplishèd / With that we lack' (3.4.60–2) – is based on a clear distinction between appearance and reality. When Nerissa, however jokingly, broaches the issue of transformation ('Why, shall we turn to men?' [3.4.79]), Portia's bawdy retort ('Fie, what a question's that / If thou wert near a lewd interpreter!' [3.4.80–1]) reinterprets the question to replace the fear of mutability with a reassertion of the pair's fundamental female sexuality. This certainty is challenged, however, by the events of the trial scene. Portia is not, of course, biologically transformed, but unlike her successors Rosalind and Viola, she assumes not simply a male costume but male power – legal expertise – in the male realm of socioeconomic activity. Moreover, she wields that power in court with a skill and authority that belie her earlier self-description as 'an unlessoned girl, unschooled, unpractisèd' (3.2.159) – so much so that it is this skill and authority, rather than her costume or the female body that lies beneath it, that becomes the focus of the scene, and the momentary essence of Portia's identity.[8] So successful is her transformation that it is jarring when, at the height of the trial as Portia is about to render her judgment, Bassanio's reply to Antonio's farewell speech ('life itself, my wife, and all the world / Are not with me esteemed above thy life' [4.2.279–80]) reasserts Portia's status as woman and wife. The dramatic irony of Portia's response – 'Your wife would give you little thanks for that / If she were by to hear you make the offer' (4.2.283–4) – further redirects our attention to her disguise and the identity beneath it.

The moment, however disconcerting, passes, and Portia's double trap – the drop of blood quibble and the law governing aliens – is sprung; in springing it, however, she shifts authority from herself to Antonio and the Duke, to whom the law gives power over Shylock's life and living. Of the ensuing thirty-eight lines preceding Shylock's exit, Portia speaks only four; and with Shylock's departure, the trial plot gives way to the ring plot, the ground for which was prepared in the earlier exchange on the relative value of Portia and Antonio.

Like the trial, the ring plot is orchestrated by Portia; but while the former takes place in the male domains of law and finance and revolves less around Portia's disguise than her forensic ability, the latter shifts the field to the female realm of marriage and family, and its humor hinges on the discrepancy between the wives' male disguises and their 'true' female identities (as in Portia's ironic assertion that 'I'll die for't but some woman had the ring' [5.1.207]). Moreover, while in the trial Portia wields the authority of the law, in the ring plot her weapons of choice are the twin threats of sexual withholding ('By heaven, I will ne'er come in your bed / Until I see the ring' [5.1.189–90]) and sexual promiscuity ('I'll have that doctor for my bedfellow' [5.1.232]), underlining the fundamental nature of her biological sex and the gendered traits associated with it in the period's familiar misogynist discourse. Portia's device is, of course, successful, and having extracted from Bassanio the assurance she requires for their happy future together (conventionally understood as a promise to value the bonds of marriage over those of both male friendship and finance) she reveals her imposture and retracts the threat of cuckoldry. If Portia's use of disguise brings her power in the marital realm, however, it does so by containing her within it, and within an essentialized femininity that can be temporarily disguised but ultimately not repudiated. But try as it may, the play's ending cannot completely silence the echoes of the trial scene and its suggestion of an identity not rooted in biology, and of women who can 'turn to men' by escaping the essentialism of gendered interiority.

If *The Merchant of Venice* offers a qualified endorsement of the utility of a concealable gender identity by restricting its range and grounding it in an essentialized interiority unaffected by exterior alteration, *As You Like It* underscores both the endorsement and its qualifications. While *Merchant*'s fifth act must work to contain the ramifications of Portia's successful intervention in the Venetian public sphere by returning her to Belmont and the domestic, *As You Like It* empowers Rosalind only when she flees from the corrupt public world of Duke Frederick's court to the idealized private realm of the forest.[9] Her power there, though formidable, is exercised solely over her fellow lovers in the arranging of suitable marriages, and is renounced with her disguise when in her final lines she pointedly reasserts her identity as woman, daughter, and wife:

> [to the Duke] I'll have no father if you be not he.
> [to Orlando] I'll have no husband if you be not he,
> [to Phoebe] Nor ne'er wed woman if you be not she.
>
> (5.4.111–13)

It is Jaques de Bois, not Rosalind, who finally clears away the play's political obstacles and facilitates the company's return to court (Park 1980: 107–8; Erickson 1985: 31). Similarly, if Portia's ability to wield the law permits a momentary slippage of an otherwise insistent feminine interiority, Rosalind is allowed no such ambiguity: for all her quicksilver transitions from Rosalind to Ganymede to 'Rosalind', we are never allowed to forget who – or what – she really is. Like Portia, Rosalind predicates her initial description of her disguise on a carefully maintained distinction between an exterior masculinity ('We'll have a swashing and a martial outside' [1.3.114]) and an interior – and inferior – femininity ('Lie there [in my heart] what hidden woman's fear there will' [1.3.113]); her comparison of her own plan to the practice of 'other mannish cowards' who 'outface it with their semblances' (1.3.115–16) identifies her as a dissembler while establishing a standard of 'true' masculinity to be fulfilled by Orlando at the play's end. The play insists throughout on the female body and – more importantly – the feminine nature beneath Rosalind's costume: the very first time we see her as Ganymede, she immediately acknowledges that 'I could find it in my heart to disgrace my man's apparel and to cry like a woman. But I must comfort the weaker vessel, as doublet and hose ought to show itself courageous to petticoat' (2.4.3–6; cf. 3.2.178–80; 3.2.227–8; 3.4.1–3; 3.5.73–4; 4.1.173–4; 4.3.163–74).

A number of critics, however, have suggested that the subversiveness of Rosalind's gender-play lies not in an attempt to usurp male power or identity, but in the denaturalizing of gender identity itself. Her mockery of Orlando's by-the-book pseudo-Petrarchan verses and sentiments (3.2.143–63, 4.1.59–92), of Silvius' literary-pastoral rhetoric of praise and prostration and Phoebe's corresponding coldness (3.5.36–81), and of her own invocation of misogynist stereotypes of women as fickle, jealous, and unfaithful (3.3.365–79, 4.1.45–151) are read as revealing the artificiality of conventional gender roles (Kimbrough 1982: 25; Grady 1996: 199–203). That much of this takes place while Rosalind-Ganymede-'Rosalind' in effect plays herself further underlines the theatricality of identity (Howard 1988: 435; Belsey 1985a: 180–5; Grady 1996: 202). In this way, Rosalind's denaturalizing practice would appear to have much in common with Elizabeth's theatricalization and convention-alization of her own supposed feminine interiority. The ontological problem posed by Elizabeth's exteriorization of her femininity, how-ever, lay in its emptying out of the space of interiority, posing the threat of an individual with no fixed or essential self, who could not only *seem*, but also *become* – and perhaps force others to become – whatever suited her needs. Rosalind's exposure of the theatricality of identity stops short of Elizabeth's practice in that behind each of the personae she assumes and/or exposes as artificial lies a more fundamental, natural identity which the text takes pains to authenti-cate and endorse. Her performance of 'Rosalind' as the misogynist stereotype of a cuckolding, shrewish wife in 4.1 is immediately followed by a glimpse beneath the disguise: 'O coz, coz, coz, my pretty little coz, that thou didst know how many fathom deep I am in love. . . . I cannot be out of the sight of Orlando. I'll go find a shadow and sigh till he come' (4.1.175–6, 185–6). The genuineness of this devoted, loving Rosalind is attested to in the play's most notorious moment of self-revelation, her involuntary swoon at the sight of Orlando's blood, testimony to an essential femininity which she vainly tries to pass off as 'counterfeiting' (4.3.156–80). In this light, Rosalind offers an analogue for a reassuringly modern inter-pretation of Elizabeth as a woman who may *act* like a man who acts like a woman, but is fundamentally – biologically and tempera-mentally – female. Similarly, Rosalind's derision of Orlando's conventional romantic postures is in the service of effecting his 'cure' – not the deconstruction of his subjectivity but rather the paring away of affectation and confusion to reveal the 'natural' nobility that rescues the undeserving Oliver (4.3.126–31) and pro-duces the wiser but still ardent lover who finally 'can live no longer by thinking' (i.e., by accepting 'Rosalind' for Rosalind [5.2.45]). If Rosalind's own gender-play affects the identity of the men in her thrall, it is not, as was feared of Elizabeth, to transform them into women, but to help them realize their 'true' masculinity.

As this most self-consciously theatrical play draws to a close, however, there remains one final imposture to be revealed. The Epilogue's exposure of the male actor behind the fictive Rosalind has been read as everything from a final demonstration of the instability of the boundaries between genders (Howard 1988: 435; Belsey 1985a: 180–5) to a concluding erasure of the lingering threat of female agency (Erickson 1985: 35; Orgel 1996: 63). Read in the context of the play's – and the period's – understanding of identity in terms of disguise and transformation, however, the Epilogue would appear to fall somewhere in between, neither radically destabilizing nor conservatively patriarchal. In its ironic self-deprecation, which invites us to disagree by acknowledging our appreciation with applause, the Epilogue celebrates the power and pleasure of theatricality – a theatricality that the play itself reminds us is not contained by the walls of the theater. At the same time, the Epilogue's insistence on a biological essentialism that ultimately determines social and sexual behavior ('If I were a woman, I would kiss as many of you as had beards that pleased me' [14–16]) limits the power of costume by insisting that the boy actor, however convincing in 'the woman's part', is not transformed by it. Marcus (1988) has suggested that not only the transvestite comic heroine, but also the boy actor who plays her, can be seen as an analogue of Elizabeth's layering of gender identities: a fundamental male self that appears to be female (whether on the theatrical or political stage) and self-consciously plays a male role (Marcus 1988: 100–1). It is the nature of that 'fundamental male self', however, that marks the difference between Shakespeare's practice and Elizabeth's: while *As You Like It*'s Epilogue locates a stable gendered body at the heart of the theatrical enterprise's playful dissimulation, Elizabeth's interiorization of a political masculinity and exteriorization of her 'natural' gender identity deconstructed the emerging modern hierarchization of public and private, exterior and interior, and in so doing challenged the very notion of an essential subjectivity. If Elizabeth's self-fashioning threatened to expose the *necessary* artificiality of *all* identity, the comedies' impostures reveal the *possible* (and at times useful) artificiality of *some* identities, whether culturally constructed or individually improvised, while shielding these modern notions of subjectivity from the more radical threat of Elizabethan 'postmodernity'.

## Notes

1  On the latter, see the excellent work by Maus (1995) and Hanson (1998).
2  Marcus (1988: 55) notes that with the exception of her reported appearance in partial armor at Tilbury, Elizabeth was never known to dress as a man. Susan Frye (1992) has argued that the Tilbury story may itself be apocryphal.
3  The critical literature on both anti-theatricality and crossdressing is copious. The major work on anti-theatricality is still Barish (1981); also

important, especially to my argument, is Levine (1994). On cross-dressing, see the long bibliographic note in Howard (1988: 419), as well as Howard's essay itself; other important works include Garber (1992) and Orgel (1996). On the relation between the two in early modern discussions of misrepresentation and sociopolitical order, see Orgel (1996: esp. ch. 4), Levine (1994: 10–25), Barish (1981: chs. 4 and 6), and Rackin (1987: 35).

4  It is perhaps no coincidence that despite the increased use of sumptuary legislation under Elizabeth, no laws specifically governing male–female or female–male crossdressing were ever passed (Orgel 1996: 96–8).

5  On the transformative potential of acting, particularly in relation to the boy actor, see Stallybrass (1992: 74–6), Orgel (1996: 26–30), and especially Levine (1994: 10–25), to which my entire discussion of the fear of transformation is very much indebted.

6  'Progressive' is, of course, a relative term: as numerous critics have noted, the comedies expand but uphold the social order, providing opportunities for the impoverished Bassanio and the younger son Orlando as well as allowing Portia and Rosalind to improve their marital lots, while still preserving primogeniture and patriarchal marriage.

7  All references to Shakespeare's plays are from *The Norton Shakespeare* (Greenblatt 1997).

8  Marcus (1988: 98–9) notes that Portia's admission of the infirmities of her sex and subsequent exercise of masculine authority is reminiscent of Elizabeth's rhetorical practice – the more so, I would add, in her ability at least in the trial scene to make her authority seem more fundamental than her femininity.

9  On the Forest of Arden's relation to the modern construction of the private, see Grady (1996: 184–8). The question of Rosalind's empowerment over others as well as over her own identity, and its ramifications for the play's gender politics, has been much debated; see Grady (1996: 199, note 28) for bibliography and discussion. I hope to shed new light on the issue by differentiating between Rosalind's ability to disguise and to transform her gender identity, and exploring the politics of each.

# 3

# Ante-aesthetics

## Towards a theory of early modern audience response

## CHARLES WHITNEY

The neo-classical consensus was that Shakespeare and other Renaissance English dramatists achieved what they did despite their crass audiences. In 1902 A. C. Bradley found Shakespeare's audience an interesting but peripheral topic, since everything important about his work was almost entirely independent of it: they wanted a clown and he gave them the Gravedigger (Bradley 1909: 365). In 1941 Alfred Harbage came to the opposite conclusion, finding early modern audiences superior in themselves and significant partners in the creative process: 'Shakespeare's audience . . . thrived for a time, it passed quickly, and its like has never existed since. It must be given much of the credit for the greatness of Shakespeare's plays' (Harbage 1941: 3).

The fundamental reason why Harbage made his claim, the unique social diversity of early modern public amphitheater audiences, has also seemed to a number of later scholars to have been crucial to the development of early modern drama: that heterogeneous audiences prompted dramatists to address the most important subjects from a multiplicity of sometimes contradictory viewpoints and understandings (Hattaway 1982: 1; Butler 1984: 306; Bruster 1992: 3). Harbage himself overestimated this diversity,[1] but nevertheless a theater audience so diverse 'has never existed since', and so the amphitheater audiences of the Shakespearean period can be seen, as Harbage suggested, to provide in some sense a democratic precedent and perspective for modern drama and literature, and even to comprise or contribute to an early modern public sphere, to become part of artistic, social, and political narratives of modernity. Any such large claims for the importance of these audiences in the creative process and in modernity, however, are balanced by the extremely fragmentary record of actual audience response. The gulf is at least as wide as that between the plays themselves and the underachieving dramatic criticism of the period. There simply are no detailed accounts of response; the great majority are brief remarks and offhand comments that have been collected in compendia like the *Shakspere Allusion-Book* (Munro 1932). Because the upper levels of society did most of the publishing and kept most of the records, extant evidence is skewed toward the upper end of the playgoing social spectrum. How then can the nature and importance of early modern amphitheater audiences be understood and evaluated in any meaningful way?

Partly in response to the scant record, most studies of audience response have been performance-oriented readings of the plays themselves, to discover how playwrights masterfully constructed and guided their audiences (Rabkin 1967; Honigmann 1976; Howard 1984; Cartwright 1991). Within the limits of their method, which seeks to define a response valid for all competent audience members, and sometimes for audiences of any time period as well, the contribution of these studies has been immense. Some classic historicist studies that approach drama as cultural expression rather than the creation of autonomous authors also assume, as Stephen Greenblatt puts it, that the theater 'manifestly addresses its audience as a collectivity' (Greenblatt 1988a: 5) and that therefore, for instance, a play's preponderant hegemonic or subversive impression on that unified audience can be meaningfully determined. Such assumptions secure the audience's pivotal role at the expense of its authority and its heterogeneity: the social diversity of audiences becomes primarily a challenge, and Shakespeare in particular is sometimes seen to rise Coleridgeanly to this challenge by finding ways to reconcile disparate elements, that is, interests, viewpoints, tastes, genders, social ranks, and practices. Critics' licenses to interpret pluralistically are seldom extended to the early playgoers whose responses are the subject of interpretation. Such views of the dynamics of audience response may themselves reflect modern critical ideals, but cannot fully address the dialogism of audience response, where interpretive communities actively construct meaning. Nor do they address the implications of historicist and materialist scholarship itself – that cultural forms circulate and can be re-appropriated diversely by individuals or groups. The question then is whether any historically grounded notion of early modern audiences can be developed that recognizes the tremendous achievements of playwrights at the beginning of commercial theater in molding a responsive and sensitive audience out of a crowd and guiding their theatrical experience, and yet also recognizes some of the ways a diverse audience expressed and negotiated its own interests and sensibilities through playgoing, thereby stimulating and guiding a theater that disseminated meaning as well as controlled it.

My concern here is not with the changing tastes of the period or the clientele at different venues;[2] it is almost entirely limited to the public theaters of the Shakespearean period that continued to draw socially diverse audiences. I propose first to view pertinent aspects of the theater, literary criticism, and certain reading habits of the Shakespearean period in a very broad historical perspective, one that assesses their relation to modern aesthetics and their status as early modern. The significance of particular surviving responses, especially Simon Forman's (1974a), can then become more legible, as can the nature of the audience's active contribution to the creative process. Audience response rather than the plays themselves was the central element in the early modern theater. And to a greater extent than has been recognized, response was ante-aesthetic, that is, productive, purposeful, and performative, linking the world of the play to the world beyond and to the lives of playgoers, rather than referable primarily to an aesthetic dimension. Not that the aesthetic character of early modern drama is merely the projection of later ages: 'ante' means 'anticipatory' as well as 'prior to' – here, anticipatory of the later differentiation of a distinct aesthetic dimension of experience as the focus of poetic creation and appreciation. But a fully developed aesthetic sensibility lends a glare that does not well illuminate many surviving early modern responses. Hence my emphasis here on theatricality and rhetoric rather than aesthetics. The Romantic period produced a powerful way of understanding Shakespearean aesthetics that continues to resonate; here I wish to examine the particular authority and performative agency of early modern audiences with a kind of Shakespearean pragmatics.

The aesthetic dimension of modernity emerged at a particular moment of history. The invention of 'the fine arts' and the inclusion of separate arts such as poetry, painting, and music together under this rubric took place only in the late eighteenth century (Kristeller

1970). Founding texts of aesthetic modernity such as David Hume's 'Of the Standard of Taste' (1757) and Immanuel Kant's *Critique of Judgment* (1790) attempted to provide a philosophical basis for distinctively aesthetic production, experience, and judgment. Hume argued that the judgment of sensitive, cultivated, and unprejudiced individuals approximates a standard of taste that deserves general acceptance. Starting from the evident truth that artistic productions must in some sense exceed or turn away from immediate sensual gratification and practical use, Kant founded one of the major modern grand narratives by defining the special world of fine art as that of autonomous objects that are to be contemplated disinterestedly. He defined aesthetic experience as disinterested appreciation of 'purposefulness without purpose', which is supposed to lead to judgments of taste that are universal. Aesthetic judgment therefore requires that the spectator look completely beyond his or her desire, pleasure, and practical interests to contemplate the art object, using the particular mental faculty assigned to art, the imagination. Art is autonomous, that is, it has a value in and of itself: aesthetic pleasure does involve a moral sensitivity, but it arises from the form of the work.

With the help of such philosophical underpinnings, a distinctive aesthetic sphere of production and experience evolved at this time to provide a haven for serious work against increasing commercialization. Purporting to rise above the status of the tawdry commodity, this sphere on the one hand provided a basis for Romantic visions of human possibility and critiques of industrial society, but on the other reinforced social distinction and, with or without the license of Kantian austerity, supplied the potential within modernity for a disenfranchisement of art as a self-isolated, specialized activity whose universals belong to another universe.

The category of the aesthetic in this way became in its origin – and has often remained – deeply problematic. But early on and with the guidance of Kant, Samuel Taylor Coleridge praised Shakespeare's genius as a model for the creative intellect and helped establish the poet's commanding place in the canon. The activities of literary interpretation and analysis have themselves developed partly because of the emphasis the creation of a modern aesthetic dimension puts on formal analysis of the art object (Tompkins 1980: 205–6). Therefore, while modern aesthetics generated new dimensions of meanings in classic works, in an important sense Shakespearean drama is pre-modern, or modern in a non-aesthetic way, although carrying elements latterly-to-be-known-as 'aesthetic'. Criticism has embedded some unexamined anachronisms into study and appreciation of early modern drama.

What was early modern drama if it was not part of a special 'aesthetic' realm? Perhaps no single word can encompass it, but the one that comes close is 'recreation', a kind of pastime, sport, or play. 'Honest recreations', as John Redford's interlude *Wit and Science* put it (Peterson 1988: 67), give pleasure but also instruct. In 1572 the Queen's Counsel tried vainly to persuade City officials to allow more play performances in order 'to represse vyce & extoll vertue, for the recreacion of the people, & thereby to drawe them from sundrye worser exercyses' (quoted in Chambers 1923: vol. 4, 269); Henry Chettle defended plays as 'honest recreation' in 1592 and the anti-theatrical Joseph Hall disdained them as 'recreation' in 1608 (Chettle 1592: 43; Hall quoted in Gurr 1996: 230). In his preface to the collected plays of Francis Beaumont and John Fletcher in 1647, James Shirley praised the dramatic poet for his 'transcendent abilities', for 'a soul miraculously knowing and conversing with all mankind', yet still referred to plays as 'Recreations' (Beaumont and Fletcher 1905: vol. 1, xi; see also Mullaney 1988).

The focus of recreation remains much more on the life-world of audience members than the focus of many versions of aesthetic experience. Recreation connects rather than detaches dramatic response from popular entertainment, from the wrestling that Ben Jonson in *Timber* complained some groundlings might as well be attending, to the art of conversation. Playgoing was one among many commercial leisure-time activities, such as bowling and the bearbaiting that directly competed with plays and that was staged in similar amphitheaters. Playgoers' boisterous deportment and the variety of activities commonly practiced in theaters, from smoking to courtship to prostitution, complement the theater's recreative function. On a bad day at the theater different audience segments might get in a shouting match, or turn on the players; on a good day with a large and enthusiastic crowd, 'All is so pester'd', as Leonard Digges put it in 1623, commending Shakespeare's First Folio (quoted in Gurr 1996: 244).

Many plays of Shakespeare and other playwrights depict characters engaging in various forms of recreation, tricks, and high jinx, the audiences' recreation being to watch the characters at recreation. Sometimes, as in *A Mad World My Masters*, *Twelfth Night*, the Henry IV plays, and *The Tempest*, such recreation forms the basis of much of the plot, encompassing moral trials and reflections, as well as personal discovery (Peterson 1988). Such earnest tricksters as Faustus, Hieronymo, Hamlet, and Iago can also be viewed as following this model. Prince Hal distances himself from 'playing holidays' in his first scene in *1 Henry IV* (Greenblatt 1997: 1164). But though recreation, festivity, and mirth could be interrogated as themes in particular plays, and though players struggled for respectability, the early modern public theater itself was never reinvented as something clearly distinct from a space of recreation (see e.g. Weimann 1989).

The popular character of the public theater as a commercial institution was one reason why no hegemonic standard of taste could develop as it did under the leadership of John Dryden at the end of the century, to be philosophically grounded in the next. Whereas the category of the aesthetic was founded on a distinction between it and popular entertainment, the public amphitheaters were part of popular entertainment. Theater-as-recreation included an extraordinary mingling of folk and learned, rough and respectable, or little and great traditions of culture, a mingling to be increasingly repressed later (Burke 1985). Given the diversity of the audiences, playwrights had to appeal to diverse tastes and backgrounds in what Thomas Dekker in 1609 called 'the poet's Royal Exchange' (Dekker 1968: 98). Acknowledgements of playgoers' diverse tastes, expectations, judgments, or mental compositions are common in dramatic prefaces, ranging from John Lyly's address to a 'hodge-podge' audience for which a dramatic 'gallimaufrey' and 'mingle-mangle' are necessary (*Midas* 1590) to statements by Thomas Heywood (*Four Prentices of London* 1594), Beaumont (*Knight of the Burning Pestle* 1607), John Day (*The Isle of Gulls* 1607), Jonson (*Epicoene* 1609; *Bartholomew Fair* 1614), Thomas Dekker and Thomas Middleton (*The Roaring Girl* 1611), Middleton (*No Wit, No Help Like a Woman's* 1612), and Fletcher and Shakespeare (*Henry VIII* 1613), among others. In these prefaces diversity is often perceived as a novel problem, the result of the new commercial medium of drama, but it is not to be solved simply by appeal to some shared standard.

Likewise there did not exist a 'general' public guided by such standards, let alone by theater critics. The 'men of better palate' to whom Thomas Carew appealed in his 1641 preface to D'Avenant's *The Wits* (D'Avenant 1964: vol. 2, 116) had never been arbiters of taste in the Shakespearean period, though many of Shakespeare's younger contemporaries, notably Jonson, made special appeals to 'the judicious', that is to theater connoisseurs from the court, law schools, or elsewhere who possessed cultural capital and whose qualifications included liking the play in question. The period during which the sophisticated boys' private theaters thrived (1599–1609) stimulated the popularity of this concept. Shakespeare himself referred to this group only through his character Hamlet, whose use of it represents 'an extra touch of fastidiousness, even a hint of up-to-the-minute fashionable affectation' referable to the character not the author (Salingar 1991: 210–11, 217). If the prescribers of taste represented a vanguard, then, Shakespeare held a conservative position. His work remained in some sense, as the First Folio dedication put it, for 'the great Variety of Readers' and playgoers.

On the other hand, Jonson's goal to 'raise the despised head of poetry again . . . and render her worthy to be embraced and kissed of all the great and master-spirits of our world' (Jonson 1925–52: vol. 4, 20–1) suffered the disillusionment registered in his poem 'Come Leave the Lothed Stage'. Thomas Heywood in his *An Apology for Actors* (1612) attributes no unique identity to the theater as a fine art. Rather it is the theater's rhetorical power to move its audience to good and its civic and economic contribution to the nation that is the basis of his defense. And over a hundred years later, Joseph Addison in his essays on how to spend one's leisure time profitably, 'The Pleasures of the Imagination', still views the arts as 'a refined spectator sport' (Woodmansee 1994: 6).

But if dramatic experience in Shakespeare's time was not distinctively aesthetic in the sense defined here, it was certainly theatrical in complex ways. There must be a distinction between the stage world and the world of the audience in order for theater to work. But some of the ways Shakespearean theater worked could also powerfully link life in and outside of the playhouse. Elizabethan dramatists crafted self-contained plays that still acknowledged the audience in asides, soliloquies, plays-within-plays, and other self-referential devices, such as the thematic staging of recreation itself noted above, or *The Winter's Tale*'s beautiful sculpture of Hermione that comes to life, amazing both characters and spectators. This connection was appropriate to amphitheaters with stages thrust out into the midst of the audience, the stages with no scenery, the audiences illuminated by daylight as much as or more than the actors, and the actors often wearing not specially made costumes but botched outfits acquired from patrons and dealers in second-hand clothes. There developed a complex alternation of audience engagement with the illusory stage world and the audience's detached awareness of the play as a play. In the playhouse that involvement could be complexly audible and visible, but in any case it provided an opportunity for registering of playgoers' feelings, perceptions, inferences, applications, and meta-theatrical questionings; it helped insure that the audience's role was not obscured in an illusion of representation behind an invisible fourth wall, such as the proscenium stage later enforced. This was not merely a sophisticated awareness reserved for the educated, but also a question of who wielded what authority in the playhouse; groundlings knew well enough that in the theater not only the players spoke. Playgoers expressed pleasure in the illusion of representation, in Richard Burbage's remarkably lifelike portrayals, for instance, but stage conditions, requiring a continual effort of the imagination from the audience, insured that the meta-theatrical awareness of the signifier remained vital. Characters' identities were constructed and deconstructed.

The early modern theater in this way discourages standard modern philosophical dichotomies between a knowing subject with a fixed standpoint and a fixed object of knowledge – an opposition that aesthetics helped install in the act of appreciation. Its complex theatricality instead invites playgoers to participate in a play of resemblances between life and art involving eventually their own identities,[3] because it 'subvert[s] the place of our own look' and 'answer[s] to our paradoxical desire to see how we cannot see ourselves seeing' (Freedman 1991: 5, 4). Our identities too are put in question. Something like Bertolt Brecht's 'alienation effect' must have been instrinsic (Gurr 1996: 106), that logically could lead to reflection on religion and society as well as the self. The urgent meta-theatrical possibility broached by the motto traditionally ascribed to the Globe Theatre, 'Totus mundus agit histrionem', 'All the world' plays the actor', is that characters, players, and playgoers are all encompassed in one articulated theatrical continuum, not entirely divided into knower and known, and that life can be seen as a series of performances and improvisations. That perception that all the men and women are merely players encourages interpretation and analysis of an art object less than it does the theatricalization of life, the application of theatrical experience to one's own life, the conscious modeling of the stage world in one's life (see e.g. Montrose 1996). Heywood's (1841) introductory myth in *An Apology for Actors* concerns a primordial theater of the muses that shows heroes the models for their subsequent history-inaugurating achievements.

The early modern theater's status as recreation, its lack of effective standards of taste, and its distinctive theatricality are all related to its rhetorical character. The tradition of criticism from at least the time of Plato through most of the eighteenth century is rhetorical because it emphasizes that writing connects with and affects audience members more than it represents reality for its own sake, expresses the ideas and feelings of the writer, or presents the text as an object of study in itself. The goal is rather more 'pragmatic' than 'mimetic', 'expressive' or 'formal' (Abrams 1953: 14–21), and poetry is not usually severed from the rhetoric that could heighten its effect upon the audience.

The anti-theatrical controversy comprised most of the commentary on drama of the early modern period, and it had one focus: whether stage-plays and the environment they created harmed playgoers and the commonwealth morally, politically, economically, medically, and damnably. Responding to charges that plays corrupted audiences, Philip Sidney, Thomas Nashe, and Thomas Heywood supply the major statements of the period concerning the type of refreshment and improvement offered by recreational playgoing. These apologists suggest that early modern players and playgoers approached plays as ways of affecting audiences in pleasantly moral and civic-minded ways, as if plays were primarily vehicles for producing response. Here Nashe focuses on politics (1592):

> The policy of plays is very necessary . . . They show the ill
> success of treason, the fall of hasty climbers, the
> wretched end of usurpers, the misery of civil dissension,
> and how just God is evermore in punishing of murder.
> (Nashe 1966: 211–13)

And Heywood on personal morals, suggesting here that plays address audience members differentially according to their particular faults (1612):

> art thou addicted to prodigallity, envy, cruelty, perjury,
> flattery, or rage? our scenes affoord thee store of men

to shape your lives by, who be frugall, loving, gentle,
trusty, without soothing, and in all things temperate.

(Heywood 1841: 56)

It is fundamental to the arguments of both writers in defense of the
stage that this kind of civic and ethical effect operates in one way or
another on all segments of the audience, although some members of
each segment may not be in the frame of mind to receive it. For a
major anti-theatrical argument was that plays perverted the base-
born. John Taylor, himself a working man turned poet, suggests
that those who avoid moral improvement may tend to be of low
degree, but his sense is simply that by resisting or contesting moral
application playgoers reveal themselves to be morally low:

> A self-wise foole, that sees his wits out-stript,
> Or any vice that feeles it selfe but nipt . . .
> But straight the poyson of their envious tongues,
> Breakes out in vollyes of calumnious wronges,
> and then a tinker, or a dray-man sweares,
> I would the house were fir'd about their eares.
>
> (in Heywood 1841: 12)

Even this offended tinker or drayman who wishes the theater were
burned down is quite as sensitive at least about registering moral
content relevant to himself as his betters should be. But if Taylor
actually witnessed such responses from playgoers of low degree,
they might also have arisen from a broader perception that the play
in question was hostile to the class interests of workers. After all, as
Peter Burke warns, when the higher culture addresses a low audience, do not expect 'the message transmitted was necessarily the
message received' (Burke 1985: 32).

The many examples of individual response that emphasize the
importance of moral instruction, however, do come from educated
playgoers. Student Richard West wrote in the memorial volume for
Ben Jonson (*Jonsonus Virbius*, 1638), 'Thy scaenes are precepts,
every verse doth give/Counsel, and teach us not to laugh, but live'
(Craig 1990: 208–9). Many playgoers wrote down lines as 'precepts'
in commonplace books, such as Francis Bacon's 'Promus of Formu-
laries and Elegancies' or the 'tables' in which Hamlet is immediately
compelled to record the moral he draws from Claudius's murder of
his father (Greenblatt 1997: 1686). The practice reinforced the

tendency of some playgoers to seize upon wise saws, extracting them from their dramatic contexts and relating them to a body of received wisdom. Here the play becomes a catalyst for the playgoer's inventive recycling; it is the playgoer's experience and needs that take precedence. On the Roman crowd's fickleness in turning against Shakespeare's Brutus, the judicious aficionado John Weever riffed in 1601, 'Man's memorie, with new, forgets the old, One tale is good, until another's told' (Munro 1932: vol. 1, 94). In the same year, William Cornwallis's *Discourses Upon Seneca the Tragedian* takes this kind of reception to an extreme, as essayistic commentary is provided on very brief passages removed completely from the context of the plays.

Yet perhaps at no time was literary criticism, especially of tragedy, as inadequate both to its subject matter and to what must have been actual responses. The doctrine that poetry supports prevailing, unified, and stable ethical values; the emphasis on positive and negative examples (which one finds expressed even in *Hamlet*, that plays should 'show virtue her own feature, scorn her own image' [Greenblatt 1997: 1708]), seem to deny that tragedies can be 'open-ended explorations of crises and struggles . . . interrogative forms that test traditional values' (Gellrich 1988: 197). Exactly what moral precepts is one supposed to deduce from seeing, for instance, how an adulterous wife wastes away to death under solitary confinement by her husband in Heywood's own *A Woman Killed with Kindness*? Why did criticism fail to address exploratory and interrogative aspects of response significantly? Precisely because a public sphere of comment had not significantly extended to print from the playhouse and from lived experience. In a culture of patronage in which licit discourse about culture tended toward celebration of the patron as public benefactor, little space existed for acknowledging the possibility that drama could stimulate controversy or disseminate meaning promiscuously rather than measure and control it. Heywood's *Apology* is primarily a work of public relations, claiming on the one hand that the established acting companies in 1612 were respectable, predictable, and willing to serve the interests of their patrons, members of the royal family all, and on the other hand that they were a major resource of a great city.

An analogous situation can be found in comments on the other goal of stage-plays, pleasure. In the late sixteenth century and after, the didactic goal sometimes dropped out of prologues to comedy, leaving only 'mirth', 'delight', or 'to make you laugh'

(Klein 1910: 9–10, 55–7, 166–70); Shakespeare's rare epilogues mention only pleasure. A strong emphasis on audience response – yet a generic, cultural, or politic barrier against addressing the controversy invited by that emphasis – is evident in perhaps the most detailed description of the pleasure of spectatorship, the anonymous 'On Worthy Master Shakespeare and his Poems', one of the Second Folio's commendatory verses (1632). With its lively appreciation of Shakespeare's ability to design complex plot reversals that play on different emotions of playgoers, it recalls though it does not mention the notion of catharsis, which was widely discussed by sixteenth-century Italian critics. One can see how its substantial description of theatrical recreation or 'pastime' could have been developed, in a later age, as an analysis of previously elusive and intangible aesthetic components, though the focus would have been on the aesthetics of audience response rather than that of stage or page.

> *Yet so to temper passion, that our eares*
> *Take pleasure in their paine; And eyes in teares*
> *Both weepe and smile; fearefull at plots so sad,*
> *Then, laughing at our feare; abus'd, and glad*
> *To be abus'd, affected with that truth*
> *Which we perceive is false; pleas'd in that ruth*
> *At which we start; and by elaborate play*
> *Tortur'd and tickled; by a crablike way*
> *Time past made pastime.*
>
> (Anon. 1909: B1r)

As in this passage, extant response of the period often admires a good plot and the emotions it elicits (R. Levin 1980); this poem takes the view that the audience, desiring to be passively molded, to be *'Stolne from our selves'*, enters under the total control of the dramatist, a 'Plebeian *Impe from lofty throne*', who in his plays also paradoxically makes *'Kings his subjects'* by staging them. The controversial social and political implications of attributing such power to the dramatist are not developed. Yet one may discern that the playgoer still represents himself as active in the sense that his praise finds in the author a radical power to do what anti-theatrical writers feared the theater would do, 'make proud majesty a subject', and 'deconsecrate sovereignty' (Kastan 1986), so that not only the playwright but also the playgoers could scrutinize and judge rulers, as well as identify or sympathize with them.

Given the limitations of literary criticism at this time, before considering in detail responses of individual playgoers let us consider other evidence that might help prepare us to construe those responses. Humanist education supplies an important context for understanding the moral content of plays. One intriguing area is the note-taking practice of keeping commonplace books recently explored by Mary Thomas Crane and alluded to by Richard West's comment on Jonson quoted above. The widespread activity of 'gathering' quotable quotes and 'framing' or organizing them under headings had a creative aspect and provided a matrix of assimilated material from classical and contemporary sources that could be adapted for a range of uses, from moral touchstones of general applicability to proving one had the rhetorical and literary savvy to get a professional job, to teaching, corresponding, transacting business, managing, governing, and writing love sonnets. Commonplace books therefore provided an opportunity for the development and elaboration of public and private selves, fashioning selfhood as autonomous or as grounded in tradition and culture (Crane 1993). Plays must be open and adaptable for appropriation by these tools – they must invite playgoers to engage in a continuing dialogue of *sententiae*. Such a responsive practice empowers playgoers by giving them the authority to interpret and apply unimpeachable wisdom – wisdom that could be used to question and test as well as to support existing institutions and practices. Playgoing becomes an exchange of cultural capital, but the playgoer is more than a consumer – he or she can re-create the product.

Techniques of rhetorical elaboration defined by Erasmus in *De Copia* offer more tangible possibilities for complex and even diverse response, as Marion Trousdale has shown. Here readers copiously invent their own glosses on a story or saying. In plays this would have been done, often, following the prompting of characters' own moralizing, that 'Ripeness is all' and 'The lunatic, the lover, and the poet Are of imagination all compact'. The method of rhetorical elaboration must have been one of exploration and meditation, both interpretive of the story and prescriptive toward the life-world of the audience. The degree to which this method was established in grammar-school curricula made it easy for playwrights to accommodate playgoers' knowledge of it, empowering them to take the ball (Trousdale 1982: 45, 133). The majority of most amphitheater audiences would have had some grammar-school education, not just the privileged.

Rhetorical elaboration would also have been an active kind of reception producing diverse responses, with different playgoers coming to different, even contradictory, conclusions about the moral significance of the same action. The method itself aimed to exploit a story's possibilities for generating moral commentary, not necessarily to render the commentary consistent. For instance, George Sandys's commentary on Ovid's *Metamorphoses* (1632) offers a frankly contradictory interpretation of a tragic couple who disobey their parents, Pyramus and Thisbe. The story

> upbraids[s] those parents, who measure their childrens by
> their owne out-worne and deaded affections; in forcing
> them to serve thir avarice or ambition in their fatall
> mariages . . . Not considering that riches canot purchase love;
> nor threats or violence either force or restraine it.
>
> (Trousdale 1982: 130–1)

But the method of rhetorical amplification prompts Sandys on: the story also 'exemplifies the sad success of clandestine loves, and neglected parents: to whom obediance is due'. In responding to a play, audiences in this way had the opportunity to choose from among interpretive possibilities according as 'a mans sense must direct him, when he considers how aptly such a thing [story, action] would fitt with an exercise [habit, behavior] of his', as a college student put it about his reading of ancient and modern authors in a commmonplace book about 1600 (Trousdale 1982: 147), and inevitably these choices of interpretation would have differed from playgoer to playgoer. Diversity would be most evident in post-performance responses, of course, but also in the theater during those moments of detachment from the action, helping to make the rhythm of engagement and detachment also one of unity and diversity of response, or, in the terms of Roland Barthes's *Writing Degree Zero*, of the reading and the writing of the text.

The longest set of extant responses to early modern English drama, Simon Forman's (1974b) accounts of four plays that he saw at the Globe Theatre in 1611 during his sixtieth and last year, do concern three of Shakespeare's plays, but strangely enough the most significant of Forman's accounts for understanding the pro-ductive and purposeful aspects of early modern response concerns the one play not by Shakespeare. This is partly because Forman had a strong personal reaction to a particular event in the non-Shakespearean play, and perhaps partly because Shakespeare's plays were more substantial than the scope of Forman's accounts could treat, so in their cases he stuck mainly to summary of their plots, which evidently fascinated him. But even here Forman's interest, at least in the case of *Macbeth*, was not entirely focused on the play itself as an object of contemplation, but on the whole matrix of discourse about the historical Macbeth (Scragg 1973).

Forman was a London astrologer and unlicensed doctor hounded intermittently by the London College of Physicians whose clients included aristocracy as well as theater people, and even the Master of Revels, Lord Hunsdon. He liked the theater, went abroad in purple velvet and was notorious about London as a magician, having within the past two years been satirically mentioned in both *The Alchemist* and *Epicoene*. If the accounts of this consummately theatrical personage really show no 'evidence of any particular critical insight into the drama' (Cerasano 1993: 158) and 'no consciousness of possible divisions [of response, i.e. diversity of response] within the audience' (Gurr 1993: 16) as historians have concluded, we may readily despair of any other accounts doing so. The foregoing characterization of early modern response will help us locate Forman's insights, singularity, and representativeness. Forman's response is purposeful and productive of value for him, and suggests how ordinary playgoers could shape significance and ultimately the plays themselves.

Forman is an example of a playgoer who seeks and finds connections between his own life and the theater. Playgoing was part of his social world, an opportunity for many assignations with women (Cerasano 1993: 150). He was particularly interested in plays featuring specialties of his own, prognostication, magic, and medicine: in 1611 at the Globe these were *Macbeth* with its prophecies and, according to Forman, its note-taking doctor (Forman the practitioner took copious notes), *Cymbeline* with its 'sleeping Dram' that imitates death (Forman 1974b: 1842; all references are to this page), *The Winter's Tale* with its oracle and magical revival, and a lost play concerning Richard II with its seer predicting Bolingbroke's kingship. Forman's accounts also exemplify the notebook practice of recording useful material gleaned from plays. In his case this was not so much moral instruction as practical or prudential lessons about getting along in the world. 'Watch your back' typifies the kind of instruction Forman extracted, shrewd and defensive lessons that fitted his suspicious nature.

One remark in Forman's 'Bocke of Plaies' above all expresses a strong critical judgment directly related to Forman's identity and experience. It is found in his account of the play on Richard II and concerns his emphatic and defiant reaction to John of Gaunt's murder of the seer who prophesied that his son would be king: 'This was a pollicie in the common wealthes opinion. But I sai yt was a villaines parte and a Iudas kisse to hange the man. for telling him the truth.' The personal side is especially clear here: offense at the murder of a fellow oracle. Forman himself had been jailed several times during the 1590s for practicing astrology without a license. But at the same time he is also raising a *bona fide* critical issue in the evaluation of character: how should the Gaunt of this play (the Duke of Lancaster) be assessed? Is he admirably prudent, as he is for instance in Shakespeare's *Richard II*, selfish and cold, or what? This is the kind of issue Shakespeare deliberately embeds in his characters, from Prince Hal to Duke Vincentio. Forman's conclusion, that the Duke was playing 'a villain's part', also touches on dramatic structure. It is not clear whether by the 'common wealth' who approved of the murder Forman means other playgoers with divergent views or characters in the play, but it is clear that Forman would insist on his own particular interpretation about this matter whatever those of others might be, and that he considers disagreement a distinct possibility. His comment thus illustrates the active manner in which early modern playgoers could discover meaning that had a particular relevance to their own lives, as well as diverse response on an interpretive issue.

Actually, Forman's entire account of the lost play on Richard II offers a coherent thematic interpretation, though its interpretation is aimed toward practical application, not analysis of an aesthetic artifact, just as one would expect. For Forman, the dramatic conflicts in the play are fomented by self-serving deceivers in positions of power, including King Richard himself. The maxim of common policy he draws from the seer's murder by the duke concludes the account of the play and in effect sums it up: 'Beware by this Example of noble men/and of their fair wordes & sai lyttel to them, lest they doe the Like by thee for thy good will.'

Forman's anti-aristocratic response to this play contrasts with the emphasis of Heywood's *Apology*, published in the same year. It recalls the well-worn question of the degree to which early modern plays could subvert hegemonic power. This spectator hardly takes a monarch's viewpoint of this King's Men's play. In this case his sympathies are not engaged by the sufferings of the mighty as are those of the author of 'On Worthy Master Shakespeare'; rather, his subject position is aligned with that of their potential victims. This includes not only the seer but the plebeian rebel Jack Straw, whom Forman faults only for his naïveté, and from whose failure he even draws a cautionary precept of common policy. Forman's response does not rise to the level of abstract class analysis or critique of contemporary society as Brecht might have hoped, but it does register a certain disgusted alienation from the world of the play, one which finds concrete and direct application in Forman's England and in his own performance of life.

Forman spent a year at Oxford, but his formal education was slight. He was 11 when his father died and he was forced to become an apprentice for a shopkeeper (Forman 1974a: 271). His points of common policy are not appeals to a timeless body of scholarly wisdom, but personal opinions framed in his own idiom. Perhaps the form as well as the social viewpoint of these opinions exemplify others from playgoers with modest education and social rank. At any rate, reading Forman's 'Bocke of Plaies' illustrates basic features about early modern audience response: the lack of aesthetic disinterest, the improvisatory emphasis not on what the play means but on what playgoers can discover from the play and how they can profit from it, diversity of taste and response that can be connected to habitus, and the theater's ability not only to dispense and control meaning, but also to disseminate it productively.

Briefer comments by other playgoers underscore the importance of these features. Plays or sundry other practices regularly carried on in the theater are found to be productive and to catalyze performances. 'Every mechanical mate', complained Nashe in 1589, 'abhors the English he was borne to', preferring 'servile imitations of vainglorious Tragedians' and their 'bragging blank verse' (Nashe 1966: vol. 3, 311). For law student Henry Fitzgeffrey, the types of self-fashioning playgoers provided a more entertaining spectacle than the plays – yet one that was similar (Fitzgeffrey 1617). Amelia Lanyer attributed a special power to the figure of Cleopatra, addressing her with great intimacy in her poem, as if finding in her a way to help define her values and identity. Cleopatra's devotion to sexual love becomes the significant counter-example to the life of religious devotion Lanyer and her patron pursue, a new life that followed Lanyer's own compromising erotic experiences (Lanyer 1993: 59–60, 111–13). Bedridden Joan Drake's improvised defense against the tiresome exhortations of a visiting minister was to liken him to one of Jonson's Puritan butts in *The Alchemist* (Pritchard 1994). James Shirley's praise of Beaumont and Fletcher focuses on their educative usefulness for the 'hopeful young heir' and 'discoursing dining wits' (Beaumont and Fletcher 1905: vol. 1, xi). Ex-sailor's apprentice Richard Norwood found that his addictive 1612 visits to the Fortune Theatre distracted him totally from his study of mathematics and navigation and stimulated him to try writing his own play. Because they powerfully drew him toward a range of worldly desires and occupations, he later blamed plays for helping to turn him against God (Norwood 1945: 42–3). And that avid playgoer Lord Hamlet formulates the *Mousetrap* while brooding on the relevance to his own predicament of the First Player's dramatic recitation. The *Mousetrap* itself depends on Claudius's own idiopathic response.

Two factualistic poems exemplify a particularly rich area of conjunction of stage and world, how Shakespeare's plays affected love-making and the construction of desire. The theaters both staged love and provided opportunity for amorous encounters among play-goers – in the anonymous Cambridge play *1 The Return from Parnassus* (1600), for instance, Gullio's conversation is a patchwork of Shakespeare because he has reinvented himself as a real-life surro-gate of a Shakespearean lover (Greenblatt 1997: 3325–6). Anthony Scolokar in his 1604 mock-epic *Daiphantus* seems to have imitated Hamlet's serio-comic performance of madness as a cathartic means of overcoming melancholy and gaining perspective on a failed love relationship. Robert Tofte's Petrarchan love-sonnet sequence *Alba* (1598) carries a good deal of factuality; in one poem its speaker is dragged to *Love's Labor's Lost* by his beloved, apparently discovers in the play desperate lovers like himself and takes hope his beloved will therefore take pity on him, then realizes the play is actually making fun of such lovers, goes into a funk, and is subsequently rejected by his disgusted companion. 'This Play no Play, but Plague was vnto me, For ther I lost the Loue I liked most' (Tofte 1994: 175). A further implication here is that Shakespeare's comedies may have articulated the interests of women caught up in Petrarchan rituals, and could actually intervene to their advantage, just as with *As You Like It* Shakespeare seems to address women's experience of love (Dusinberre 1994).

Such responses show how plays were productive, answering audiences' purposes diversely and actuating behavior and identity. Early modern playgoers had the ability to shape diverse responses from plays that, as commercial products and as sites of popular authority, disseminated meaning liberally and variably. This kind of authority suggests an answer to the question broached at the beginning of this chapter about the role of the audience in shaping early modern drama. Audiences may have influenced dramatists to write diacritically, that is, such that their plays encouraged or at least accommodated differential response, opening themselves to appropriation and contingency. By a diacritical work I mean one that accommodates multiple implied readers, audience segments, or subject positions, either to tailor one complex meaning or effect differentially, or to enable the reception of different meanings or effects by different audience segments. Such a work would allow individuals and groups to find their own interests and concerns challenged or supported as it attempts to accommodate and even stimulate divergent response. In a rhetorical age, meeting the diacritical necessity to cater to a many-headed and unpredictable public monster lent power and depth to plays.

The emphasis on identifying a unitarian response for early modern audiences has the effect, especially in the case of Shakespeare the 'multiconscious' and 'myriad-minded' writer, of loading the fully adequate playgoer with the task of apprehending a vortex of ambivalences that surrounds contradictory characters like Shylock or Henry V, preventing the attainment of a definite conclusion about them, and prompting the embrace of ambiguity, uncertainty, or compromise. This state of arrest defines a kind of proto-modern aesthetic wisdom. It is worth asking, though, whether the emphasis originally was not rather on accommodating more diverse and more partial responses – an emphasis explored by Burnett (1997) and Findlay (1999), among others – and has become shifted with the rise of modern aesthetic orientations toward analytic elaboration of all-inclusive significances.

Let us glance at the case of *Romeo and Juliet*. The play offers different perspectives on Petrarchan love passion and the duty of children. Sandys's copious treatment of the Pyramus and Thisbe story (quoted above), which finds it offering support for both eloping offspring and for match-making parents, provides an example showing how the play could provoke contradictory interpretations. But according to a unitarian thesis, response should ideally rise to become a rigorous appreciation of Shakespeare's sublimely inclusive vision, an appreciation of all the mutual qualifications that warn playgoers not to come to any simple conclusions about what does happen to be a major issue on the cultural agenda in 1596, the prerogative of parents versus the demands of Petrarchan love. The ideal playgoer can be imagined here in a state not dissimilar to aesthetic disinterest. According to the diacritical thesis, the play empowers rather than dissuades, by making available a range of more partial and more vigorous receptions to different audience segments. Surely the play provides a sense that particular judgments are subject to qualification by others, but there is also an emphasis on supplying grounds for a variety of affirmations of particular viewpoints toward the lovers and their parents. This would occur in something like the way a writer using the method of amplification to invent matter would then select from that matter to frame some particular argument.

Or so it seems to have happened. Robert Burton, in the second (1624) edition of *The Anatomy of Melancholy*, offers a distinctively anti-romantic reading, appropriating these lines from the prologue to help support his argument that love melancholy and madness lead to destruction and death: 'Who ever heard a story of more woe, Then that of *Juliet* and her *Romeo*' (Burton 1989–94: vol. 3, 199). But a few years earlier a fellow Oxford divine, one Mr. Richardson, minister of St. Mary's Church in Magdalene College, devised a very different application. In sermons of 1620 and 1621 he quoted from Shakespeare, comparing Juliet's care that Romeo leave her before morning discovers him to 'God's loue to his Saints either hurt with sinne, or aduersity[,] neuer forsaking them' (Munro 1932: vol. 1, 279 [Bodleian MS. eng. misc. d. 28, p. 359, col. 705]). By allegorizing their carnal love as God's love for his saints, Richardson takes a much more respectful and affectionate view of the pair's love than Burton (though, interestingly, both view the love as an absolute force). It is true that in the phrase 'either hurt with sinne, or aduersity' Richardson hesitates a bit in his degree of admiration. It might be said that this is because the question of whether the lovers are blameworthy or simply star-crossed is rendered sublimely undecidable in the play, and that is surely a valid position; the diacritical perspective would add that the play also licenses a choice between sin and adversity in its judgment of the lovers, and that in his sermon perhaps the preacher was hedging so as to maintain solidarity with the devotes of stage love he was trying to reach, a segment of the congregation who might have made a firm decision against the sinful reading. Perhaps *Romeo and Juliet* figured in a wider debate about love at Oxford in the 1620s.

The early modern audience was an unprecedented and diverse public engaged with subjects of wide significance, and hence important in the history of modernity. The evidence suggests that this audience entertained and helped create the theater's shaping fantasies. Its pluralistic dimensions may be relevant to some of the many important manifestations of pluralism today, and its theatrical transactions might be fruitfully compared or contrasted to the circulation of language, feeling, and identity between today's producers and consumers of mass entertainment (Fiske 1987), especially given the mixture of high and low and the skeptical and pragmatic forms of (post-)modernity current in both eras (Blumenberg 1983; Toulmin 1990). The deep appreciation of *Romeo and Juliet* expressed by Mr. Richardson underscores the relevance of modern aesthetics to early modern drama and the double meaning of 'ante-' as 'anticipatory' as well as 'prior'. The uses of art, or the relation of aesthetic experience to the life-world, is a major issue in studies of modernity and in postmodern criticism (Horkheimer and Adorno 1972; Foster 1983; Barthes 1975; Danto 1986): the ante-aesthetic, rhetorical, and complexly theatrical and performative character of early modern dramatic transactions may offer a valuable perspective, and vice versa. Concepts of performance, improvisation, and surrogation help us understand the social construction of race, gender, and subjectivity today (Roach 1996); the early modern theater audience seems to have widely explored such conjunctions between stage and world.

## Notes

1  Cook (1981); Cook also emphasizes diversity of interest and outlook in early modern theater audiences, but locates much of it within her broadly defined category of the 'privileged'.
2  Gurr (1996) provides the indispensable guide to audiences in this period, making it possible to address questions such as the present one.
3  On the distinction between life and art see Foucault (1970: 17–77).

# 4

# Shakespeare, modernity and the aesthetic

## Art, truth and judgement in *The Winter's Tale*

### JOHN J. JOUGHIN

Any discussion of the literary or artistic merit of Shakespeare's plays is almost bound to arouse suspicion. For most radical critics, aesthetics still tends to be discarded as part of the 'problem' rather than part of the 'solution', all too reminiscent of a brand of outdated idealism which privileged notions of refined sensibility and the immutability of 'literary value'. As a consequence, contemporary political and historicist criticism has tended to regard a 'commitment to the literary' as 'one of the major limitations' of traditionalist approaches to the playwright's work (Hawkes 1996b: 11). Yet more recently, the emergence in a British context of a critical formation, sometimes pejoratively labelled 'new aestheticist' in its orientation, has foregrounded the need to give some further consideration to the transformative potential of the aesthetic.

In the course of resituating some of the assumptions of post-structuralist thought in relation to the philosophical analysis of modernity offered by the Frankfurt School tradition of Critical Theory, philosophers like Jay Bernstein (1992), Andrew Bowie (1990; 1997a), Howard Caygill (1989) and Peter Dews (1987; 1995) have enabled a reconsideration of key issues concerning aesthetic validity which were often neglected in the first stage development of literary theory.[1] I want to argue that this work has also indirectly paved the way to the revival of the aesthetic as a politically critical category in English studies. Rather than ceding the question of aesthetic value as the exclusive preserve of the political Right, this chapter aims to demonstrate that the time is now ripe for a re-examination of the idea of the aesthetic in materialist criticism.

Of course the danger of a return to an old-style aestheticism in Shakespeare studies remains a constant threat, as Harold Bloom's (1999) celebration of 'Shakespeare's universalism' testifies. Bloom complains that, in relying on 'ideologically imposed contextualization', recent critical approaches like cultural materialism and new historicism tend to 'value theory over the literature itself'. For these critics, Bloom reflects sadly, 'the aesthetic stance is itself an ideology' (Bloom 1999: 9). But in some sense, even as he is prone to overstate the case, Bloom is partly right. Cultural materialism usefully draws our attention to the fact that the question of aesthetic value is a politically loaded issue and not a neutral one. Yet while the deployment of Shakespeare is clearly open to 'ideological misuse', surely Bloom also has a point when he implies that the endurance of Shakespeare's texts cannot be reduced solely to the question of their ideological function in any given period.

Nor, I might add (and this is where Bloom partly misses the point himself), is this necessarily a position which recent critical approaches would wholly resist: after all, as the bulk of recent work on the cultural production and reception of Shakespeare's plays has demonstrated, historically speaking at least, the striking thing about the playwright's texts is their continued refusal to be exhausted by their continued appropriation and counter-appropriation in an endless variety of contexts (see e.g. G. Taylor 1991; Marsden 1991). This is not to say that the playwright's work is somehow of 'timeless' significance, nor is it to deny the value of work which has revealed the playwright's involvement in securing regimes which have deployed Shakespeare for their own oppressive ideological ends. There can be no doubt that the revival of certain plays, at specific moments, in particular contexts, usefully alerts us to the manipulation of Shakespeare as an instrument of social control. Yet the enduring longevity of the dramatist's work is also clearly related to its ability to sustain interpretations which are often contestable or diametrically opposed. Cultural materialism allows for precisely this type of contestation, yet as Andrew Bowie observes:

> the failure [of radical criticism] to engage with the most powerful works of bourgeois culture . . . beyond revealing their indisput-

able relations to barbarism, means we do not understand why such works are enduringly powerful in ways which cannot finally be grasped by the category of ideology and which cannot be merely a function of their roots in barbarism.

(Bowie 1997a: 7)

Bowie offers us a more nuanced and effective defence of the aesthetic than Bloom can possibly muster, yet his point also implicitly echoes Bloom's complaint, that one of the limitations of ideology critique is that it fails satisfactorily to explain why it is that, in most circumstances, even once they are demythologized or problematized, outside of their immediate ideological function, certain canonical texts like Shakespeare's continue to remain meaningful and authoritative.

For Bloom the 'ultimate use' of Shakespeare is in teaching us 'whatever truth you can sustain without perishing' (Bloom 1999: 10). Yet paradoxically, as I have already implied, it appears as if Shakespeare's very survival as a literary text is less a product of the type of meaningful repleteness Bloom alludes to than a result of its resistance to ever being clearly understood (cf. Bowie 1997a: 11). Moreover, as I hope to demonstrate, the question of Shakespeare's ireducibility to interpretation actually offers a fruitful resource for critical thought and has a direct bearing on our understanding of the relationship that obtains between *literary* interpretation and the question of *its* validity. In these and in other respects, an over-restrictively functionalist account of Shakespeare's involvement in sustaining the reductions and inequities of canon formation falls short of a more reflective acknowledgement that Shakespeare's 'literary' distinction is actually entwined with a more complex intellectual legacy: one which raises pressing philosophical as well as political questions. Again, Bowie puts the case still more succinctly, as he reminds us that:

The rise of 'literature' and the rise of philosophical aesthetics – of a new philosophical concern with understanding the nature of art – are inseparable phenomena, which are vitally connected to changes in conceptions of truth in modern thought.

(Bowie 1997a: 1)

Clearly, the specificity of literature's cognitive significance and the critical potential these 'literary' issues have in relation to canonical texts like Shakespeare is not something we can merely side-step or wish away. By way of developing Bowie's thesis, I want to argue for a reconceived understanding of the aesthetic in relation to Shakespeare's plays. The practical aspect of this argument will be to develop a reading of the closing scene of Shakespeare's *The Winter's Tale* (5.3), where I will be particularly concerned with unravelling the significance of the competing truth claims which surround Hermione's unlikely restoration at the end of the play. But the theoretical issues raised by Bowie also merit further consideration in their own right, and I will want to argue that they also have an explicit bearing upon our understanding of Shakespeare in its 'modern' context. In many ways, the 'changing conception of truth in modern thought' that Bowie alludes to goes to the very root of the formation of 'Eng. lit.' as a discipline and continues to sustain the claims to cognitive validity on which it continues to rely. While this 'modern' aesthetic distinction arguably post-dates the 'original' production of Shakespeare's texts, it nevertheless continues to mediate the tradition of Shakespeare's critical heritage in a powerfully influential fashion. A more critically nuanced and discriminative sense of the role that aesthetics plays in Shakespeare criticism reawakens a series of key issues concerning the broader consensual and regulative criteria which continue to govern our understanding of the plays themselves.

## A brief excursus on art and truth

Traditionalist viewpoints which uncritically endorse the 'superior validity' of Shakespeare's plays, to the exclusion of all other considerations, often claim that they are politically neutral. Excepting the qualifications I have outlined above, the major contribution of ideology critique in Shakespeare studies has been in unmasking this stance of polite disinterestedness, and in revealing the extent to which it effectively conceals a series of tendentious presumptions concerning the 'truth' of the human condition, the overall tenor of which Terence Hawkes helpfully summarizes in the following fashion:

> That, in short, Shakespeare's plays present us with nothing less than the truth, the whole truth and nothing but the truth about the most fundamental matters of human existence: birth, death and the life that comes between.

> (Hawkes 1996b: 9)

For all its self-evident transparency this 'common sense' view of literature actually secretes its own theoretical agenda, underpinning an approach to interpretation which Catherine Belsey helpfully characterizes as 'expressive realist' in its overall connotation:

> expressive realism . . . is the theory that literature reflects the *reality* of experience as it is perceived by one (especially gifted) individual, who *expresses* it in a discourse which enables other individuals to recognise it as true.
>
> (Belsey 1980: 7, Belsey's emphasis)

As Belsey argues, this apparently 'natural way of reading' actually presupposes a rather fixed understanding of the value of literary texts and their claim to authenticity.

Crucially, 'expressive realism' presumes a practice of reading literature which is founded on what philosophers would categorize as a *correspondence model of truth*. In other words, literature's relationship to the world is conceived in terms of a naive mimeticism which posits the truth of an anterior or predetermined ideal reality, of which literature is correspondingly a 'true' re-presentation. Furthermore, as Belsey's statement implies, empirical-idealist variants of lit. crit. locate their premise on the assumption that the origination, reception and knowledge of these 'truths' is generally accessible to experience and self-evident – although more so to some than others, and especially to the more refined sensibilities of 'high and solitary minds'. In effect, literary texts are treated as if they were physical phenomena whose very existence serves to verify clear and testable ideas. In the case of its neo-classical variants, literary criticism reimposes an understanding of art as corresponding with the pre-existent uniformity of nature itself.

As Belsey, Hawkes, and a host of other critics have demonstrated, recent developments in literary theory have revealed just how restrictive these 'rational' truth claims actually are. Materialist approaches to the plays demonstrate that the 'meaning' of a text is historically determined and is dependent on its cultural context. In turn, a poststructuralist critique of metaphysics has produced a healthy climate of hermeneutic suspicion, both in disclosing the complicity between truth, reason and domination, and in revealing language itself to be 'perpetually in process' and productive of a potential plurality of meanings (cf. Belsey 1980: 19–20). Yet, in taking an exclusively linguistic and culturalist turn, recent criticism also runs the risk of excluding from its consideration the distinctively qualitative aspects of literary meaning. In short, as Bowie observes, *literary* theorists are often effectively in danger of being 'without a valid way of talking about "literature"' (Bowie 1997a: 5). While poststructuralism usefully focuses on the reader's role in the constitution of meaning and allows for the possibility that texts are open to a number of interpretations, it tends to neglect the truth-potential of the particular transformation wrought by the aesthetic experience itself. For new aestheticists like Bowie, our understanding of the relationship between art, truth and interpretation is not merely dependent on an openness to the fact that literary texts transform meaning, but is also equally concerned with asking precisely *how* this revelation is to be construed (Bowie 1997a: 5). Understood in relation to more conventional truth claims, the distinctive articulation of truth in works of art – in being truer than empirical or mimetic 'truth' – underpins what Bowie terms a 'disclosive' literary distinction, which he characterizes in the following terms:

> rather than truth being the revelation of a pre-existing reality, it [art's truth status] is in fact a creative process of 'disclosure'. Artworks, in this view, reveal aspects of the world which would not emerge if there were no such disclosure: truth 'happens' – it does not imitate or represent.
>
> (Bowie 1992: 33)

Such moments could conceivably be construed purely in formal or 'linguistic terms', in relation to overturning conventional expectations or in breaking with existing rules. Yet the revelatory potential of aesthetic disclosure suggests that it also needs to be understood as a more participatory and consensual event, in the course of which, as Bowie puts it, in defamiliarizing habitual perceptions: 'something comes to be seen as something in a new way' (Bowie 1997a: 301).

Crucially, the relationship between the 'happening' of aesthetic disclosure and the interplay by which we understand it to 'be' a distinctively *literary* happening throws a new light on the question of interpretation and enables us to retain a sense of the creative and evaluative dimension which informs judgement (aesthetic or otherwise), without then merely lapsing back into the restrictions which obtain to the more traditionalist truth claims of essentialism or empiricism. Instead, in developing a Heideggerian sense of the disclosive capacity of the aesthetic (without wanting to restrict

'disclosure' to uncovering 'some kind of already present essence'),
Bowie persuasively locates 'seeing as' as a constitutive experience
which effectively: '"discloses" the world in new ways . . . rather
than copying or representing what is known to be already there'
(Bowie 1997a: 5, 301). I shall want to return to these distinctions
during my reading of *The Winter's Tale*.

## Art, truth and judgement in *The Winter's Tale*

For mainstream criticism much of the attendant moral outrage at
the apparent sundering of the link between art and truth in radical
criticism has tended to oscillate rather reductively between two
extreme polarities. On the one hand, traditionalist critics complain
that, if claims to knowledge are not grounded in a fixed or absolute way, but are endlessly contingent and uncertain, the lure of
epistemological relativism will ensure that a type of critical nihilism
will ensue as a result. In short, meaninglessness rather than mean-
ingfulness will be the order of the day. Somewhat contradictorily,
this accusation of critical relativism tends to chime intermittently
with the complaint of critical reductionism; so that, for Bloom,
recent approaches move in from the outside 'on the poor play'.
Radical critics are 'gender-and-power freaks' whose insidious act of
cultural imperialism is to 'shape Shakespeare' by imposing in
advance their own prescriptive brand of cultural politics (Bloom
1999: 9–10).

I have to say that my own experience of teaching Shakespeare is at
once more mundane and more revealing. For most students, on first
studying Shakespeare at university level, the empirical and essentialist truth claims underpinning traditionalist approaches to the
playwright's work are often already residually in place. These
assumptions are fairly easily overturned, yet even while students
are willing to take a more relativistic view of Shakespeare's plays,
they are still drawn back to the assertion that Shakespeare's texts
are somehow qualitatively distinctive. There is a resistance to the
cultural reductionism which Bloom caricatures as the pedagogical
norm, though, as yet, there is often a lack of a developed critical
lexicon by which to explore the issue of literary value. As a result,
students often 'cope' with the singularity of the Shakespeare text in
a rather vague and unsituated fashion.[2]

In practice, the closing scene of Shakespeare's *The Winter's Tale*
tends to operate as a type of critical degree zero for locating some of

these issues in a more critical context. In its eloquent silence and unfathomable recovery, the puzzle of Hermione's restoration at the end of the play immediately invites idealization, and often does so precisely in terms of those old-style critical unities which would endorse a sense of the literary artefact as the source of some unsullied or immanent value. As she steps down from her pedestal, somewhere between automaton and living being, the 'resurrection' of Hermione has tended to double as a *tableau vivant* for Shakespearicity itself – that impossible thing, 'a living monument'. Yet, crucially of course, Hermione's unlikely transformation during the scene in question remains 'meaningful', only insofar as she is *not* restored to what she once was. Leontes is quick enough to point this out for himself on first seeing the statue:

> But yet, Paulina,
> Hermione was not so much wrinkled, nothing
> So aged as this seems.
>
> (5.3.27–9)

Almost by default, Leontes' momentary regret here indirectly confirms the essentialist-type error that he had already implicitly committed moments earlier when, indulging in a kind of wish-fulfilment, on first seeing his daughter Perdita, he is immediately reminded of his wife – 'I thought of her/Even in these looks I made' (5.1.226–7) – and against which the shrewd counsellor Paulina anticipates a sharp reproof (cf. 5.1.223–5).

It is precisely because of these and other 'inconsistencies' that the statue scene is the one episode in the whole of Shakespeare which in confounding expectations simultaneously throws a 'common sense' understanding of the relationship between art and 'truth' into sharp relief. In my experience of teaching the play, the provocation presented by the scene's manifest improbability immediately tempts students to restrict matters to the 'status quo' of empiricism. On paying closer attention to the text, they insist that it is clear that 'She didn't really die' – their case often unwittingly hinging on the probability or otherwise of (that old critical chestnut), Hermione's 'voluntary concealment' (5.3.126–9). Yet curiously, as the discussion proceeds, it is clear that Hermione's recovery is not explicable in these 'evidentiary' terms: after all, the point remains that even if we were to judge matters in terms of the most restrictive truth-only criteria, earlier on, at least, the play is certain enough about the 'fact' of Hermione's death (cf. 3.2.201–5, 232–4; 3.3.15–18).[3]

My point, of course, is that the statue scene remains meaningful while also flouting most of our conventional criteria for understanding. And for this reason, a brief flick through the play's 'critical heritage' is enough to confirm the students' intuition that the question of Hermione's restoration constitutes the key interpretative dilemma of the play, as, from Dryden onwards, the critical consensus consistently maintains that *The Winter's Tale* is, in effect, 'grounded on impossibilities' (Vickers 1995, vol. 1: 145). We might say that Hermione's unforeseen recovery unwittingly confirms the unsettling effect of a meaningful temporal dis-continuity. Nor, of course, is this the first instance in the play when the audience is suddenly alerted to the transformative potential of a dramatic recontextualization. Earlier on, at a related moment of incongruity, Time's interpolation (4.1) itself ensures that the action 'slide(s)/O'er sixteen years' (4.1.5–6). Each episode produces a conjunctural clash of past and present which, in remaining resistant to interpretation, has remained critically significant ever since.[4]

These improbabilities and temporal dislocations have clearly served to focus issues relating to the validity of past interpretations of the play; yet coming to a more reflective understanding of the particular transformation wrought by Hermione's restoration, depends precisely on *how* we address the question of its 'meaning'. As I have already implied, it is pointless to somehow try to 'fix' the meaning of the statue scene, either by attempting to pluck out the kernel of its 'truth', or by skewing the 'evidence' so that it somehow fits with our quest for certain knowledge. Each of these moves produces an over-reductively schematic and distortedly unified account of particular events.

Interestingly of course, it was precisely this type of *mis*judgement which ensured that Leontes remained such a bad judge during the early stages of the play, where, plagued by certainty, and in his determination to prove truths irrefutably, he quickly emerges as an early prototype of the dogmatic 'systems thinker' whom Theodor Adorno has in mind as he outlines 'Idealism as Rage' in *Negative Dialectics* (1990):

The system in which the sovereign mind imagined itself transfigured, has its primal history in the pre-mental, the animal life of the species . . . The more completely his actions [the 'rational animal's'] follow the law of self-preservation, the less can he admit the primacy of that law to himself and others . . . The system is the belly turned mind, and rage is the mark of each and every idealism.

(Adorno 1990: 22–3)

The 'belly turned mind' would serve as a more than adequate description of the destructive yet ravenous incorporative rage which Leontes exemplifies in the totalitarian state that was the first half of the play. Leontes' behaviour here is typical of the type of 'identity-thinking' which, in its 'progressive' domination of nature, would reduce all particulars to conceptual generalization and ensures that in a 'systematized' post-Enlightenment society, 'the sublimation of this anthropological schema extends all the way to epistemology' (Adorno 1990: 22). Jay Bernstein (1991) offers a useful clarification of this aspect of Adorno's critique of 'enlightened' reason:

[S]uch a rationality must treat unlike (unequal) things as like (equal), and subsume objects under (the unreflective drives of) subjects. Subsumption, then, is domination in the conceptual realm. The purpose of subsumption is to allow for conceptual and technical mastery. When subsumptive rationality came to be considered the whole of reason . . . the ends for the sake of which the path of enlightened rationality was undertaken became occluded. Without the possibility of judging particulars and rationally considering ends and goals, the reason which was to be the means to satisfying human ends becomes its own end, and thereby turns against the true aims of Enlightenment: freedom and happiness.

(Bernstein 1991: 4)

For Adorno then, instrumental reason (reason which effectively becomes a means to its own end) excludes the 'cognition of the particular in its own right' (cf. Bernstein 1991: 4). Any interpretative paradigm which is governed by these assumptions tends to fix the meaning 'which already lies behind the question' (Adorno 1977: 127), so that, as Adorno himself puts it: 'The things philosophy has yet to judge are postulated before it begins' (Adorno 1990: 24).[5]

Yet, in contrast, during the statue scene, Leontes' habitual tendency to foreclose on his interpretative options in advance undergoes an abrupt and remarkable transformation. Suddenly his capacity for 'judgment' confirms itself as a newly dynamic and creative process, which involves an open-ended awareness of participating in the sensuous particularity of the 'truths' that are unfolding before him. The experience of suffering Hermione's restoration opens out on to a series of qualitative distinctions which, fittingly enough (for Leontes at least), proceed to constellate themselves around the metaphor of ingestion itself, the expression of which is now freshly modulated and comparative: 'this affliction has a taste *as* sweet / *As* any cordial comfort' (5.3.76–7), 'let it be art / Lawful *as* eating' (5.3.110–11, my emphases). In terms of the reflective capacity of judgement we broached earlier on, this productive ability to 'see more in things than they are' constitutes what Adorno terms 'aesthetic behaviour':

> Aesthetic behaviour is the ability to see more in things than they are. It is the gaze that transforms empirical being into imagery. The empirical world has no trouble exposing the inadequacy of aesthetic behaviour, and yet it is aesthetic behaviour alone which is able to experience that world.
>
> (Adorno 1984: 453)

Like the reconciliation scene which precedes it, Hermione's restoration proceeds largely in silence; and as 'a sight which was to be / seen, cannot be spoken of' (5.2.38–9), its 'world-disclosing' capacity cannot be reduced to paraphrase, as art itself 'renders reality visible':[6]

> *Paulina:*                              That she is living,
>              Were it but told you, should be hooted at
>              Like an old tale. But it appears she lives,
>              Though yet she speak not. Mark a little while.
>                                              (5.3.116–19)

Beyond any correspondent sense of a 'true' representation, in Bowie's terms 'something comes to be seen as something in a new way' during the statue scene. That which 'appears' as true cannot be proven to be true: 'truth "happens" – it does not imitate or represent' (Bowie 1990: 5; 1992: 33). Indeed, during the process of Hermione's 'recovery' *disclosure* appears as still more complex and overdetermined precisely in ways that place an emphasis on the non-representational rather than the formally coherent, or mimetic aspects of art. Music, silence, and most decisively of all of course, ruination itself, are very much to the fore, as, beyond mere recovery, 'existing meanings are most decisively transformed . . . to the point of the *destruction* of those meanings'(cf. Bowie on Adorno: Bowie 1997a: 25, Bowie's emphasis) – or as Leontes himself has it: 'Hermione was not so much wrinkled'.

In short, it is precisely because Hermione's restoration is 'newly fixed' (5.3.48) that it undoes attempts to unify meaning. The key to understanding aesthetic judgement in the statue scene then is to see that it proceeds on uncertain grounds, or 'begins in the middle' so to speak (cf. Bowie 1997a: 104–6). It is certainly *not* the unifyingly fulfilling or unreflectively transcendental category of the aesthetic caricatured and maligned by so much early 'radical' cultural criticism.

## Shakespeare, modernity and the aesthetic

In order to develop the significance of the distinctions I have raised so far, I want to move on now to consider the relation of Shakespeare to the aesthetic in its 'modern' context. As I hope my brief analysis of *The Winter's Tale* has demonstrated, the statue scene discloses the potential to constitute new meanings which, in their refusal to submit to existing rules, are 'self-validating' in their own right. In its modern form, this independent truth potential of art to 'give the law to itself' is often discussed in terms of the notion of 'aesthetic autonomy'(Bowie 1992: 33–7).

Doubtless, for many, the very idea of aesthetic autonomy risks contamination by the residual idealism of 'Eng. lit.', insofar as it tends to evoke ideas concerning the ahistorical fixity and 'autotelic' self-sufficiency of the 'text in itself' – an outmoded approach to the question of aesthetic validity which was favoured by the old New Critics and others, but which was effectively overturned by the first-wave theorization of Shakespeare studies (see e.g. Barker and Hulme 1985: 192). Yet literature's becoming merely self-sufficient or, as poststructuralists might prefer its 'lack of a referent', actually serves only to underpin its historical and political significance within modernity. In the course of breaking its ties with tradition, it is precisely because literature is forced back on its 'own' resources that, in its autonomous 'exceeding moment', it provides new means of expression and accommodates the creative potential for new forms of social cognition, not least around the related question of subjectivity.[7] This proto-political potential of the aesthetic to unleash 'unrealized possibilities' for 'human emancipation' is of particular importance to Marxist theorists of the Frankfurt School of Critical Theory, and is linked in complex fashion to their critique of the more dominative aspects of enlightened modernity (cf. Bowie 1997a: 14–15). In its qualitative independence, autonomous art resists subsumption within the instrumentalist logic of capital production and offers an enclave for the articulation of alternative values. In this form, aesthetics is not a rejection of reason; indeed, as Andrew Bowie observes: 'it becomes the location in which what has been repressed by a limited conception of reason can be articulated' (Bowie 1990: 4). The appearance of a separate aesthetic domain during the eighteenth century proceeds to provide a compensatory site for the evaluation of our experience of those sensuous particulars, which are now also increasingly denied to us in our newly 'alienated' modern condition. And in this respect, the survival of canonical texts like Shakespeare continue to confirm their significance in manifesting the potential to play a crucial role in reconfiguring our understanding of modern society. Tied to actuality, in ways that cannot be reduced to the empirical, the emergence of literature serves as a type of 'non-empirical record', which allows for the creation of 'possible-worlds' (Bowie 1997a: 16–27) beyond but also within the regulated sphere of its 'new' bourgeois confinement.

Coinciding as it does with the emergence of what Habermas (1992) would term the public sphere, the ground-breaking utopian potential of art to 'move beyond the world of what there is to a world of as yet unrealised possibility' (Bowie 1997a: 14) has theoretical as well as practical implications. In the context of an enlightened modernity, aesthetic discourse provides new concepts and tools of analysis with which to challenge existing conceptual frameworks. In this respect, just as the modern division between distinct spheres of 'knowledge' itself becomes increasingly restrictive and specialized, the 'intellectual' pursuits of art and literature also begin to have potentially far reaching effects.[8]

Yet crucially of course, the relegatory shift of art to the relative exclusivity of an autonomous realm (within which the assimilation of Shakespeare is evidently implicated at a very early stage) also, in the same process, proceeds to produce a formative practical dilemma for literary criticism. On the one hand aesthetic autonomy ensures art's significance as a potentially transgressive or 'critical' location. On the other hand art's 'untheorizable excess' also promotes suspicion, insofar as the distinctiveness of art's newly autonomous 'self-regulating' truth claim is perceived to present an alternative to those restrictive notions of empirical truth which continue to govern neo-classical literary criticism itself in its early emergence, and against which contemporary literary theorists have so consistently railed.[9]

As the early antecedents of aesthetic theory and literary criticism become increasingly 'institutionalized', the relation of literature to the criticism which attempts to explain or understand it serves to sustain literature's claim to validity. Yet, paradoxically, as I have already suggested, it is only because Shakespeare evades any finite sense of conceptual determination that, in resisting appropriation and in stirring debate, the playwright's work continues to offer us such a valuable resource for critical thought. This distinctive 'excessive' quality is clearly at the heart of canon formation itself, so that, as Bowie observes: 'texts which retain a productive ambiguity in thoroughly different contexts over long periods seem to be those to which the name literature is now often attached' (Bowie 1997a: 7). Yet the categorical separation of 'artistic truth' from other kinds of philosophical truth in modernity has also necessarily proceeded to haunt the convergence of a secularized literature and its criticism ever since. Bernstein formulates the dilemma in the following theoretical terms:

> If art is taken as lying outside of truth and reason then if art speaks in its own voice it does not speak truthfully or rationally; while if one defends art from within the confines of the language of truth-only cognition one belies the claim that art is more truthful than that truth-only cognition.
>
> (Bernstein 1992: 2)

In a nutshell then, the problem, as David Wood incisively puts it, is that: 'poetic discourse may be able to say what philosophy can know it cannot' (Wood 1990: 2). In this sense of course, the very notion of 'aesthetic theory' is something of a contradiction in terms. Indeed, as more than one commentator has suggested, the title of

Adorno's last major unfinished work *Aesthetic Theory* itself implicitly constitutes its own form of ironical epitaph, in that, as Adorno himself observes: 'What is called philosophy of art usually lacks one of two things: either the philosophy or the art' (Adorno 1984: 498; also see Zuidervaart 1991: 3). It is in confronting this situation that, as Bernstein argues, more recent 'post-aestheticist' philosophies of art like Adorno's actually take art's critical potential seriously by 'employ[ing] art to challenge truth-only cognition', while also facing the dilemma that 'philosophy cannot say what is true without abandoning itself to that which it would criticise' (Bernstein 1992: 4–9).

It is possible to extend the significance of the implications of Bernstein's thesis on the critical potential of art in terms of its related impact on recent trends within cultural criticism and literary theory. Key paradigm shifts in contemporary variants of Shakespearean criticism are clearly themselves indirectly reliant on the transformative cognitive potential of the aesthetic. Consider, for example, the 'disclosive' aspects of new historicism's more general recontextualization of anecdotal material, drawn from a variety of non-literary contexts and freshly deployed in 'illuminating' re-readings of canonical texts. These and other interpretative procedures produce precisely the type of unsettling interpretative ambiguities which Russian Formalists, at least, would have still recognized as 'literary' (cf. Bowie 1997a: 4–13). Yet while ambiguous faultlines, ruptures, fissures, crises in representation and so on, litter the corpus of cultural criticism, and frequently provide the foci for its activity, there is often an overall lack of any reflective engagement concerning the cognitive implications of such excesses, or, indeed, concerning the relationship between such moments of 'textual excess' and the emancipatory politics they implicitly promise as a payload (also see Middleton 1998: 152). The disclosive power of the aesthetic has implicitly enabled cultural critics to open up 'a world which was hidden by existing forms of articulation' (Bowie 1992: 36), yet crucially, in its attempt to break with the prescriptive 'truth-only' formality of traditional 'Eng. lit.', this reconciliatory impulse still necessarily 'hibernates' only within the confines of the very metaphysical hierarchy it would seek to overcome (see Bernstein 1992: 9). It follows that literary criticism is necessarily caught in a double bind of its own making, insofar as its relative 'freedom' and the autonomous truth potential which sustains its critique are wholly dependent on the rigid categorical distinctions which simultaneously 'prohibit the fulfilment' of its goals (cf. Bernstein 1992: 1–7). Viewed in this light, the newer formations of cultural criticism in literary studies could be viewed as 'post-aestheticist' in Bernstein's sense of the term: that is to say, not merely in the weaker sense of having broken with a reductive notion of aesthetic value or in 'being' postmodern anti-aestheticisms – but also in the potentially stronger sense that cultural criticism continues to deploy the cognitive import of the truth potential of the aesthetic against its own implication in disciplinary division, but has not itself always faced up to the divisive implications of its own interpretative procedures. The particular lure (and simultaneous frustration) of institutionally central or canonical texts like Shakespeare's is that they accommodate a form of critical displacement which is valid and 'meaningful' only insofar as they tend to accentuate the very institutional limits that continue to make critique possible, but which then also deny its realization as a meaningful form of political praxis. Indeed, when it is conceived within, as well as against, the oppressive constraints of the instrumental rationality of which it is part, the 'meaning' of 'dissidence', in its very displacement, might actually serve to symptomatize 'the absence of a truly political domain' (see Bernstein 1992: 3). A position which has been inadvertently confirmed and consolidated during the recent past as, since the 1960s or so, the rising stock of non-traditional cultural critique within the academy has actually expanded at an inversely proportional rate to its ability to intervene against, let alone stem or prevent, the ravages of capital's advance in what remains of the public realm.

Here, as elsewhere, it is apparent that the 'fate' of art in modernity is that, inasmuch as it remains 'critical', then as Bernstein argues, it necessarily continues to 'suffer' its alienation, either as a form of betrayal or 'bereavement'. As a result, even for those who would refute nostalgia, each critical act is inevitably, in some sense, a displaced form of memorial. In short, cultural criticism becomes an act of testimony or remembrance, or as Bernstein puts it:

> every conception of the alienation of art from truth is simultaneously a work of remembrance, a work of mourning and grief, even for those philosophers who doubt that such an 'original' state of union ever existed. In modernity beauty is not only alienated from truth, but grieves its loss; modernity is the site of beauty bereaved – bereaved of truth.
>
> (Bernstein 1992: 4)

In this sense, as Bernstein's comments serve to suggest, our reliance on the thwarted aesthetic potential of Renaissance or early modern texts might actually be reconstrued as a conventionally 'modern' predicament. If there were time to do so here, alongside new historicism's ill-fated desire to speak with the dead, it would be tempting to survey the melancholic *fort-da* game that cultural materialism has enacted in its continued allegorization of a lost 'corpus' or body of truth in Renaissance 'literature'. From the initial intensity of its disavowal of the organic community of Tillyard onwards, in its encounter with Renaissance texts, cultural materialism enacts a type of 'memorial aesthetics' which centres on representations of dead bodies or on images of their dismemberment.[10] Yet it seems to me, that the issue of memorial surfaces as the key conceptual register for Renaissance criticism in recent years *only* insofar as it begins to function in its very displacement as a 'sign of modernity' (see Bernstein 1992: 4). And to this extent, our need to 'remember' is also an indirect symptom of a failure to come to terms with what Bernstein rightly identifies as the 'discordance' between art and truth in a modern secular society.

## Shakespeare and de-traditionalization

Modernity, as Adorno reminds us, is 'a qualitative, not a chronological category' (Adorno 1978: 218; also cited in Osborne 1995: 9). In this respect, as Peter Osborne suggests, 'modernity' situates itself as a temporal determinant of a 'very specific kind'; indeed the German term for modernity, *Neuzeit*, locates precisely this sense of its fuller significance, as a *new* or different 'kind of time' (Osborne 1995: 9, 5, 1–29). During the Enlightenment, as Osborne observes, this 'qualitative claim about the newness of the times' manifests itself 'in the sense of their being "completely other . . . than what has gone before"' (Osborne 1995: 10, citing Koselleck 1985: 238). As we have seen, the emergence of an independent aesthetic sphere is clearly caught up in this distinctive shift in the temporal matrix: both in the form of the newly distinctive experience of modernity it engenders, but also in relation to its attempt to transform its historical consciousness of this transition into a 'general model of social experience' (Osborne 1995: 12).

Yet this sense of the qualitative newness of a 'modern' aesthetic distinction or, indeed, of the 'aestheticization' of modernity itself, also needs some further qualification. The question of aesthetic autonomy only arises *as a question* when in the course of its progressive secularization, culture effects its own act of self-legitimation. Which is to say that, in understanding itself to be distinctively 'modern', and in the course of dislodging a God-centred universe, culture somewhat contradictorily installs itself as 'the *tradition* of the new' – a tradition which in *being* modern is simultaneously without tradition (see Rose 1992: 3, my emphasis). As such, modernity could be said to inaugurate itself as a tradition of de-traditionalization; indeed as Simon Critchley argues:

> [I]t could be claimed that the consciousness of tradition *as such* only occurs in the process of its destruction, that is to say, with the emergence of a *modernity* as that which places in question the evidence of tradition.
>
> (Critchley 1995: 20, original italics)[11]

The overall consequence of de-traditionalization for a modern cultural criticism is double-edged. On the one hand the innovative aspect of de-traditionalization enables a newly critical sense of engagement with the past and could be said to encourage an affirmative stance, engendering a sense of autonomy and freedom: a liberation from the religious constraints which preceded it. On the other hand, the post-theological world can be a solitary place: one which locates the finiteness of the human condition and amplifies our sense of its contingency and inherent 'meaninglessness'. As Andrew Bowie (1990) observes, either response to modernity – liberatory or nihilistic – inevitably attaches an enormous significance to a secular aesthetic: 'either as an image of what the world could look like if we were to realise our freedom, or as the only means of creating an illusion which would enable us to face an otherwise meaningless existence' (Bowie 1990: 3).

It follows that, in confronting secular disenchantment, art's transformative potential is clearly closely linked to an utopian impulse: the felt need to overcome the limitations of the present. Yet in this sense, as we have seen, the encounter of most cultural criticism with modernity could also be said to be exclusively 'tragic', as in relativizing the question of authority it then fails to deliver us from the consequence of doing so. In its moment of overturning or undermining its precursors, a critical engagement with tradition often locates a type of ironic discomfort which alerts us to the deleterious consequence of a break with the past. In this sense, as Gerald Bruns observes, an encounter with tradition is potentially:

> an event that exposes us to our own blindness or the limits of our historicality and extracts from us *an acknowledgement of our belongingness to something different,* reversing what we had thought.
> (Bruns 1992, cited in Critchley 1995: 21, Critchley's emphasis)

As a result, as I have already implied above, in relativizing tradition, contemporary forms of de-traditionalization can all too easily enshrine a form of melancholic entrapment or memorial: an indeterminate form of 'self-definition through difference' (again also see Osborne 1995: 14), which endlessly intensifies a meaningful sense of loss in the present, without offering the possibility of redemption in the future.

Interestingly of course, Leontes is presented with a roughly analogous dilemma mid-way through *The Winter's Tale* as, in regretting the past, he recognizes his own, non-redemptive future as a form of eternal return:

> The causes of their death appear, unto
> Our shame perpetual. Once a day I'll visit
> The chapel where they lie, and tears shed there
> Shall be my recreation.
>
> (3.2.235–8)

Yet significantly, during the statue scene, Leontes moves toward a renewed conceptualization of his former misdemeanours by engaging in a more reflective sense of remembrance. Crucially, this newly evaluative understanding of his historical situation, which manifests itself as an openness to the other, depends on his willingness to concede his continuing involvement in upholding the very process he would now seek to overcome. The moment of transformation effectively pivots on Leontes' critical ability to recognize the fuller extent and deleterious consequence of his own past misrecognition:

> O, thus she stood,
> Even with such life of majesty – warm life,
> As now it coldly stands – when first I wooed her.
> I am ashamed. Does not the stone rebuke me

> For being more stone than it? O royal piece!
> There's magic in thy majesty, which has
> My evils conjured to remembrance
>
> (5.3.34–40)

Intriguingly, of course, when it is viewed in these terms Leontes' admission of guilt and complicity resonates with the key 'procedural dilemma' of cultural criticism itself, which we might now shorthand as the perennial problem of 'how to overcome authority without claiming authority'.[12] In the course of coming to terms with the question of self-implication – 'my evils conjured to remembrance' – Leontes might be said to follow 'the path of self-reflection' opened up by critical theory – a process which Bernstein helpfully glosses in the following terms:

> Adornoesque critical theory is a continuation of the modern pro-ject of self-reflection beyond all transcendental understanding. Self-reflection without transcendental reflection is the ethical act of self-consciousness that brings the subject before and into his or her historical situation . . . in Adorno's act of self-implication: he is part of the barbarism that he is seeking to understand and over-come. Only through the confession of guilt can immanence be achieved; that guilt is the guilt of self-reflection's totalization of experience: the history it recounts and the explanations it offers. When the totality is reflected and challenged in the same thought, ethical action begins to surmount itself toward the political world whose absence calls it into being.
>
> (Bernstein 1992: 16)

In surmounting self-reflection by conceding 'reflection from within experience', Leontes learns to live with the consequence of historical difference as well as remaining open to its potential affinities. In yielding to affinity through distance, and conjuring the possibility of reconciliation into being, the transformative potential of Leontes' moment of acknowledgement is in implication structurally comic rather than tragic.

Yet such 'traditional' transactions are not indicative of a mere point of closure nor is the achievement of reconciliation without considerable risk. In this respect the statue scene remains, in every sense, ground-breaking: narrowly treading the line between oppres-sive reimposition and newly created consensus on the one hand and the accusation of illegitimacy on the other. Indeed it is precisely because the statue scene is law making (canonical even?), just as it is simultaneously indeterminate and law breaking, that in its untheorizable excess it arouses suspicion, mistrust and 'dread':

> *Paulina:*                    you'll think –
> Which I protest against – I am assisted
> By wicked powers.
>
> (5.3.89–91)
>
> . . . my spell is lawful.
>
> (5.3.105)

Faced with the intractability of tradition, the temptation for cultural criticism will either be to wager away its implication within tradition, or, as I have argued elsewhere, to merely remain melancholically enchanted by its productive failure to conjure tradition (Joughin 1997b: 290). Yet, as I have tried to make clear, it is not merely a matter of reconciling ourselves to the tragic discomforts which accrue to our persistent attempts to de-traditionalize Shakespeare, but also, rather, attempting to overcome them – in the process of doing so, we will need to remain alert to tradition's moment of truth. As Adorno's work serves to remind us, a more reflective engagement with remembrance does not merely collapse the past with the present – either by fetishizing a 'contemporaneous' sense of its alienated detachment from the past, or alternatively by endorsing a more reductive sense of a metaphysical continuity between past and present. Rather cultural critics need to achieve what Adorno terms 'an attitude which raises tradition to consciousness without succumbing to it'. This means remaining open to the 'past that persists' in those works which (like Hermione's statue) refuse to 'be restored to what they once were' (Adorno 1993/4: 78–80). In this form at least, as *The Winter's Tale* serves to remind us, the sedimented truths of aesthetic disclosure continue to be historically substantiated, even insofar as they are 'newly performed':

> So much the more our carver's excellence,
> Which lets go by some sixteen years and makes her
> As she lived now
>
> (5.3.30–2)

## Conclusion

Revisiting the question of aesthetic autonomy in Shakespeare studies need not entail a return to the uncritical uniformities which informed the bad aestheticisms of the past. Yet rethinking Shakespeare in aesthetical terms will require an altogether more rigorous form of correspondence with the past: one which resists the lure of nostalgic recuperation in either its radical or conservative forms, in maintaining a more reflective attitude toward tradition. Such a stance would remain attuned to what Adorno terms in his own reflection 'On tradition' – 'affinity through distance' (Adorno 1993/4: 79–80): the more substantial risk of which, we, like Leontes, might yet learn to live with.

In the course of becoming aesthetical and in disclosing truths which are 'truer than truth-only cognition', Shakespearean texts clearly manifest the transformative potential to sustain a critique of modernity, while also presenting the possibility of producing what Bernstein terms a 'non-neutral' defence of rationality. While there are evidently moral, political and aesthetic implications entailed in lifting Shakespeare's plays out of their immediate seventeenth-century milieu, the virtue of reconceptualizing Shakespeare in relation to a later 'middling' definition of modernity lies in acknowledging the mediating categories of modern Shakespearean reception as 'our own'.[13] Just as Shakespeare seems to anticipate a 'modern' secular culture, he does so for us only by continuing to reside within its constraints. In their attempts to challenge the dominant rationality assumptions of disciplinary division, recent advances in cultural and literary criticism have inevitably continued to rely on the transformative power of the aesthetic. As a result, the cognitive and revelatory potential of the aesthetic has already proved crucially informative, not merely in productively accommodating the discontents of 'Lit. crit.'s' insular dislocation, but also in tacitly reshaping the direction cultural and literary studies have taken in recent years.[14] A newly conceived reappraisal of the qualitative significance of the aesthetic in Shakespeare criticism is now overdue. A more reflective materialist approach to the Shakespearean aesthetic will enable us to come to a fuller understanding of the determinants which currently govern our own displaced late modern compulsion to engage with the thwarted truth-potential of Renaissance texts, accommodating a fresh understanding of the playwright's significance for critical thought, even as it discloses new opportunities for interpretation.

## Notes

1  My indebtedness to these thinkers will be evident throughout, but I am particularly grateful to Bowie, on whom I draw heavily here and below, and whose exploration of the philosophical origins of literary theory has proved especially informative (see esp. Bowie 1997a: 1–27). For more on the emergent debate surrounding 'new aestheticism' in its British context see Beech and Roberts (1996), Bernstein (1997) and Bowie (1997b).

2  For more on 'the haunting singularity of the literary text' and for an incisive reassessment of the question of literary value in its post-theoretical context and in relation to Bloom on Shakespeare, see Bennett and Royle (1999: 44–53, esp. 50–3).

3  I am grateful to Howard Felperin for illuminating this point for me.

4  I am partially indebted here to Robert Weimann, for his suggestive treatment of the fuller interpretative consequence of conjunctural historicity in relation to a reflective account of his own contribution to Shakespearean criticism in its 'German' context (Weimann 1997, see esp. 187).

5  Or as Leontes might put it: – 'Say it be, 'tis true' (1.2.300); 'How blest am I/In my just censure, in my true opinion!' (2.1.38–9); 'No. If I mistake/In those foundations which I build upon,/The centre is not big enough to bear/A schoolboy's top' (2.1.102–5). And so on.

6  This last dictum on art belongs, of course, to Paul Klee. Also cited in Bowie (1997a: 5).

7  I am grateful to Terry Eagleton for clarifying these distinctions in the course of a panel discussion on 'The uses of literature' at the symposium on 'The Value of Literature' held at the Kaetsu Centre, New Hall, Cambridge on 3–4 July 1998. On the emergence of the aesthetic as the site for an alternative conceptualization of the 'self' within modernity see also Bowie (1990) and C. Taylor (1989).

8  In short, the institutionalization of literary criticism and the early pre-cursors of aesthetic and literary theory are, from the start, also implicitly caught up in 'a questioning of the borders between differing disciplines' (Bowie 1997a: 13–16).

9  From its very beginning then, the rationalization of the Shakespearean corpus, and the attendant editorial apparatus which quickly grows up around his work, is actually snared on the hook of a characteristically ambiguous dilemma. And in their 'British' context, the pressure of situating these variant truth claims in relation to Shakespeare's work in some part serves to locate the inherently contradictory formation of an emergent 'national literary criticism' itself. Such, as Christopher Norris (1985) reminds us, is the 'paradoxical consequence' of Dr Johnson's early editorial project that:

> On the one hand Shakespeare has to be accommodated to the eighteenth-century idea of a proper, self-regulating discourse which would finally create a rational correspondence between words and things, language and reality . . . On the other hand, allowances have to be made for the luxuriant native wildness of Shakespeare's genius, its refusal to brook the 'rules' laid down by more decorous traditions like that of French neo-classicism.
>
> (Norris 1985: 49)

10  Again I have reappropriated the phrase 'memorial aesthetics' from Bernstein's *The Fate of Art* (1992), where he develops the philosophical and artistic significance of the term in specific relation to a re-reading of the implications of Kant's third *Critique*.

11  For a provocative interrogation of some of the key procedural features of de-traditionalization which differs from my own reading in its deconstructive emphasis, but which nonetheless provides an extremely persuasive account of the philosophical tradition as a tradition of de-traditionalization, compare Critchley (1995).

12  The formulation is Rorty's (Rorty 1989, cited in Bowie 1997a: 86), though the inference is my own.

13  If it is not already apparent, by a 'middling' definition of modernity I mean to imply a shift away from a preoccupation with the 'early-modern' with its emphasis on Shakespeare's liminal placement between feudal and modern, in order to hasten the reconceptualization of a *modern* sense of a Shakespearean aesthetic and its criticism, in more direct relation to the categorical differentiation between value spheres that is itself *constitutive of* an enlightened modernity (see Bernstein 1992: 2).

14  There is not enough time to unravel the full complexity of this formation here. But, briefly, one could point immediately to the performative dimension of gender studies and queer aestheticism; cultural criticism's persistent allegorization of the body and its concern with the libidinal intensities, affectivities, pulses, flows, rhythms, and becomings which inform any properly 'materialist' sense of our understanding of the significance of culture; Black Atlanticism and the aesthetics of alterity and post-colonialism; work on the creativity of counter cultures, the carnivalesque, subcultures of resistance, and so on.

# 5

# *Measure for Measure* and modernity
## The problem of the sceptic's authority
### LARS ENGLE

If intellectual modernity begins with the movements toward scientific and philosophical method inaugurated by Galileo, Bacon, and Descartes, then Shakespeare is pre-modern. But if modernity also has a more general historical beginning in disenchantment with the older meaning-giving myths and structures, structures that science and rational philosophy seek to displace, then Shakespeare may be modern or incipiently modern when he gives undermining or satirical descriptions of the meaning-bearing traditions of his time. Of course where one interpreter sees an undermining representation of a foundational discourse, another may see an admiring recital of a fundamental truth. Shakespeare embeds general ideas in their particular enactments with such complexity that his taste for embeddedness itself might be seen as an implicit critique of methodical philosophy and pure science, a critique that arises just before those discourses get started. This view offers a way of taking seriously Shakespeare and other sixteenth-century thinkers, notably Montaigne, as prior correctives to modernity. As such, these thinkers may have special relevance for postmoderns who are disenchanted with the universality claims of philosophy and science, now seen as myths of modernity. This way of valuing sixteenth-century thought as akin to late-twentieth-century thought has been advanced by Stephen Toulmin (1990: 42–4). Toulmin has in turn been invoked by several books which attempt to situate Shakespeare as a modern thinker through discussing ways in which he handles relations between foundationalist, absolutist, idealist, or metaphysical thinking on one hand, and anti-foundationalist, contingent, materialist, or historically located thinking on the other (see Engle 1993: 8–10; Grady 1996: 15–20). Modern literary criticism and theory makes a great deal of this general opposition, which seems quite an obvious way of mapping intellectual terrain to us; it is I think an interesting question how, and indeed whether, this opposition would have appeared to Shakespeare.

The most obvious early modern discourse which might model anti-foundationalism for Shakespeare is scepticism, which enjoyed a vigorous revival in the sixteenth century. As he typically does in working with intellectual materials, Shakespeare treats scepticism by weaving it into a fabric of socially situated motive and explanation. In several plays he embodies scepticism in social practice partly in order to show how awkwardly it performs there, in effect treating scepticism itself rather sceptically. A case in point is the Jacobean comedy, *Measure for Measure*.

## A fable

Suppose you are a sceptic who suspects that public morality inheres in the habits and beliefs of communities, and only there. Suppose also that you are the supreme moral authority in your community, which, under your tolerant leadership, has acquired dismaying moral habits and appears also to be acquiring some dismaying tentative beliefs. One such belief, linked to the moral habits you find loose and bad, is the belief that morality, especially sexual morality, is entirely conventional. As a concerned ruler, you want to lead or force one set of habits to revert or give way to another; you do not, however, want to appear arbitrary and inconsistent with your past self; and you do not yourself believe that there is an absolute standard of morality (or at least of sexual morality) which you can invoke to ground the changes you wish to enforce.

One solution to this problem might be to substitute for yourself a person who does believe in absolute morality, and to give that person power to act in your stead. Your absolutist substitute would both enforce laws strongly and exemplify authoritative certainty about the firm bases of laws. Moreover, such an authority might well be welcomed by many. Since one of the beliefs you know to be circulating in your community (alongside the loosening, centrifugal, and perhaps emergent one about the conventionality of morality) is a centripetal and perhaps residual belief in morality as God-given and absolute, you know that an absolutist holding such a belief will at any rate not encounter full-hearted resistance. Your substitute, then, can enforce morality with a conscientiousness derived from a belief-structure you do not entirely share but think is a good thing for an enforcer of morality to have and to insist on, at least for a while.

Now suppose further that you are not always a relaxed self-confident sceptic, but are at times a querulous unhappy sceptic who wishes there were some firm truths around to lean on. Given this, your absolutist substitute represents an alter ego: forms of behavior that have emptied themselves into formality for you (religious ritual for instance, or the public administration of justice) are for him apparently full of luminous meaning. Your substitute may be someone you would rather be, but you are not sure his rectitude and metaphysical confidence would survive the experiences which have led to your own scepticism. And you are generally sceptical about metaphysical confidence in others, especially when it is socially assertive. So you would not be entirely unhappy to see him fail, even as for your community you hope he will succeed.

### *Measure for Measure* **and scepticism**

In this chapter I explore relations between the abstract proposal I have just offered and Shakespeare's *Measure for Measure*, which begins with a transfer of power from Duke Vincentio to Lord Angelo that resembles in some ways the story I have just told.[1] I argue below that *Measure for Measure* presents a case study of authority issues in a community strongly influenced by Renaissance scepticism. In fact I think this way of looking at the play clarifies not only its beginning but also its ending, the collapse into quick fixes by way of forced marriages that has disappointed and puzzled commentators.

What I am calling Renaissance scepticism is the kind exemplified by Montaigne's *An Apology for Raymond Sebond*. While no indisputable allusions to Montaigne occur in Shakespeare prior to *The Tempest*, the *Apology* has long seemed close in spirit to *Hamlet* and thus to be known to Shakespeare,[2] and since, as Richard Popkin (1988) comments, in the *Apology* 'Montaigne showed his contemporaries that sceptical difficulties would prevent them from justifying any particular rule of faith, any particular set of human opinions and alleged claims of scientific knowledge' (Popkin 1988: 683–4), I use the

*Apology* below as a source-text for Renaissance scepticism to set alongside the scepticism I find in *Measure for Measure*. Victoria Kahn remarks that in Montaigne (and Erasmus) 'we see a questioning of the early humanist belief in the compatibility of scepticism and prudence, cognitive doubt and practical certainty' (Kahn 1985: 52–3). My fable above, and the Montaignean reading of *Measure for Measure* that follows, see the play as sharing what Kahn calls Montaigne's concern 'with forcing the reader to reflect on how praxis can be and, in some cases, *whether* it can be' (Kahn 1985: 54, original italics). I suggest that Duke Vincentio is a sceptic who acts as he does because he fears the social consequences of authoritative scepticism, and because he sees (as do readers and auditors of *Measure for Measure*) sceptical conventionalism about morality, law, and religion as emergent in Vienna in disturbing ways. Even, perhaps especially, in his friar's robes, I shall argue, Vincentio acts and sounds like a sceptic, and the play in a variety of ways stages encounters between moral authority and resistant subjects that can plausibly be described as clashes between absolutism and scepticism, or as clashes between disguised sceptics attempting to invoke absolutes and open sceptics resisting their invocation. I believe, but will not argue, that this kind of issue is of general interest to Shakespeare around the time he writes *Measure for Measure*.[3]

Let me begin by talking about scepticism as Shakespeare more generally seems to me to manifest it. One of its hallmarks is perspectival thinking, what we might, following Richard Rorty, call an appetite for competitive redescription (see Rorty 1989: 39 and *passim*). Such redescription thwarts or bypasses available stabilizing hierarchies of description, raises the possibility that of dialogic redescription there can be no end, and thus forces one to think of truth as a mutable human commodity rather than a natural or God-given certainty. When such redescription is a feature of the treatment of religious discourse, then it amounts to religious scepticism as well. I find this pervasively in Montaigne and Shakespeare, and it is an aspect of something I have elsewhere called Shakespearean pragmatism (see Engle 1993: 1–24). In tragedy, Stanley Cavell has argued, moments of violent sundering, in which a doubt (usually a doubt of someone else's love) leads to a radical breach in one's life-world, may enact the philosophical violence of Cartesian doubt, so that Shakespeare both stages and frames a concerted philosophical attack on available claims to knowledge or certainty (see

Cavell 1987: 7 and *passim*). A more comic scepticism is, I suggest, being worked through in *Measure for Measure*. Shakespeare's comic scepticism tends to issue in comments like Parolles' in *All's Well That Ends Well*: 'Simply the thing I am/Shall make me live' (4.3.310) – or Dumain's: 'The web of our life is of a mingled yarn, good and ill together' (4.3.69) – that is, an acknowledgement of the impure negotiation of purposes that renders any final judgment on anything questionable, and an apparent disposition to take some comfort from that acknowledgement.[4] One of the features that makes the so-called Problem Plays a plausible generic grouping is their shared concern with the social consequences and opportunities brought by pervasive scepticism or pragmatism; *Troilus and Cressida* is more like *King Lear* or *Othello* or the first half of *The Winter's Tale* in pushing issues about doubt and belief toward an epistemological crisis, while in *All's Well That Ends Well* redescription is seen mostly as a redemptive set of opportunities, most fully seized by Helena. *Measure for Measure* sits between the two.

Habits of redescription pervade *Measure for Measure*. On sex and morality the play's second scene gives us a virtuoso display of redescription, inaugurating what Katharine Eisaman Maus calls its care for 'specifying an extraordinary diversity of attitudes toward sexuality' (Maus 1995: 171). Consider the act for which Claudio is condemned:

> *Mistress Overdone*: Well, what has he done?
> *Pompey*: A woman.
> *Mistress Overdone*: But what's his offense?
> *Pompey*: Groping for trouts in a peculiar river.
> *Mistress Overdone*: What, is there a maid with child by him?
> *Pompey*: No, but there's a woman with maid by him.
>
> (Bevington 1992 1.2.86)[5]

> *Lucio:*      Whence comes this restraint?
> *Claudio:*   From too much liberty, my Lucio, liberty.
>             As surfeit is the father of much fast,
>             So every scope, by the immoderate use,
>             Turns to restraint. Our natures do pursue,
>             Like rats that raven down their proper bane,
>             A thirsty evil; and when we drink, we die.
>
> (1.2.104)

*Lucio:*      What's thy offense, Claudio?
*Claudio:*   What but to speak of would offend again.
*Lucio:*      What, is't murder?
*Claudio:*                          No.
*Lucio:*                                      Lechery?
*Claudio:*                                                   Call it so.

(1.2.114)

*Claudio:*                          But it chances
              The stealth of our most mutual entertainment
              With character too gross is writ on Juliet.

(1.2.130)

*Lucio:*      . . . I would be sorry [thy life] should be thus foolishly
              lost at a game of tick-tack.

(1.2.167)

Most of these widely variable descriptions of sex have some discernible social purpose. In Lucio's case, or Pompey's, the purpose is to treat the act as unworthy of such a grave fuss; in Claudio's comment on restraint and immoderation, as I shall discuss below, the purpose may be to make some moral sense of the fuss that authority has made. Pompey also, with his 'groping for trouts' metaphor, likens Claudio's act to poaching and thus implicitly likens Angelo's response to a general upper-class defense of particular privileges against the transgressive needs and desires of others. (Claudio expresses the same idea more philosophically in his reflection on how 'liberty' provokes 'restraint.') The notion that the sexual act serves or is sponsored by nature, implicit in Pompey's comments, is made explicit shortly after in Lucio's announcement of Juliet's pregnancy to Isabella:

              Fewness and truth, 'tis thus:
       Your brother and his lover have embraced.
       As those that feed grow full, as blossoming time
       That from the seedness the bare fallow brings
       To teeming foison, even so her plenteous womb
       Expresseth his full tilth and husbandry.

(1.4.38)

Pompey's anti-authoritarianism and Lucio's claim that Claudio and Juliet were simply following a natural program both reappear in Lucio's first conversation with the disguised Duke Vincentio, culminating in two further redescriptions of sex:

> *Lucio:* It was a mad fantastical trick of [the Duke] to steal from the state, and usurp the beggary he was never born to. Lord Angelo dukes it well in his absence; he puts transgression to't.
> *Duke:* He does well in't.
> *Lucio:* A little more lenity to lechery would do no harm in him. Something too crabbed that way, friar.
> *Duke:* It is too general a vice, and severity must cure it.
> *Lucio:* Yes, in good sooth, the vice is of a great kindred, it is well allied. But it is impossible to extirp it quite, friar, till eating and drinking be put down . . . Why, what a ruthless thing is this in [Angelo], for the rebellion of a codpiece to take away the life of a man!
>
> (3.1.340)

> *Lucio:* Canst thou tell if Claudio die tomorrow or no?
> *Duke:* Why should he die, sir?
> *Lucio:* Why? For filling a bottle with a tundish.
>
> (3.2.403)

Lucio, like Pompey, is a fount of sexual redescription, and his sexual redescriptions treat social authority in sexual matters as a blundering ineffective agent of personal repression.

So what? one might ask. Of course *Measure for Measure* sets authority and repression and justice in opposition to nature and sex and liberty; of course the play sets articulate representatives of urban lowlife and the lower bodily stratum (as signaled by names, e.g. 'Pompey Bum') in dialogue with representatives of personal and social restraint and the ideal body ('Angelo'), often to the discomfiture of the latter.[6] Angelo is no more thrown from his declared positions by his sexual desire for Isabella than Vincentio is thrown from his sense of self by his dialogue with Lucio. We all know that this is the sort of thing *Measure for Measure* does, and arguments to this effect do not advance the claim that *Measure* is about scepticism very far: the redescribability of sex does not, after all, entail the redescribability of everything else, nor does a general fashion for redescription in Vienna entail the impossibility of final or true descriptions there, though the fashion may be a symptom of the weakness of inherited final descriptions.

Not only sex and allied issues about public morality, however, are subject to redescriptive play in the early parts of *Measure For Measure*. Lucio, joking with fellow soldiers about venereal disease in the second scene, also makes very articulately the Montaignean point that we carve our religion to suit our purposes:

> *First gentleman:* Heaven grant us its peace, but not the King of Hungary's!
> *Second gentleman:* Amen.
> *Lucio:* Thou concludest like the sanctimonious pirate that went to sea with the Ten Commandments, but scraped one out of the table.
> *Second gentleman:* 'Thou shalt not steal'?
> *Lucio:* Ay, that he razed.
> *First gentleman:* Why, 'twas a commandment to command the captain and all the rest from their functions: they put forth to steal. There's not a soldier of us all that in the thanksgiving before meat do relish the petition well that prays for peace.
>
> (1.2.4)

J. W. Lever's Arden edition cites Montaigne: 'No Souldier is pleased with the peace of his Citie' (quoted in Eccles 1980: 22), and we might cite also Montaigne's darker remark that 'It is evident to me that we only willingly carry out those religious duties which flatter our passions. Christians excel at hating enemies' (Montaigne 1987: 495). A little further in the *Apology*, Montaigne makes the more general point that French adherence to Catholic or Protestant Christianity has little to do with the divine truth of one of these creeds, but rather with custom and/or expedience: 'we accept our religion only as we would fashion it, only from our own hands – no differently from the way other religions gain acceptance' (Montaigne 1987: 497). In a similar way, we see these gentlemen relativizing religion to suit professional imperatives – and not only doing this, but asserting that such relativizing is normal – even as they give testimony to the problems of public health that a loose relativizing attitude about sexual morality may lead to in condoning or justifying the sex professions:

> *Lucio:* Behold, behold, where Madam Mitigation comes! I have purchased as many diseases under her roof as come to –

*Second gentleman:* To what, I pray?
*Lucio:* Judge.
*Second gentleman:* To three thousand dolours a year.

(1.2.40)

Lucio has also, quite casually, mentioned the conflict among Christians about the nature of grace: 'Grace is grace despite of all controversy' (1.2.23). The play casually puts forward a quite extensive set of sceptical arguments or proto-arguments, and hints that what holds things together is a universal negotiation in which systems of restraint give way to human desire. In this Madam Mitigation is akin to the sanctimonious pirate who erased 'Thou shalt not steal' from the ten commandments: mitigation is the consequence when desire encounters a system of moral restraint like the Ten Commandments or Vienna's anti-fornication statute.

Justice, enforcement, and mitigation come together again just before the first trial scene. Escalus makes a mitigating plea for Claudio's life, claiming both social privilege (Claudio 'had a most noble father' [2.1.7]) and that it is natural for desire to overcome restraint in sexual matters:

> Let but your honor know
> Whom I believe to be most strait in virtue,
> That, in the working of your own affections,
> Had time cohered with place, or place with wishing,
> Or that the resolute acting of your blood
> Could have attained th' effect of your own purpose,
> Whether you had not sometime in your life
> Erred in this point which now you censure him,
> And pulled the law upon you.

(2.1.8)

In this plea for clemency, Escalus palters between subjunctive and active moods. He does not know whether Angelo has ever done something like this – that is, he does not know whether or not the unmarried Angelo is a virgin (Angelo's past history with Mariana, unmentioned to this point in the play, may be hovering in Escalus's or Shakespeare's mind) – but it will support his arguments if Angelo's internal system of restraint has felt the mitigating pull of sexual desire. It is human to mitigate, Escalus feels. Angelo, setting himself precisely against the idea that law should become comfortable through 'custom'(2.1.3), counters that in order for law to be terrifying and real it must, in an impersonal way, operate freely as a set of authoritative descriptions: 'What's open made to justice, / That justice seizes'(2.1.22).[7] He rejects Escalus's attempt to probe his moral psychology as irrelevant. Angelo wishes, as he says later in a compromised context to Isabella, to be 'the voice of the recorded law' (2.4.61). Angelo's impersonality claim, moreover, at least partly persuades Escalus, who says later to the disguised Duke: 'my brother justice I have found so severe that he hath forced me to tell him he is indeed Justice' (3.1.473).

Claudio and Juliet do not deny their act, and Juliet is visibly pregnant so some such act is undeniable. When Escalus and Angelo sit in judgment over a more typical vice trial, however, little is 'open made to justice' and so almost nothing is seized. Constable Elbow's incompetence as an accuser meets Pompey's adeptness at filibuster and provocation, so that Master Froth's assault on or obscene proposition to the pregnant Mistress Elbow never emerges in testimony. What does emerge, again, is an economy of partly competing and partly collaborating desires: Mistress Elbow's and Master Froth's for stewed prunes, Master Froth's for the other unspecified objects of desire that Pompey can provide, Pompey's for the 'fourscore pound a year' that Master Froth inherited when his father died on Halloween, Constable Elbow's for vengeance, Escalus's for usable testimony, Angelo's for 'good cause to whip them all' (2.1.125). The trial proper comes to a comic climax (again over the definition of an action: Pompey asks, 'if his face be the worst thing about him, how could Master Froth do the constable's wife any harm?' [2.1.141]):

> *Escalus:* He's in the right, constable; what say you to it?
> *Elbow:* First, an it like you, the house is a respected house; next, this is a respected fellow; and his mistress is a respected woman.
> *Pompey:* By this hand, sir, his wife is a more respected person than any of us all.
> *Elbow:* Varlet, thou liest; thou liest, wicked varlet. The time is yet to come that she was ever respected with man, woman, or child.
> *Pompey:* Sir, she was respected with him before he married with her.

> *Escalus:* Which is the wiser here, Justice or Iniquity? Is this true?
> *Elbow:* O thou caitiff, O thou varlet, O thou wicked Hannibal! I
> respected with her before I was married to her? If ever I was
> respected with her, or she with me, let not your worship think
> me the poor Duke's officer.
>
> (2.1.144)

Part of the charm of these malapropisms – which lie open to Pompey,
and on which he seizes – derives from a prevailing willingness to
entertain the idea that the Elbows have been respected with each
other before their marriage (as were Claudio and Juliet), an idea
articulated more gravely by the Provost: 'All sects, all ages smack of
this vice – and he / To die for't' (2.2.5). As Escalus's earlier question
to Angelo shows, everyone is suspected of and, if male, even possibly
in some circumstances respected for premarital sex. Iniquity may
be wiser than Justice here, even if we factor out Elbow's incompetence, since while surely Mistress Elbow should be able to request
stewed prunes in a bathhouse without sexual harassment, it is less
clear that a Vienna entirely without non-marital sex is possible or
desirable. A sharp exchange between Escalus and Pompey underlines the point.

> *Escalus:* Pompey, you are partly a bawd . . . are you not? . . .
> *Pompey:* Truly, sir, I am a poor fellow that would live.
> *Escalus:* How would you live, Pompey? By being a bawd? What
> do you think of the trade, Pompey? Is it a lawful trade?
> *Pompey:* If the law would allow it, sir.
>
> (2.1.195)

Viennese law clearly has allowed prostitution until very recently;
Angelo's ban on brothels has taken initial hold in the suburbs but
not in the city (see 1.2.76–81). Pompey's general claim that the
legality or illegality of prostitution is a matter of convention, not
nature, is never disputed by Escalus, who simply argues that conventions are now changed:

> *Escalus:* But the law will not allow it, Pompey; nor it shall not be
> allowed in Vienna.
> *Pompey:* Does your worship mean to geld and spay all the youth of
> the city?

> *Escalus:* No, Pompey.
> *Pompey:* Truly, sir, in my poor opinion they will to't then. If your worship will take order for the drabs and the knaves, you need not to fear the bawds.
>
> (2.1.203)

I noted above that Escalus has his own way with modal verbs. Here his comment on the law, which will not allow it, and his apparently logically unnecessary 'nor it shall not be allowed in Vienna', bespeak his awareness that a whole array of positions exists along the line which links having a law, attempting to enforce a law, and succeeding in doing away with an interdicted social activity. Escalus here tries on for size the impersonal 'voice of the recorded law' Angelo mentions elsewhere. But he gets nowhere with it – indeed his confusing transitional 'nor' (which suggests that what the law allows is one thing, but what is being allowed is in fact another) rather undermines the force of his attempt.

In the trial itself, Escalus has a logically related enforcement problem, one which is both an object of sceptical commentary on justice (of the kind Pompey has just given) and a consequence of judicial scepticism. He is trying to promote a change in the social order which he himself has reservations about (certainly insofar as it condemns Claudio), and one which the agents of law at his disposal are unable properly to define. Moreover, lying behind this local problem in ways I have been hinting at is the general issue of the law's uncertain relation to morality and social convention. Montaigne comments:

> Nothing keeps changing so continuously as the Law. Since I was born I have seen our neighbours, the English, chopping and changing theirs three or four times, not only on political matters (where we may wish to do without constancy) but on the most important subject there ever can be: religion . . .
>
> And closer to home, I have seen capital offences made lawful . . .
>
> But what has Philosophy to teach us in this plight? Why, that we should follow the laws of our country! – laws which are but an uncertain sea of opinions deriving from peoples or princes, who will paint it in as many different colours and present it, reformed, under as many different faces as they have changes of heart. I cannot make my judgement as flexible as that. What

kind of Good can it be, which was honoured yesterday but not today!

(Montaigne 1987: 653)

Both Escalus and Vincentio suffer from awareness of this problem, and both seek some absolute positions to enforce amid a puddle of linguistic slippage, social change, and moral relativity, but find none. Both are left issuing warnings and threats, and attempting to promote redescriptions which their subjects are reluctant to internalize.

In this scene, since Escalus cannot deliver judgment without having an explicit crime before him, confessed or at least attested by witnesses (rather than merely 'detested' as by Elbow), he brings the formal trial to a close at this point:

> *Elbow:* What is't your worship's pleasure I shall do with this wicked caitiff?
> *Escalus:* Truly, officer, because he hath some offenses in him that thou wouldst discover if thou couldst, let him continue in his courses till thou knowest what they are.
> *Elbow:* Marry, I thank your worship for it. – Thou seest, thou wicked varlet now, what's come upon thee: thou art to continue now, thou varlet, thou art to continue.
>
> (2.1.164)

A sceptical authority finds himself condemning others to continue what they are doing until they understand how and why it is so bad. The authority attempts to promote this understanding by redescribing the activity while threatening also to punish it. Duke Vincentio, whose problematic exercise of authority drives the play, also frequently condemns others to continue.

## Vincentio's enforcement problem: 'I will not die today, for any man's persuasion'

Vincentio is a disguised sceptic as, for much of the play, he is a disguised Duke. He is known to be philosophical, indeed Socratic: as Escalus remarks (to the disguised Vincentio, who is seeking reassurance that he is not as described by Lucio), the Duke has been 'One that, above all other strifes, contended especially to know himself' (3.1.456).[8] It is suggestive of scepticism that when he assumes the role of a friar, he uses that role in an almost entirely secular way, to gain a platform for his philosophical and political handling of problems in this life. 'Here comes a man of comfort, whose advice / Hath often stilled my brawling discontent' (4.1.8), as Mariana says, suggesting surprisingly that the Duke has an off-stage history of religious role-playing. This presentation of religion as a way of 'stilling' social discontent (and Mariana's strong word 'brawling' allies her own grief incongruously with streetfighting) is one Montaigne finds in the ancient philosophers, who, he says, did not critique ancient religion because, on their account, such practice:

> was simply designed to meet the social needs of the general public . . . With this in mind it was reasonable not to strip popularly held opinions of their living feathers. They had no wish to spawn ideas which would disturb the people's obedience to the laws and customs of their land.
>
> (Montaigne 1987: 571)

Vincentio's handling of religion fits this pattern.

Moreover, a sceptic of the sort I have described will have a problem with enforcement that is part of a more general problem concerning social authority. He will regard his authority as provisional, granted by a network of social customs and legitimized by a habit of consent: both network and habit are mutable, and thus authority is vulnerable, particularly vulnerable if it is invoked unsuccessfully. Machiavelli, writing of the uses of violence by rulers (and meaning by violence a use of force unsanctioned by anything other than the ruler's own authority and motivated by the ruler's expediency) advises that such uses be rare, quick, final, and above all successful. 'It should be noted that one must either pamper or do away with men, for they will avenge themselves for minor offenses while for more serious ones they cannot; so that any harm done to a man must be the kind that removes any fear of revenge' (Bondanella and Musa 1979: 83). Vincentio has in the past evidently tried to follow Machiavelli in dealing with condemned persons: his prisoners have ever been promptly 'delivered to . . . liberty or executed' (4.2.122).

Enforcement of laws by an established ruler is obviously less risky than the new-princely mayhem Machiavelli writes of, since the laws are a formalization of the network of customs which upholds the authority of a ruler. Nonetheless, to a prince philosophically sensitive to these matters, even simple law enforcement raises fraught issues which can only be safely dealt with by a mechanism of social consultation (like a jury trial) or, better yet, by the consent of the offender to his or her punishment.

*Measure for Measure* is full of attempts (sometimes partly successful) to obtain the consent of the offender to his or her punishment, and Duke Vincentio is particularly assiduous in attempting to obtain them. But even before Vincentio is directly involved, the Viennese seem prone to accept and internalize their punishments (see Maus 1997a: 2021–2). Claudio, feeling the first impact of the new moral regime as he parades in irons through the streets to deter others from fornication, provides an example.

> *Claudio:*  Fellow, why dost thou show me thus to th' world?
> Bear me to prison, where I am committed.
> *Provost:*  I do it not in evil disposition,
> But from Lord Angelo by special charge.
> *Claudio:*  Thus can the demigod Authority
> Make us pay down for our offence, by weight,
> The bonds of heaven. On whom it will, it will;
> On whom it will not, so; yet still 'tis just.
>
> (1.2.96)

Claudio, willing to see in Angelo a questionable demigod who alienates to his own ends bonds due to heaven, also accepts that he himself has done something which deserves the punishment he is about to receive. And he has clearly been reflecting on the nature of his act as a measure of his internal character, as he shows when Lucio accosts him in a passage already quoted:

> *Lucio:*  Why how now, Claudio? Whence comes this restraint?
> *Claudio:*  From too much liberty, my Lucio, liberty.
>
> (1.2.104)

Claudio, then, initially seems an authority's dream subject: one in whom punishment inspires not resistance or the unravelling of a social fabric, but rather reflective justification of the punishment and attendant moral commentary on the natural evils of the self which make exercises of supervisory authority necessary.

Nor is Claudio the only such subject. Duke Vincentio in disguise as a friar receives the same sort of cooperation from Juliet:

> *Duke:*   Repent you, fair one, of the sin you carry?
> *Juliet:*  I do, and bear the shame most patiently.
> *Duke:*   I'll teach you how you shall arraign your conscience,
>     And try your penitence if it be sound
>     Or hollowly put on.
> *Juliet:*                          I'll gladly learn.
> *Duke:*   Love you the man that wronged you?
> *Juliet:*  Yes, as I love the woman that wronged him.
> *Duke:*   So it seems your most offenceful act
>     Was mutually committed?
> *Juliet:*                          Mutually.
> *Duke:*   Then was your sin of heavier kind than his.
> *Juliet:*  I do confess it, and repent it, Father.
> *Duke:*   'Tis meet so, daughter. But lest you do repent
>     As that the sin hath brought you to this shame –
>     Which sorrow is always toward ourselves, not heaven,
>     Showing we would not spare heaven as we love it,
>     But as we stand in fear –
> *Juliet:*  I do repent me as it is an evil,
>     And take the shame with joy.
> *Duke:*                          There rest.
>
> (2.3.20)

Juliet's interruption may express understandable impatience with this catechism, but Vincentio's need to carry it through to the end displays sceptical anxiety about the degree to which an exercise of authority in the name of divine absolutes has worked in her case. It turns out that it has worked very well: she accepts (or says she accepts) her punishment with joy.[9] Vincentio's elaborate prudential argument that Claudio should 'be absolute for death' yields a similar result:

> *Duke:*                          What's in this
>     That bears the name of life? Yet in this life
>     Lie hid more thousand deaths; yet death we fear
>     That makes these odds all even.
> *Claudio:*                          I humbly thank you.

> To sue to live, I find I seek to die,
> And seeking death, find life. Let it come on.
>
> (3.1.38)

But each of these interventions is only a temporary success, soon reversed when death comes closer. And Vincentio fails spectacularly when he comes to Barnardine, whose head he seeks to substitute for Claudio's as he has substituted Mariana's maidenhead for Isabella's:

> *Duke:* Sir, induced by my charity, and hearing how hastily you are to depart, I am come to advise you, comfort you, and pray with you.
>
> *Barnardine:* Friar, not I. I have been drinking hard all night, and I will have more time to prepare me, or they shall beat out my brains with billets. I will not consent to die this day, that's certain.
>
> *Duke:* O, sir, you must; and therefore I beseech you, Look forward on the journey you shall go.
>
> *Barnardine:* I swear I will not die today, for any man's persuasion.
>
> (4.3.43)

Thus the play underlines a plausible general boundary to the sceptic's attempt to float his judicial authority to punish on the religious consent of subjects: you can persuade them to feel guilty, but not to will their own deaths. Saved by Ragozine's timely fever, the Duke spares Barnardine rather than crossing this boundary, and brings the play to its odd denouement in a series of forced marriages, denying even Angelo the death he deserves and seeks, and limiting Ducal vengeance on Lucio to life as husband to Kate Keepdown.

The ending of the play, which disappoints many readers – Richard Wheeler (1981: 139) comments that 'Shakespeare strands Vincentio in a kind of allegorical no-man's-land' – is less puzzling if it is seen as the result of a sceptic's failed experiment in the invocation of an absolute. Having seen Angelo relativized, and having seen Isabella herself turning on principle to plead for him, Vincentio imposes a universal sentence (applying unexpectedly to Isabella and himself as well as others), one that illustrates the sceptic's general problem in enforcing social reform. It is a sentence already proclaimed by Constable Elbow: 'Marry, I thank you . . . Thou art to continue, thou varlet, thou art to continue' (2.1.169).

## Conclusion

In closing, I return briefly to my fable. How has it fared? Some of the problems that the Duke has as a ruler, and the solution he attempts, and its failure, may be successfully accounted for as aspects of the partly paradoxical situation of the sceptic in social authority. Indeed, this approach goes some way toward explaining why it is that, as Harry Berger Jr. puts it, the Duke is just 'weird' (Berger 1997: 339), even though Berger intends the adjective as an index of the difficulty systematic criticism has in explaining the Duke. If the Duke is inconsistent, self-preoccupied, tetchy and unctuous by turns as he uses his assumed religious office to make instruments of others, hypersensitive to the reports on his own sexual and moral character he eagerly solicits, Pompey-like in setting up the bed-trick, Angelo-like in his breathtaking final proposal to Isabella, which seems both a personal use or abuse of office to gain sexual companionship and a final social attempt to herd the full range of Viennese positions on morality into the corral of marriage and social continuance: does not all this further qualify him as an exemplar of the discomfort of the sceptic in a position of moral leadership?

The Duke's weirdness may be Shakespeare's extended registration of the partial contradiction which arises when sceptics involve themselves in social enforcement. And the Duke's agitation may be part of a more general registration of discomfort in Renaissance scepticism. We should not, after all, expect Renaissance scepticism to be serene, as if it could secure itself in a conviction that it constituted a vanguard of emergent modernity; at the turn of the seventeenth century holy severity and religious intolerance seemed at least as emergent as scepticism. Montaigne's serenity, such as it is, comes from his explicit abjuration of leadership. Montaigne remarks at the end of 'On Experience', the last of the *Essays*, that 'upon the highest throne in the world, we are seated, still, upon our arses' (Montaigne 1987: 1269). Such a seat offers no universal foundation for the enforcement of justice, particularly if the sitter shares some of Montaigne's scepticism, as, I have argued, Vincentio does. Vincentio responds at the end by remaking Vienna as a marriage bed for himself and his subjects to lie in. Modern readers cannot imagine that this solution leads to lasting comfort, but *Measure for Measure* prefigures modernity precisely by exploring how difficult it is to repose on the instability of truth.

## Acknowledgements

This chapter was drafted for an SAA seminar on Shakespeare and Scepticism led by Lawrence Rhu. I am grateful for his comments and those of others at the seminar, for questions and suggestions from audiences who heard later versions of it at the University of Houston and the University of California, Irvine, and for shaping commentary from David Bevington, Hugh Grady and Holly Laird.

## Notes

1 Surprisingly, this way of looking at *Measure for Measure* has not to my knowledge been explored before. See, however, Bradshaw (1987: 178) for discussion of Isabella and Angelo as 'youthfully zealous moral absolutists' committed to ethical systems, 'unlike the capriciously pragmatic, fudging Duke'.

2 See Jenkins (1982: 108–10). For verbal echoes of Montaigne in *Measure for Measure*, including two from the *Apology*, see Eccles (1980: 543) under 'Montaigne' in the index. Because Montaigne himself is such an echo-chamber of classical and Renaissance commonplaces, it is often hard to be sure what counts as a borrowing and what may simply be use of a shared source.

3 Hamlet, like Vincentio, tries to show his opponents what they are in order to gain their permission for what he will do to them, and this is an intelligent sceptic's response to the problem of authority. In assessing Montaigne's influence at this period in Shakespeare's career, it may be relevant that the verb 'to assay' and the noun 'assay' and their cognates cluster in *Measure for Measure*, which has three instances, *Othello*, also with three, and *Hamlet*, which has five. No other play has more than one. See Spevack (1973: 67, 362–3). Shakespeare rarely uses the word 'essay'.

4 Parenthetical citations from *The Norton Shakespeare* (Greenblatt 1997); I have also regularly consulted and once cited Bevington (1992) (see note 5).

5 *The Norton Shakespeare*, following a theory of the Oxford editors, omits this passage as having been intended for deletion (though Shakespearean) when, as the Oxford editors believe, Middleton revised the text (see Greenblatt 1997: 2087; Wells *et al.* 1987: 468). I am unpersuaded by the Oxford/Norton arguments for revision here, and so I cite Bevington (1992), who follows the Folio, keeps the passage, and treats the entire scene as Shakespearean.

6 See, for example, Wheeler (1981: 9): '[Isabella's] characterization is part of an intricate dramatic network of interrelated conflicts – authority/ sexuality; order/liberty; justice/mercy; virtue/vice; self-awareness/self-deception – that intersect in her experience.'

7 For an interesting account of this exchange as an illustration that Angelo does not recognize his own inwardness, and treats Escalus's question as if

it raised a problem about secret versus known actions rather than a problem about intentions versus actions, see Maus (1995: 162).

8 On this, however, see Harry Berger's (1997) commentary (which develops a point of Marc Shell's):

> Is there any indication that he *wants* to know himself? . . . His peremptory flight from ducal responsibility and enthusiastic performance of a friar's role and offices suggest that above all other strifes he struggles to control the self-representation that will convince others of his goodness so that their conviction may shore up his own. The Duke contends especially to justify himself.
>
> (Berger 1997: 340, original italics)

9 Stephen Greenblatt (1988a), drawing a parallel between Vincentio's strategies and those of Renaissance princes, writes of this exchange as part of a general effort by Vincentio to arouse salutary anxiety in his subjects, and indeed takes up a number of the same examples I treat in this chapter. But his account does not, I think, explain Vincentio's unwillingness when personally involved to execute *any* recalcitrant subject, something for which Renaissance princes were not noted. See Greenblatt (1988a: 136–42).

# 6

# '*Jew*. Shylock is my name'

## Speech prefixes in *The Merchant of Venice* as symptoms of the early modern

### JOHN DRAKAKIS

In 1935 in what has become a well-known article, the bibliographer R. B. McKerrow (1997) drew attention to the fact that in early play-texts there were both regularities and variations in the setting of speech prefixes. He posed the question: 'What, then, is the meaning of this difference between regularity and irregularity in the way in which speakers' names are shown?'(McKerrow 1997: 5). McKerrow's concern here was with the bibliographical details of early play-texts, and the scope of his inquiry was limited to what these details disclosed about the 'authority' of the manuscript that lay behind printed copy. His response to the question he posed was disarmingly simple: 'a play in which the names are irregular was printed from the author's original MS.', while 'one in which they are regular and uniform is more likely to have been printed from some sort of fair copy, perhaps made by a professional scribe' (McKerrow 1997: 5). At no stage in McKerrow's inquiry was he concerned to investigate the semiotic significance or the *cultural* value that might be derived from such bibliographical variation. In an interesting revision of McKerrow's thesis, designed to separate authorial, theatrical and compositorial fact from editorial fiction, William B. Long (1997: 25) advanced the view that 'varying speech-heads may be a kind of vestigial remains of the planning, left by the playwright and used by the players.' Beginning from the claim made in Alexander Pope's preface to the 1723 edition of *The Works of Mr William Shakespeare* that 'every single character in

Shakespeare is as much an Individual as those in life itself', and that 'had all the Speeches been printed without the very names of the Persons, I believe one might have applied them with certainty to every speaker', Random Cloud (1997) proffers another kind of challenge to McKerrow's thesis. Taking Romeo's speech at the end of 2.1, and the Friar's at the beginning of 2.2 in the 1599 quarto of *Romeo and Juliet*, Cloud argues that the repetitions may be interpreted as details that are '*dramatically* or *scenically* functional, and not unmediatedly *mimetic* or redolent of the *Personal* character of Life itself' (Cloud 1997: 135). He cites a further example from *All's Well That Ends Well* in which the Countess is referred to as '*Cou.*' and '*Old Cou.*' and he concludes that first, 'once an actress intones the words of Shakespeare's dialogue, they become her own, as it were, in the service of the role that she performs', but also, 'The residual variant speech tags, however, remain behind in Shakespeare's "voice", for surely they are all his vocatives' (Cloud 1997: 135). Isolating the variations *Mother*, *Countess*, *Old Countess*, *Lady* and *Old Lady* as examples in *All's Well That Ends Well*, Cloud concludes: 'One of the simplest explanations for the repeated and augmented speech-tag is that it marks a seam in the layering of composition', although a much more provocative conclusion follows from what seems at this stage to be a regression to a version of McKerrow's original thesis; he continues:

> The ideal unity we *read into* such a text runs up against a fragmentation or a multiplicity that we actually *read*. It is a problem of interpretation whether such supposed traces of construction are to be swept under the rug in production, as if they were mere noise, or whether they are to be attended to as messages – as discontinuities in tone, or in action, or in what interests me most here, individual characterisation.
>
> (Cloud 1997: 136–7, original italics)

Cloud has nothing to say about *The Merchant of Venice*, whereas McKerrow does; the latter mentions the existence of unstable speech prefix forms in two other plays printed by James Roberts in 1600, *A Midsummer Night's Dream* and *Titus Andronicus* Q2. Of *A Midsummer Night's Dream* he notes that 'Bottom is sometimes called "*Clowne*." (The word seems to have been regularly applied to the principal "funny man" and is so used in other plays as an alternative to the personal name)'. Of *The Merchant of Venice* he observes,

'There is comparatively little opportunity for variation of names in this play, but the following may be noticed: Shylock is often called "*Iew.*" Launcelot is often "*Clowne*"'(McKerrow 1997: 4–5). McKerrow also has nothing whatsoever to say about a further set of variations, involving the clown, where at 2.2.3 the Clown refers to himself as '*Iobbe, Launcelet Jobbe,* good *Launcelet,* or good *Iobbe*'. The extent to which details of this kind continue to attract little attention can be gauged from Anne Barton's *The Names of Comedy* (1990), where she concludes that the issue here simply involved the dramatist's failure to make up his mind.[1]

In a much more recent challenge to the bibliographical content of McKerrow's thesis, Richard F. Kennedy (1998) steers the discussion away from questions of what we might call 'the layering of composition' to consider the possible contribution of the variations of speech prefixes made by compositorial practice to the process of textual production. That is, he considers the *material* questions involved in the business of setting a text into type by one or more compositors, and he looks closely at what types might have been available for the business of text setting. Specifically, Kennedy plots the shortages of lower and upper case italic types disclosed in the printed quarto text of *A Midsummer Night's Dream* (1600), and then proceeds to examine the quarto of *The Merchant of Venice* (1600). He tabulates a series of shortages, of italic cap *I* types, as well as of a number of roman cap types, and draws the conclusion that Shakespeare's manuscript contained throughout the forms *Iewe.* and *Clowne.*, but that type shortages forced the two compositors who worked on the quarto text to set *Shy./Shyl.* and *Launcelet./Launce* (Kennedy 1998: 191–202). Kennedy takes the view that in the case of *Clowne./Launcelet.* these were the only two alternatives available (Kennedy 1998: 202); he does not consider the possibility that the speech prefixes for the two roles that we have come to know through editorial normalization as *Launcelot* and *Gobbo* might conceivably disguise a further problem concerned with a possible instability emanating from Q1's initial spelling *Iobbe* and the accompanying shortages of cap *I* sorts.[2] In short, Kennedy remains within certain recognizable bibliographical parameters in his concern to establish the features of a hypothetical manuscript that is assumed to lie behind the printed text. What he and other bibliographical scholars refrain from doing is raising questions about the 'textual' articulations of that subjectivity that familiarity has communicated to us as 'the author'.

I begin with reference to the empirical bibliographical evidence, and some of the interpretations to which it has given rise, because it seems to me that, at least in the case of the *Iewe./Shy./Shyl.* and possibly in the *Gobbo/Iobbe* substitutions, further levels of meaning and cultural value may well be at issue that extend well beyond the straightforward causal logic that has hitherto underpinned bibliographical inquiry. I wish to draw a distinction between the phrase 'levels of meaning', and Cloud's (1997) 'layering of composition', since my concern is not to posit an authorial source for this instability. Rather, I want to suggest that these alternative inscriptions may well submit to a symptomatic reading of, among other things, the very process of the construction of authority itself. Here compositorial reading – and there is evidence that Roberts' compositors could both read and write – is contingent upon a reading formation which is mediated in the text of the play, where what might be called the move to individuation is shown to conflict with details that are both dramatically functional and culturally significant. Such details are not the products of an intention, compositorial or authorial, but rather unintended consequences of a series of practical printing-house decisions whose meanings we can retrospectively construct. Questions which involve the 'author' as origin, or which seek to establish the essential 'humanity' of a dramatic character are, I suggest, in this context, secondary to other kinds of inquiry which expand the terms of mimetic reference to include the notion of encroaching individuation, along with questions of temporality, and the issue of periodization, parts of an intricate discursive field which lies behind this deceptively complex re-presentation. In this the evidence left by the compositors may be interpreted in accordance with the protocols of more than one discursive regime. In short, I want to argue that these bibliographical details permit a reading that locates the text on the threshold of modernity, where questions of type (both literally and figuratively), stereotype and function are in the process of giving way to a more historically specific individuated form of dramatic characterization. Placed in a wider epistemological context we may perceive modernity in the words of the Italian philosopher Gianni Vattimo (1988) as an 'era of history'. Vattimo approaches the problem of modernity from the standpoint of the postmodern, hence his dependency on the philosophy of Nietzsche and Heidegger rather than upon Marxist historicism, and upon a nihilism that challenges all systems of reason. However, his comments on the nature of modernity are provocative and are delivered in a vein that is pertinent to any discussion of *The Merchant of Venice*; for example, Vattimo observes:

> Only modernity, in developing and elaborating in strictly worldly and secular terms the Judeo-Christian heritage – i.e., the idea of history as the history of salvation, articulated in terms of creation, sin, redemption, and waiting for the Last Judgement – gives ontological weight to history and a determining sense of our position within it.
>
> (Vattimo 1988: 3–4)

Before focusing directly on this aspect of the play itself, it is worth teasing out some of the issues that Vattimo raises here in a little more detail.

We have become used to the related questions of authority and authorship and the ways in which they impinge upon our readings of Shakespearean texts, and the earlier examples afforded by McKerrow (1997) and Barton (1990) exemplify the ease with which commentators slip from one category to the other. We are inclined habitually to assume that behind each printed text is a manuscript whose authority or otherwise – that is to say the extent to which the writing itself might reveal the articulating 'voice' of the poet – may be established according to a series of investigative protocols. We make an assumption that the primary practice of the poet/dramatist is the process of composition, and that the result, the poet/dramatist's distinctive voice, is the source of an utterance to which we accord an absolute authority. In doing so we replay a sequence of cause-and-effect in an attempt to return to a lost origin, 'creation', and to a subsequent descent into 'history', thus ensuring a linearity in the course of events. Or to put the matter another way, one which is more pertinent to the present inquiry, we construct a scene of Shakespearean writing. This scene, like others, seems to require, as Jonathan Goldberg (1990: 287) has argued, 'some originary impulse that is not reducible to a calligraphic urge, but to an ideality and a humanity that would appear to precede the act of inscription, or to be generated from it.' Goldberg derives his account in part from the Derridean questioning of the plenitude that has traditionally been located at the point of *presence*, in the interests of inscribing a 'differance' there that combines both a deferring and a division:

> To say that *différance* is originary is simultaneously to erase the
> myth of a present origin. Which is why 'originary' must be under-
> stood has having been *crossed out*, without which *différance* would
> be derived from an original plenitude. It is a non-origin which is
> originary.
>
> (Derrida 1978: 203)

If we were to posit unproblematically for *The Merchant of Venice* an
authorial manuscript that lies directly behind the Quarto of 1600,
as a number of modern editors have done,[3] then we would also
open ourselves to the risk of falling into that process of the repression
of 'writing' that according to Derrida (1978: 197) is 'the repression
of that which threatens presence and the mastering of absence'. In
this instance what we may posit as Shakespeare's hand, the hypothetical manuscript that is thought to lie behind the first printed
text of the play, may be perceived as a reading involved in its own
mechanism of repression, which, taken together, constitute a body
of symptoms that we may read as indications of an Elizabethan
cultural unconscious. For the writer 'Shakespeare', and indeed for
Elizabethan culture generally, the figure of 'the Jew' had become a
focus for a range of marginal fiscal practices which had become of
central symbolic significance to the definition of certain material
social practices. The matter is further complicated if we consider
the material practice of the Elizabethan compositor whose own
artisanal concerns may be said to contribute to the act of writing
itself insofar as particular combinations of type generate certain
meanings that may signify a return of the repressed. The oscillation
between 'Jew' and 'Shylock', while having its practical cause in a
series of identifiable type-shortages, traverses also the gulf between
stereotype and individuated 'character' which in part signals the
birth of the modern. All this is to propose a Shakespeare as something other than the repository of a metaphysically validated truth,
an 'inventor of the human' (Bloom 1999), and a history of interiority
unfettered to a blinkered empiricism, and to resist the temptation
to perceive the dramatist, the compositors who set his plays, or the
dramatic characters to which the Elizabethan theatre gave birth, as
'selves' or 'moral agents' (Bloom 1999: 4) all of whom act with a freedom and an autonomy that is absolute. We are dealing here not so
much with a layering of composition as with a sedimentation of
over-determined signifying practices whose roots are firmly located
within a complex historicity. It is that historicity that is the mark of

modernity, that is to say, that mode of awareness of objective process that we call 'history' (Vattimo 1998: 5), and this is emphatically not a Shakespearean invention so much as a movement of which Shakespearean texts in the forms in which we have them are symptoms. Let us now turn specifically to *The Merchant of Venice* as a text that exemplifies a culture on the cusp of modernity.

In his book *Shakespeare among the Moderns*, Richard Halpern proposes to read *The Merchant of Venice* 'through the lens of modernism' (1997: 163). He cites Portia's question at 4.1.170: 'Which is the merchant here? and which the Jew?', a question which immediately precedes the line which, in Q1 and the Folio, conflates the name Shylock with the functional role 'Jew'. In an argument whose general contours Stephen Greenblatt (1990: 43) had earlier advanced, Halpern proposes that Portia's question suggests 'that Shylock and Antonio are basically indistinguishable, that Shylock is the *Judenspiegel* in which Christian society may view itself. Yet this relation of supposed equivalence still leaves the Jew in an exposed position' (Halpern 1997: 161). That momentary confusion is clarified two lines later in the separation of 'merchant' from 'Jew'. But it is a clarification that points in two opposing directions: it points backwards to that demonic figure that was the constitutive 'other' of medieval Christianity, but it also points forward to those economic practices which lay the foundation for what we have come to know as modern capitalism. It is also a reminder of the Judeo-Christian heritage of history as 'the history of salvation' (Vattimo 1988: 4) where 'sin' is associated in the play with an economic practice (usury) emblematic of 'the fall', and where redemption resides in a Christian history of 'judgment'. In the capitalist future that the play glimpses, a paradox emerges between the alienation from self that fiduciary exchange inaugurates as a consequence of the economic necessity of borrowing money, and the desire to retain forms of law underwritten by a divinely sanctioned authority. Here the figure of the Jew always exists on the cusp of the division between the medieval and the modern. He incorporates into his being an irrationality sustained through forms of religious and quasi-religious prejudice projected with extraordinary power into modernity, and a secular critical rationality which threatens to expose the hitherto mystified operations of economic practice that represent the challenge of the modern. That challenge in the sphere of the economic begins with the development of mercantilism, a process of finance and exchange that demanded a systematic borrowing of capital for investment while at the same time prohibiting the charging of 'interest'. That money-lending had always been practised, even during the medieval period, is well known, but the specific charging of interest, associated with the figure of 'the Jew' who became the exemplar of this practice, and who was demonized for it, accelerated the movement towards a modernity where individualism could challenge collectivity, and where traditional social hierarchies and the obligations that reinforced them were gradually modified, if not supplanted. To this extent, the coexistence of name and function represents an articulation of the division between patriarch and offspring which objectively figures forth the struggle between Christianity and Judaism in the play, and which simultaneously directs our attention inwards to the very social process of the formation of a modern subjectivity. The Jew is a composite figure representing both the Oedipal father who shapes the contours of desire, *and* the repressed that always threatens to return. That the play should both name and un-name 'Shylock' by representing him as an 'individual' *and* as a Jew testifies to a cultural nervousness that the compositors in Roberts' printing-house inadvertently highlight for reasons that have nothing to do with the semiotic value of these typographical details. It is, perhaps, a supreme irony that this textual instability, explicable in practical artisanal terms, should also represent a form of labour expropriated by the printer in the name of an economic practice, an embryonic capitalism, that by the end of the sixteenth century had already become integral for the printer James Roberts to the business of printing.

This formulation, however, is in need of a little more unpacking, because the figure of the Jew Shylock, which is the focus of my argument, looks both backwards *and* forwards in the play. It is this double perspective that obscures what we might think of as the passage to modernity, since it both challenges *and* facilitates a secular teleology. It may be that *The Merchant of Venice* is one of those 'visions of desacralized space dramatically inscribed by Shakespeare', which we may read as an example of that body of 'prescient projections' that Hugh Grady has identified as critiques of

> the enabling structures of Western modernity: autonomous (and instrumental) reason, a nation-state system operating according to a Machiavellian logic, and a capitalist economy reinforcing in its own autonomous operations the purposeless purposiveness

that provides the characteristic, often catastrophic non-teleology of Faustian Western (now global) development.

(Grady 1996: 33)

The Jew, Shylock, is in the play both purposive *and* purposeless since his objective is the accumulation of an instrument of exchange, a pure signifier, money. But this also raises a further methodological problem concerned with our 'reading' of Renaissance texts. Either we encounter in our reading an irreducible 'otherness' of the past represented in these texts, or we perceive them in allegorical-historical terms. These two ways of approaching the writing of the past are not, I suggest, complementary but engaged in a series of irresolvable paradoxes. We objectify in the text our subjective ('modernist') concerns, and by implication impose a temporal continuity on what we continue to perceive as a flux, but at the same time we also reconcile ourselves to the irreducible fact of a radically alienated past. The one strategy pulls in the direction of instrumentalizing and homogenizing reading, while, taken to its extreme, the other leads ultimately to the impossibility of reading. I want to argue that the figure of 'the Jew/Shylock', in addition to being a harbinger of modernity, also crystallizes this methodological paradox.

Shylock, and the appellation 'Jew', which almost invariably accompanies the name in the play, performs for us the conflict between pre-Christian and Christian modes of perceiving history. Theologically the Jew prefigures the Christian, as evidenced in Bishop John Jewell's observation in his *A Replie Vnto M. Hardings Answer* (1562), where he observes:

> *Chrysostome* compareth the state of the Jewes vnto a candle: and the state of the Christians, to the Brightnesse of the Sunne. Againe he likeneth the Jewes to the first draught, or plat of an image, set out only in bare lines: and the Christians vnto the same image liuely filled vp with all due proportion, and resemblance and furniture of colours.
>
> (1611)[4]

The idea that the state of the Jew should be likened to 'the first plat of an image, set out only in bare lines' points directly to a *process* that is remarkably close to the act of composition itself. The Jew is form without content, and the Christian is content itself, 'the same image liuely filled up with all due proportion, and resemblance and furniture of colours.' In a very literal sense the Jew Shylock *is* the bare plot of *The Merchant of Venice*, but that plot is augmented by a Christian plenitude that purports to 'humanize' a law whose patriarchal tyranny proffers a threat to the 'life' of the city.

It is perhaps no accident that the etymology of Shylock's name should remain unclear, although it has been suggested, significantly in the context of the preceding argument, that its origin lies obscurely in the Old Testament book of Genesis (Bloom and Jaffa 1964: 33). Moreover, this seems to me to be only one of the spheres within which the figure of the Jew operates in *The Merchant of Venice*. Can we, perhaps, perceive the problem as an example of objective/subjective binary that Hugh Grady has located in other Shakespearean texts? In this reading the depersonalized (and perhaps 'de-humanized') Jew is, on the one hand, an embodiment of reification; he is part and parcel of a social process containing a very specific form of objective logic acting as if it 'possessed an autonomous intentionality'. On the other hand he is, at the same time, a subjectivity 'closely implicated with it' but also 'the container of all that the new objectivity has suppressed' (Grady 1996: 19). That is, Shylock simultaneously represents capitalism itself and that 'modern' subjectivity set loose in a world decentred from its old structures of meaning, so that all identities are now in question. Similarly, wherever we turn in the play, signifiers yield up excesses of meaning, and the means of signalling semantic surplus of this kind is the verbal pun.

The *OED* records the first usage of the term 'pun' in the late seventeeth century ($sb^1$), but in his *The Arte of English Poesie* (1589) George Puttenham draws attention to what he calls '*your figures Auricular that vvorke by Surplusage*' . He calls those instances of 'surplusage' that are material to his project, 'of importance to the sence or bewtie of your langauge' in that they contribute to the production of 'harmonicall speaches', and he cites those rhetorical figures of 'repetition, and iteration or amplification' as relevant. He is not specific about the other forms of 'surplusage' that he judges to be 'rather vicious then figuratiue, & therefore not melodious as shall be remembered in the chapter on viciosities or faultie speaches' (sig. V1$^v$). The nearest Puttenham gets to defining the pun is his comments on '*Prosonomasia or the* Nicknamer' (sig. Z2$^v$–Z3$^r$), which follow in part the definition offered in the Ciceronian *Ad Herennium*: 'Ye haue a figure by which ye play with a couple of words or names much resembling, and because the one seemes to answere th'other by manner of illusion, and doth as it were, nick him, I call him the *Nicknamer*.[5] Puttenham later extends this to cover a type of 'vicious speech' in which 'we speake or write doubtfully and that the sence may be taken two wayes'; he calls this 'the *ambiguous* or figure of sence incertaine' (sig. Ff3ʳ). Terence Hawkes (1975) was one of the first commentators on Shakespearean texts to draw our attention to the ways in which 'words and things, names and nature' unite in plays such as *Richard II*, and in figures such as John of Gaunt whose language 'not only touches reality, it both shapes and is shaped by it' (Hawkes 1975: 101). Hawkes cites M. M. Mahood's observation that in the Elizabethan period name puns were a serious matter because 'The bearer of a name was everything the name implied' (Hawkes 1975: 14). Puns which link identity with function, or which indicate a reduction from the human to the animal domain, effect transformations of meaning that, in a predominantly oral art form such as the Elizabethan theatre, point in the direction of 'surplusage', and may be both comic in their effect or, more seriously, may actually undermine a harmony that is explicitly linguistic, and also by extension, social. The claim I am making is that the pun in this instance *performs* that surplus of meaning that represents analogously those very troubled and troubling economic practices that are placed under scrutiny in *The Merchant of Venice*.

In the light of the foregoing argument there are certain puns upon which *The Merchant of Venice* seems to insist, which emanate from the Q1 spelling 'Iewe' and also as from other spellings such as 'Iobbe', or the formative (and submerged sexual) pun on 'purse' and 'person' (1.1.138). In a provocative study of the play Marc Shell (1982) establishes a three-fold punning connection between 'use', 'ewes' and 'Iewes' in the play; he observes:

> Shylock uses Antonio's words 'I do never use it' (1.3.66) to gener-ate by a pun an argument that would enlarge any debate about 'use' to include consideration of the human genealogy of 'Iewes' (as Shakespeare spelled *Jews*) and also the animal generation of 'ewes'. Thus he supplements the principal meaning of 'use'.
>
> (Shell 1982: 48 and *passim*)

The pun's yielding of an excess of meaning, a kind of return derived from the act of articulation, *performs* the process of interest-taking at the level of linguistic interaction; it is the 'profit' to be derived from discursive exchange, what Shell calls 'verbal usury'. In this respect both the objective appellation 'Jew' with its interactions released by a seminal pun, and the subjective appellation 'Shylock', the individualized 'name', untraceable in the discourse of typology, in one line of the two 'authoritative' printed texts of the play, might be said to perform an additional tension that arises from the actual process of reading. That tension may well be an articulation of the modern, an individualism in embryo, so to speak, a proleptic gesture towards a form of social organization that, as yet, may only be articulated within an existing religious and moral discourse. 'Shylock' is none other than a figure who represents the forces of economic production, whose very existence challenges radically existing relations. As 'Iewe' he is positioned, but as 'Shylock' he is the force of the new that threatens to bring chaos to the traditional, harmonious world of Venice.

We might also extend this logic to the complex naming associated with 'Launcelot Gobbo', or, to use Q1's spellings 'Launcelet Iobbe' and 'Clowne'. Only one text of *The Merchant of Venice*, F3 (1664) shortens the initial 'Iobbe' to 'Job' (p. 167), but even that text continues thereafter with the nonsensical speech prefix 'Gobbo'. Shell (1982) argues that the initial encounter between Launcelet and Old Gobbo parodies the biblical scene in which Jacob dispossesses Esau by stealing his father's blessing. But he also suggests that the references to Old Gobbo's blindness and Launcelot's hirsuitness extend the parody encounter with the biblical figures of Isaac and Esau respectively (Shell 1982: 52, 16). However, the spelling 'Iobbe' also echoes parodically the sufferings of the biblical Job which included, among other things, a plague of boils; the name 'Launcelet' begins to make a little more sense if we think of it in this biblical context also; he is the small lancet that will be able to alleviate his unfortunate father's suffering, and he will do so by moving from the Old Testament to the New Testament, from a commitment to the house of the Jew Shylock, to that of the house of the Christian Antonio. The long tradition (with the exception of Capell (1768)) that has individualized 'Launcelet Iobbe', assumed the surname 'Gobbo' (which would obviate the need to use an italic cap *I* in the printing), and removed any direct reference to his function as 'Clowne' in the play, has also diminished the scope of the parody that this subplot affords. It is the theatrical self-consciousness liberated by the punning on these names that editorial tradition has methodically occluded, along with a complex debate about the nature of fiscal exchange. That debate centred on the subject of 'usury', its undesirability, its capacity to generate moral corruption, and its tendency to promote acquisitiveness, to privilege the pursuit of individualism over the collective, hierarchical organization of society, and to destroy those bonds of obligation that bound different social groups to each other. It is this negotiation that focuses our attention upon certain of the transformations of social relations that this play addresses.

This revisionary reading does not, however, quite resolve all of the difficulties that we encounter in a reading of *The Merchant of Venice*. In fact, the dialectic of the play's objective logic and the forces that it would suppress do not quite seem to work along the lines of a straightforward historicist account. Or to put the matter slightly differently, to claim the play for 'modernism' without some of these caveats would be to impose yet another pattern of distortion on its substance. In order to excavate this in a little more detail we need to look more closely at the ways in which the figure of the 'Iewe' is marginalised. The suppressions in the play are both of an animality that is ascribed to the figure of the Jew: he is 'misbeliever, cut-throat, dog' (1.3.105), 'old carrion' (3.1.32), a devil capable of scriptural misquotation, and a machiavel:

> The devil can cite Scripture for his purpose, –
> An evil soul producing holy witness,
> Is like a villain with a smiling cheek,
> A goodly apple rotten at the heart.
> O what a goodly outside falsehood hath!
>
> (1.3.93–7)

If Shylock is the representative of the 'new' order in which the process of reification is dominant, why is that order articulated within a discursive field which involves a racialization and a moralization of a series of contradictions located at the heart of a dominant Protestant culture and the subjectivities to which it gives rise? Moreover, whereas among the Christian Venetians subjectivity is negotiable, and permeable, the Jew's behaviour and his identity are constrained by Law. Antonio and Bassanio are friends but they are from different social strata, and the hard fact of fiscal provision that would tie each to the other in an antagonistic relation is occluded in a bond of friendship that allows Antonio to submerge his own identity and his wealth into the quest that Bassanio undertakes. The connection between them is, in short, hegemonic, but it also modifies their respective subjectivities, in something like the same way that those of Portia, and more problematically Jessica, are modified through their multiple transformations in the play. In the case of Bassanio and Antonio we may observe this through the interactions between the Lord, in need of the material means to sustain an aristocratic position, and a merchant, whose own commercial practice does not so much mis-recognize itself as 'friendship' as link financial and emotional ties together in an unusual combination. What is the significance of Bassanio's claim from the outset that his debt to Antonio is both fiscal *and* emotional, almost as though the two were interchangeable? 'To you, Antonio, / I owe the most in money and in love' (1.1.130–1)? Moreover, how surprising is it that Antonio should respond with the faintly scandalous insistence that: 'My purse, my person, my extremest means / Lie all unlock'ed to your occasions' (1.1.138–9)? Antonio's initial revelation of a 'sadness' whose contours he is unable to articulate find its objective resonance in the demonized figure of the Jew, who is both the projection of Venice's economic anxieties and the guarantee of its future stability. Curiously, the Antonio whose misfortune in the play leads him to characterize himself as 'a tainted wether of the flock, / Meetest for death' (4.1.114–15) offers an interesting distortion of the Jew Shylock's own account of the origins of his own fiscal practices. Antonio's 'tainted wether' – that is, a young and imperfect ewe – is an anamorphic reflection of the Jew's 'parti-colour'd lambs' (1.3.83) which is articulated as an interference in 'the act of generation', in the generative operations of Nature itself.

At issue here are competing articulations of the metaphoric significance of 'the lamb'. In the case of Shylock the lamb is the sign of burgeoning economic prosperity, the result of an act of generation involving both male potency and female fecundity – the 'ram' and the 'ewe' – and capable of extension by analogy to all forms of financial (and sexual) transaction. From Antonio's perspective the relationship that Shylock disrupts is the natural bond between 'ewe' and 'lamb'; what makes the Jew a wolf is his deafness to humane importunity or to the logic of Nature:

> You may as well go question with the wolf,
> Why he hath made the ewe bleat for the lamb:

You may as well forbid the mountain pines
To wag their high tops and to make no noise
When they are fretten with the gusts of heaven:

(4.1.73–7)

We could of course expand the catalogue of differences to include
Shylock's anti-festive, anti-theatrical demeanour, which positions
him as a projection of another sort of anxiety: he is both a condition
of the play's formal progress, its 'plot', and a clog to its satisfactory
resolution in that he poses a challenge to the codes of friendship
that prevail in Venice. Shylock, who is not an ethnic Jew, but a fantasy indispensable to Venice's own self-constitution, is excavated as
a demonic spectre making the return to an idyllic past impossible.
The best that can be achieved, and it merely postpones the inevitable, is a coerced 'conversion' that will formally guarantee salvation
and redemption: the Jew will be forced to become a Christian. But
in that conversion the cure of Venice's fiscal ailments himself now
becomes the repository of its contagious disease; Antonio is returned
to health, but it is now Shylock who becomes ill: 'Give me leave to
go from hence, / I am not well' (4.1.391). His *identity* and his subjectivity are now shown to be fissured as he glimpses the ideological
burden that the imposition of a 'Christian' name confers upon him.
In fact, the trauma of the Jew's rebirth as a Christian father is
figured in the moment at which the demonized patriarch is initiated
into the unstable symbolic order of Venice, but this is emphatically
not the process of death and rebirth which is at the root of Christian
faith even though this is the form in which Venice articulates the
problem. It is the moment when the phantasmagoric is admitted
into the social structure of Venice and becomes legitimized, disclosing the fissure that it is the function of ideology to occlude.
Ironically, and in a rather bizarre act of generation, it is the
daughter Jessica who, supported by a reading of Venetian Law
administered by a Christian daughter able to transform the letter of
patriarchal law into a series of symbolically charged imperatives,
assists in the birth of her Christian father. That birth, as T. S. Eliot's
magus might have lamented, is hard and bitter for the phantasma-
gorical figure of the Jew. We might say that this is the hard and
bitter birth of modernity, not as an Enlightenment process but as a
traumatic but inevitable transformation of a harmony no longer
able to sustain the myth of its own cultural unity and now no longer

convinced of its own economic probity. The risks inherent in mercantilist practice which the play represents, the dependency upon the seemingly arbitrary forces of 'nature' that either augment the fortune of the investor or deprive him of it, require a strategy of management which depends for its efficacy upon human interference in an order perceived as 'natural'. The Jew as a necessary secular and economic force is precisely that satanic threat, resurrected from a mythologized past, laden with all of the baggage of an emergent force that the dominant ideology designates as marginal, and that can only be domesticated, or held at bay, through the structures of comedy. Those structures are familiar to us in the setting up of obstacles that a society dedicated to harmony is required to overcome. But also, the obstacles must be perceived to be 'real' in the sense that they are articulations of specific social dilemmas. If those dilemmas remain unresolved (in the fantasy of theatrical production, at any rate) then the result will be fragmentation and chaos. Here, and in this play, the viciousness of the humour, anathema to modern liberal sensibilities, is a mark of the extreme tensions that the text attempts, only partially successfully, to negotiate. In this instance, and despite the fact that 'the Iewe', 'Shylocke', the victim/demon that Venice is required to domesticate, has a voice, it is one that provides an ironic mirror; what begins as an Elizabethan comedy can now be read from the purview of the late twentieth century as a structure that inadvertently risks opening itself to ridicule. In other words, Venice 'gazes' at 'the Iewe Shylocke' who returns the gaze in which Venice sees its own self-image. That self-image requires the idealizing closure of comedy to shore up the fissures in its own ideology.

It is no small irony that print technology, the force that accelerated the internalization of the structures of authority, and that facilitated the emergence of a modern subjectivity, but that in 1600 was still unable to homogenize its output, should, in the case of the printed text of *The Merchant of Venice*, have been the vehicle for the disclosure of a particular rupture in the process of signification itself. The unstable speech prefixes in the play are symptomatic of a much larger transformation, and they enable us to read the resultant fissure in an ideology whose own, *fin-de-siècle* ontological thrust was distinctly at odds with, not to say resistant to, Enlightenment and post-Enlightenment modes of teleological thinking.

# Notes

1 Cf. Barton (1990: 88) where she notes, 'In *The Merchant of Venice*, for instance, it seems to have taken him [Shakespeare] some time to make up his mind whether the clown should be called "Gobbo" or "Iobbe".'

2 It is possible that the manuscript terminal *e* was confused with *o* and that in the stage entry on C1v: *Enter old Gobbo with a basket*. The *G* in *Gobbo* was confused with *J*. This hypothesis requires a concatenation of compositorial misreadings of the MS, complicated by the demonstrable shortage of I sorts and the need to substitute from a depleted *I* supply. See Kennedy (1998: 197–8). Florio (1598: 152) glosses *Gobbo* as 'crook-backt. Also a kind of faulkon', *Gobbe* as 'a kind of shell fish'; and *Gobba* as 'a bunch, a knob or crooke backe, a croope'. In the context of the play, the affliction from which the Clown's father suffers is that he is 'more then sand blinde, high grauell blinde' (C1v). Moreover, the name *Launcelet*, which in Florio is glossed as a derivative of 'Lancetta': 'a lancet or flame as surgeons use to let blood with' (Florio 1598: 197), makes much more sense if his surname *Iobbe* is read, as indeed it is in F3 where it is emended to *Job*, as the Italianate form of the biblical name Job. See also Brown (1955: xxii).

3 See Brown (1955: xvii–iii); see also Mahood (1987: 170).

4 Jewell (1611): sig. Gg1v. I am grateful to Adrian Streete of the Department of English Studies at Stirling for drawing my attention to this passage.

5 See Cicero (1989: 301–9). Earlier the *Ad Herenniium* identifies the 'pun' (similitudine) as a device used to 'provoke laughter' (19–20).

# 7

# The Merchant of Venice
## 'Modern' anti-Semitism and the veil of allegory

### LISA FREINKEL

> An ideology really succeeds when even the facts which at first
> sight contradict it start to function as arguments in its favor.
> (Slavoj Žižek, *The Sublime Object of Ideology*, 1989)

What, if anything, does *The Merchant of Venice* have to do with the
modern legacy of anti-Semitism? In a 1949 lecture delivered at
Stratford-upon-Avon, Nevill Coghill formulated what was to
become one of the standard post-Holocaust responses to the play.
*Merchant*, he argued, offers an allegorical presentation of religious
themes – of, in particular, the conflict between justice and mercy,
between the Old Law and the New.

> Seen thus it puts an entirely different complexion upon the
> opposition of Jew and Gentile. The two principles for which, in
> Shakespeare's play, respectively they stand are both *inherently
> right*, and they are only in conflict because, whereas God is abso-
> lutely just as He is absolutely merciful, mortal and finite man
> can only be relatively so.[1]
>
> (Coghill 1950, original italics)

Viewed from the proper perspective, there is no real opposition
between Jew and Gentile, nor between the justice and mercy they

respectively represent. Instead, the Old Law finds its completion in the New and justice is not abolished – it is, rather, fulfilled in the mercy of redemption, in the forgiveness bought on the Cross. Here Christ's words on the Mount hold sway: 'Thinke not that I am come to destroy the Law, or the Prophets. I am not come to destroy them, but to fulfill them' (Geneva Bible, Matt. 5: 17). Read from this standpoint, *The Merchant of Venice* offers nothing less than an allegory of Christian allegory *per se*: an allegory, that is, of the revisionary hermeneutics that transform the Hebrew Bible into the 'Old' Testament, taking the Law and the Prophets as prefigurations of Christian revelation. There is, then, no true opposition of Jew to Christian in *Merchant* insofar as the play represents Christianity as the authentic destiny of the Jew.

Implicit in Coghill's account is the absolute distinction between religious faith and race. According to this view, modern anti-Semitism relies upon the concept of race, and is thus for Coghill completely distinct from the medieval theological tradition that informs Shakespeare's play. And neither Coghill, nor the post-war literary criticism of *Merchant*, is alone in making such a distinction; the tendency to differentiate an 'anti-Judaic' theological tradition from a 'modern' racialized anti-Semitism has been crucial for modern historians as well. Daniel Jonah Goldhagen's much-debated book, *Hitler's Willing Executioners* (1996), offers an interesting case in point. Arguing that broad popular sentiment within Nazi Germany supported even the most virulent, eliminationist anti-Semitism, Goldhagen's book generated great controversy. However, despite such controversy, Goldhagen's overview of the *history* of anti-Semitism is entirely conventional. Anti-Semitism begins as 'a corollary of Christianity' (Goldhagen 1997: 49), he writes, 'and no matter how extreme the medieval hatred of Jews would become, it retained its theological focus: the Church wanted not to kill the Jews, for they were redeemable, but to convert them. This would reaffirm the supremacy of Christianity' (Goldhagen 1997: 53). For Goldhagen, so absolute is the difference between this conversionist, theological paradigm and the racist, paranoid culture of a modern eliminationist anti-Semitism, that his narrative cannot span the gap between the two views. Instead, a white space bisects his account, typographically dividing his discussion into a brief description of patristic and medieval attitudes and a much longer discussion of the nineteenth and early twentieth centuries. Typographically, Goldhagen thus represents an absolute gulf between the medieval view and the burgeoning race theories of the nineteenth century. An unnarratable gap, a white hole in history, divides the story of anti-Semitism into two distinct paradigms. In this way, Goldhagen does not so much recount the gradual 'evolution' of modern anti-Semitism as he describes the utter epistemic break that produced it: 'German antisemitism in the latter part of the [nineteenth] century coalesced around a new master concept: race. Race, an immutable quality, dictated that a Jew could never become a German' (Goldhagen 1997: 65). The underlying assumption here is that an essentialist notion of Jews – ultimately only available through the scientific discourse of race – is the *sine qua non* of the modern ideology.

What makes Goldhagen's argument particularly interesting for our purposes is the author's commitment to the idea of a specifically German anti-Semitism – a long-standing tradition that, Goldhagen argues, predates the Nazis and helps explain their rise to power. One would think then that Goldhagen, more than any recent historian of the Holocaust perhaps, would have a stake in linking the early modern anti-Semitism of Martin Luther to a later elimina-tionist policy. And yet, his account emphasizes instead the break rather than the continuity between the two paradigms, thereby demonstrating the tremendous difficulty which any history of anti-Semitism based on the theology/race dichotomy faces. Simply put: how can we write the pre-nineteenth-century history of anti-Semitism if what defines the phenomenon itself is a concept that did not exist *before* the nineteenth century? Reformation theologian Heiko Oberman responds to this problem in his important mono-graph, *The Roots of Anti-Semitism* (1984). Although Oberman offers a detailed and nuanced reading of early modern attitudes toward Jews, he stumbles upon the same problem as Goldhagen does: 'Strictly speaking, "anti-Semitism" did not exist prior to the race theory of the nineteenth century. Nevertheless, there are events, atti-tudes, or statements which long before the rise of the concept come very close to the reality of anti-Semitism' (Oberman 1984: xi). From the very start, Oberman's project is vexed by anachronism. If anti-Semitism is, by definition, a modern phenomenon then *strictly speaking* it has no roots. The transhistorical 'reality' Oberman invokes in order to define the legacy of race hatred remains an empty concept. Like Goldhagen, Oberman has in fact limited this 'reality' to the present; he has denied the historical existence of the very phenomenon whose roots he wants to trace. Oberman's account no less than Goldhagen's is doomed to ahistoricity.

My hope in this chapter is, in some small measure, to narrate the gap in the traditional account of anti-Semitism. In so doing I shall not try to unearth the *roots* or early modern origins of modern anti-Semitism; that task presumes an essential 'reality' of anti-Semitism and, not coincidentally, identifies that 'reality' with an essentialist picture of the Jew. Instead, I offer a small chapter in something like the *genealogy* of anti-Semitism, excavating a history of accidents, of shifting appropriations and interpretations, instead of trans-historical essences.[2] The traditional view of anti-Semitism pivots on the question of conversion, radically distinguishing between pre-modern and modern attitudes on the basis of an essentialism that only becomes available in the nineteenth century and denies the possible redemption of the Jews. If Jews are defined by their religious faith, then their difference from us is merely accident and they may be saved through conversion; they are potentially just like us – it is only their obstinacy, their refusal to convert, that renders them abhorrent. The only good Jew, such a theology might maintain, is a Christian. Conversely, if what defines the Jews is their race, 'an immutable quality' (as Goldhagen puts it), then the Jews are essentially irredeemable, and the stakes rise dramatically; at its paranoid height such ideology will proclaim that the only good Jew is a dead Jew.

To narrate the gap in the story of anti-Semitism we must question this prevailing account in several key ways. Slavoj Žižek offers a helpful starting point in the passage I have taken as my epigraph: 'An ideology really succeeds when even the facts which at first sight contradict it start to function as arguments in its favor' (Žižek 1989: 49). The paranoid belief systems of the nineteenth and twentieth centuries, I would maintain, are *not* best understood in terms of race – in terms, that is, of the way positivist discourses (like the biology of race or the ethnography of *Volk*) offer a basis for essential-ism. To understand anti-Semitism in such terms is to presume that its virulence lies in the belief that there is an 'objective' basis of Jewishness. The progressive response to a racism so construed often points out the fallacy of such 'objectivity', questioning the so-called facts or science taken to support the essentialism. And such a response routinely fails – because it fails to recognize the ways in which such science constructs its object (and its objectivity) hysteri-cally, precisely starting from the dread that there is *no* objective correlative to the Jewishness of Jews. Within such a paranoid system, indeed, the very lack of evidence becomes a *proof* of one's convictions – proof, potentially, that Jews must be eliminated if only because one cannot stabilize their identity, fix their essence, and so distinguish them from the rest of us.

We need to think beyond the dichotomization of religion and race – especially insofar as that dichotomy structures our view of the history of anti-Semitism. We cannot understand either the dynamic of modern anti-Semitism or its continuity with early modern attitudes if we perceive the development of race theory as constituting a radical paradigm shift. Race theory does not so much enable the articulation of a modern Jewish question, as it attempts to *fix* that question; that is, race theory seeks to resolve the *Judenfrage* via an essentialism that stabilizes the question of Jewish identity. In this way, essentialism is not the cause of modern anti-Semitism, but rather the effect of an earlier destabilization and decentering of Jewish identity. In other words, nineteenth-century positivism works to reassure a hysteria that derives not from the presumed immutable nature of the Jew, but rather from the anxiety – ultimately, a *theological* anxiety – that no such immutable essence exists.

It is Martin Luther who first articulates this anxiety, when he reconsiders the doctrine of justification by faith alone. Luther, and the Reformation he inspires, force a re-examination of the nature of Hebrew Law, reconceiving and reconfiguring the relationship between Jew and Christian in the process. This reconfiguration of traditional topoi and theological assumptions can be usefully sketched in brief, if we examine Luther's radical interpretation of an ancient and pedigreed image, an image central to accounts of Christian allegory dating back to St. Paul: the image of the Law as *veil*. As I argue below and elsewhere,[3] readers like Coghill are correct: the relationship between Jew and Christian in *Merchant* is indeed defined in terms of Christian allegory. But at issue here is an allegory in crisis: a post-Lutheran allegory – an allegory that has been subjected to the critique Luther brings to the image of the Pauline veil. Thus, where Coghill and others invoke allegory to distance the play from a modern anti-Semitism, we will see on the contrary that it is an allegorical crisis that finally undermines any clear distinction within *Merchant* between Judaism defined as 'theology' or defined as 'race'. As we shall see, finally, in a discussion of the 'harsh mercy' of the trial scene, the very conversion that should mark the allegorical triumph of mercy over justice, of spirit over flesh, instead marks the emergence of a Jew who exceeds all fleshly determination, and thus remains ever a threat, ever an alibi for the further, paranoid reach of the Law. 'Tarry Jew. / The Law hath yet another hold on you' (4.1.342–3).

In short, the genealogy of anti-Semitism can be written only through the history of Christian allegory. The religion/race dichotomy common both to accounts of anti-Semitism and to post-Holocaust readings of *Merchant* bespeaks conventional wisdom about the secularity of modernity. But one crucial problem attends the conventional view: the very dichotomy by means of which we distinguish between a pre-modern theological perspective and a modern secular one is itself a construction of theology. From the start, the discourse against the Jews is defined by the theological distinction of race versus faith – of flesh versus spirit. It is the same distinction by means of which the early Christians simultaneously assimilate and dismiss both Jewish history and Jewish law, allegorically refashioning the Hebrew Bible as the new *Old* Testament.

'There is neither Iew nor Grecian: there is neither bond nor free: there is neither male nor female: for ye are all one in Christ Iesus' (Gal. 3:28). The indictment of the Jews as an alien race, distinguished by their particularity and unassimilability, dates back after all to that great Jewish convert himself: the apostle Paul. Writing to his 'brothers' in Galatia, Paul celebrates Christianity's universalism, with its ability to overcome the merely fleshly distinctions of tribe, nation, status, sex. At issue is the notion of Christian liberty; Paul is at pains to dispel the Galatians' idea that one must be a Jew, devout in adherence to Mosaic law, before one can be a Christian. The crux of Paul's argument is his revision of that foundational moment of the Jewish people: Abraham's covenant with God. Paul insists that through faith in Christ – Himself a Jew rejected by Jews – even Gentiles can lay claim to the blessing that is Abraham's birthright. 'Now to Abraham and his seede were the promises made . . . And if *ye be* Christs, then are ye Abraham's seed, and heirs by promise' (Gal. 3:16, 29). The Jews are a people insofar as they can trace their lineage back to Abraham; the Christians, on the other hand, can trace their lineage back to Abraham insofar as they are a people, insofar as they are one in Christ Jesus. Faith in Christ overrides the dictates of birth and clan; Spirit supersedes the claims of the flesh. And, ultimately for Paul – and for the long-lived allegorical tradition he inaugurates – this distinction between flesh and Spirit, between race and faith, amounts to the very distinction between Jew and Christian. In this way, the dichotomy used to define a Christian anti-Semitism, the dichotomy of religious faith versus race, is ultimately the very dichotomy by means of which Christianity determines its difference from – and its supersession of – the Jews.

From the start, then, the theological argument against the Jews mobilizes a language of race versus theology: insofar as the Jews maintain a racial identity, refusing to ally themselves according to belief rather than blood, they are different from and inferior to the universal brotherhood of Christianity. 'For the flesh lusteth against the Spirit, and the Spirit against the flesh' (Gal. 5:17). If the resistance of the flesh to spirit marks the difference between Jews and Christians, it also underlies the structure of Christian allegory, mediating the ambivalent role Judaism plays *within* Christianity. As Paul and later exegetes argue, Judaism legitimizes Christianity, serving as its authorizing origin – but it is also, like Esau displaced by his younger twin Jacob, rendered illegitimate by its very successor. Allegory thus transforms ambivalence into authority, Jewish scripture into a Christian legitimizing discourse; understood as the prefiguration of Christian truth, the literal meaning of the Hebrew Bible is simultaneously negated and preserved. Taken now as the fleshly vehicle for a Christian spiritual tenor, the concrete events of Jewish sacred history and the material requirements of Mosaic Law lose both their specificity and their autonomy.

Nowhere is this dynamic of appropriation and rejection clearer than in the image of the law as *veil* – the very topos to which Luther will return in his sixteenth-century critique of Christian allegory.

> [F]or the letter killeth, but the Spirit giueth life. If then the minis-tration of death *written* with letters and ingrauen in stones, was glorious, so that the children of Israel could not behold the face of Moses, for the glory of his countenance . . . How shall not the ministration of the Spirit be more glorious. For if that which should bee abolished, *was* glorious, much more shall that which remaineth, be glorious . . . And *we are* not as Moses *which* put a vaile vpon his face, that the children of Israel should not looke vnto the end of that which should be abolished. Therefore their minds are hardened: for vntill this day remaineth the same couer-ing vntaken away in the reading of the old Testament, which *vaile* in Christ is put away. But euen vnto this day, when Moses is

read the vaile is layd ouer their hearts. Neuerthelesse, when their *heart* shall be turned to the Lord, the vaile shal be taken away.
(2 Cor. 3:6–16, original emphasis)

For Paul, the veil with which Moses covered his radiant face as he came down from Mount Sinai to deliver the Law (Exodus 34: 33–5) itself serves as an allegory *for* the Law. The veil hides even God's reflected glory from the Israelites, just as the Law in its written letters and engraved stones mediates the covenant that itself mediates a relation to God. The Israelites are at two removes from the Lord. The veil/Law keeps the children of Israel from seeing the image of God; they are blind to 'the end [*telos*] of that which should be abolished' – blind, that is, both to its completion and its purpose in Christ. Instead, they take the Law as an end in itself, failing to see even that their vision is obscured. What the Hebrews miss is that the Law, like the veil, cannot be taken at face value.

Accordingly, at least from Origen on, Paul's allegory of the veil becomes the commonplace justification for an allegorical, spiritualist interpretation of the text. The letter killeth, but the Spirit giveth life. Standing in opposition to the spirit, the letter is that fleshly, external veil that obscures a hidden immaterial truth; it is that outer form, that tough integument, that must be peeled back to reveal the inner content, the precious kernel. Christian revelation consists, in short, in unveiling the Old Testament. To reveal the Christian truth obscured in Jewish scripture is to strip away external appearances, to search out hidden meanings, to uncover the hidden reflection of God. It thus entails, in the first place, a conviction that the Law is not to be taken at its letter. In the manner of a platonic ascent from the material to the spiritual world, the literal, 'fleshly' content of the Old Testament must be disregarded.

When Martin Luther turns to the Pauline image of the veil, however, he quietly devastates over a millennium of exegetical practice. For Luther, the veil is not that mystic letter whose concrete, historical meaning must be overridden in the name of a 'lofty', nonmaterial meaning; indeed, Luther sharply critiques the allegorist's understanding of 2 Cor. 3:6 ('the letter killeth, but the Spirit giveth life'). The allegorical reader, as Luther writes in his 1519 Commentary on Galatians,

take[s] the outward form and historical account [of the Old Testament] to be the 'letter.' But the mystical and allegorical interpretation they call 'spiritual.' And they call that man 'spiritual' who understands everything in a lofty sense, and, as they say, allows nothing of the Jewish tradition . . . [But] spiritual understanding does not mean what is mystical and anagogical (in which the ungodly also excel); but in the strict sense it means life itself and the Law as it is put into actual practice . . . In short, it means that complete fulfillment which the Law commands and requires . . . We conclude, therefore, that in itself the Law is always spiritual; that is, it signifies the spirit which is its fulfill-ment. For others, however, though never for itself, it is a 'letter.'

(Luther 1955–76: 27: 312–13)

In its very historical literality, Luther argues, in its most material reality and concrete proscriptions, the Law of Moses already has a spiritual meaning, for it signals the grace which alone can truly justify us in the eyes of God. Everything that we can do of our own power or our own free will to obey the letter of God's Law will fall short of fulfilling the Law, Luther teaches. What matters for our righteousness is our obedience to God's decrees – and not just the performance of specific acts. But perfect obedience demands that, as free men, we consent to those dictates. Obedience, in other words, requires not a slavish response to the Law but rather that we respond 'gladly and willingly' to it. Yet, as Luther teaches: 'No work of law is done gladly and willingly; it is all forced and compelled' (Luther 1955–76: 35: 241). The mere fact that we act in conformity to the Law – that we seek to obey – indicates a degree of compulsion that taints our actions.

In its literal command, the Law is impossible to fulfill; but it is this impossibility itself that signals the necessity for grace. '[W]here there is no law of God, there all human reason is so blind that it cannot recognize sin'; but in its very impossibility, the Law stirs up sin, and sets it before our eyes, 'driving all our presumption into despondency and trembling and despair' until we long for grace (Luther 1955–76: 35: 242, 243). To unveil the Law is to confront the extent of our sin and the failure of our works. Such is the divine, spiritual office of the Law: it clears away blindness and pride, reveal-ing that the just can only live by faith. But we cannot unveil this spirit of the Law without first mistaking the Law for a letter. For earlier exegetes such a mistake marked the servitude of the Jew who blindly takes the Law at its face value. For Luther, however, the mis-take is essential for the Christian as well, since revelation consists not in negating the surface of the Law in the name of a higher, or deeper, or hidden meaning – but rather in reading the surface *as such*, in its naked and intolerable essence as sheer appearance. It is the nakedness of surface that, according to Luther, the Israelites could not endure; significantly, Luther interprets the radiance of Moses' face not as reflected divine glory but instead as an intolerable glare, an unbearable knowledge: the 'glare of the knowledge of our wickedness and nothingness' (Luther 1955–76: 35: 244). Such glaring truth proves too much for the Israelites; for this reason, Moses wears a veil as he descends with the tablets of the Law. In this manner, the Israelites of Exodus 34 represent

> those who attempt to fulfil the law by their own power, without grace . . . The law comes to them but they cannot endure it. They therefore put a veil over it and lead a life of hypocrisy, doing outward works of the law. Yet the law makes it all to be sin where the veil is taken off. For the law shows that our ability counts for nothing without God's grace . . . [T]hose who see Moses clearly, without a veil . . . understand the intention of the law and how it demands impossible things.
>
> (Luther 1955–76: 35: 244–5)

Christian revelation means not a turning away from the Law, but instead a turning toward it, as toward a mirror that reflects not God but rather our own sinful natures. To unveil the Law is to recognize the extent to which it is our trial and our temptation, revealing the depths of human presumption.

For Luther, to take the Law at its letter is no longer an error confined to the Jews, but instead one necessary moment in the movement of Christian revelation. The mistake reveals the infinite depth of our sin, just as our resulting despair reveals that faith alone can save us. And therein lies the end of hypocrisy and the possibility of redemption. Despair in the face of our utter worthlessness becomes the joyful confidence that Christ was given for our sins. In this way, by linking the office of the Law to a confidence in our salvation, Luther reconsiders the nature of spiritual distress itself. The fits of despair he was himself prone to throughout his life – his *Anfechtungen*, or tribulations, as he called them, when he felt himself to be an abandoned sinner – were merely preludes to his exultant joy in being saved. For Luther, despair and faith are the lub-dub of the Christian heart. As Heiko Oberman (1982: 178) puts it, for Luther 'tribulations are not a disease, so there can be no cure for them. They are a characteristic condition of Christian life'. Without the spiritual Law, as Luther sees it, there can be no Christian life; the despair it produces serves, in this manner, as the indispensable companion to our experience of the good news. 'We cannot reach heaven until we first descend into hell,' he writes in his *Grosser Katechismus*. 'We cannot be God's children unless first we are the Devil's children. Again before the world can be seen to be a lie it must first appear to be the truth' (Luther 1883–1919: 30[1] I: 249).[4]

Yet the tribulations do not stop there: since the truth emerges only once we recognize our presumption as a lie, it is always possible to mistrust that 'truth' as nothing more than renewed presumption. In arguing that the Law is a test, meant to push us to despair, Luther opens up a second-guessing hermeneutics – a hermeneutics of suspicion where every reading becomes itself the letter of a further reading. Luther's conception of the unveiled Law thus restructures the dichotomies of a traditional Christian allegory. Ultimately, in place of a teleological, allegorical narrative from Judaism to Christianity and from dead letter to living spirit, Luther's Law unveils instead an essential and ceaseless ambivalence between mutually exclusive alternatives: flesh/spirit, law/gospel, damnation/salvation, slavery/freedom. This rabbit/duck ambivalence, Luther teaches, is at play not only within the history of the Church, but also within the lives of the just.

'For the flesh lusteth against the Spirit.' The flesh is easily defined within the allegorical tradition that Luther rejects. It is the material veil that separates us from the Spirit, but understood rightly it is also the signifying vehicle that leads us *to* the Spirit. Utterly distinct from the Spirit that it either hides or signifies, the flesh (like the Law as veil) is only a problem when we take it as an end in itself. But as we have seen, Luther unsettles this view of the flesh with his doctrine of justification by faith alone. For Luther the flesh is no longer a veil – indeed it is no longer even necessarily material – but what, exactly, is it? Luther cites Romans 14:23, 'Whatever does not proceed from faith is sin', and argues that the flesh is not just the body, but is everything that is born of the flesh: 'the whole man, with body and soul, mind and sense – because everything about him longs for the flesh' (Luther 1955–76: 27: 76; 35: 371). The flesh is what cannot save us, but since it is no longer the veil-signifier that points us toward God, it cannot be stripped away either. The flesh is not the Spirit, but since we cannot peel it away from the Spirit, how exactly can we determine and overcome it? Indeed, after Luther, defining the flesh becomes a central task for sixteenth-century Protestants and Catholics; it animates almost all of the crucial doctrinal debates: iconoclasm, infant baptism, the nature of the Eucharist, and so on. And, broadly speaking, it is the problem of defining the flesh that lies at the heart of *The Merchant of Venice*, ultimately undermining the Christian triumph of mercy through the ambivalent figure of the Jewish convert.

From the start, an uneasiness, or uncertainty, about the nature of the flesh seems to generate a melancholy that pervades the play. Certainly Antonio's own contested flesh positions him as 'th'unhappy subject' around whom the 'quarrels' of the play's two main plots revolve (cf. 5.1.237), but even the 'want-wit sadness' (1.1.6) with which he opens the play seems relevant to the problem of defining the flesh:

> *Solanio:* Not in love neither? Then let us say you are sad,
> Because you are not merry, and 'twere as easy
> For you to laugh, and leap, and say you are merry,
> Because you are not sad. Now, by two-headed Janus,
> Nature hath framed strange fellows in her time:
> Some that will evermore peep through their eyes
> And laugh like parrots at a bagpiper,
> And other of such vinegar aspect
> That they'll not show their teeth in way of smile,
> Though Nestor swear the jest be laughable.
>
> (1.1.47–56)

As melancholy often works in Shakespeare, Antonio's causeless sadness seems to evacuate meaning, leaving behind the world as an empty shell – think here of Jaques, sucking melancholy out of a song 'as a weasel sucks eggs' (*As You Like It* 2.5.11–12). Solanio's figure for that shell is the two-headed Janus: the face that is always facing us, merry because it is not sad, sad because it is not merry. Structurally, Solanio's Janus presents something like the undecidable rabbit/duck ambivalence of Luther's critique of allegory, where presumption is just the other side of despair and the world must be a lie before it can be the truth. This face that is always facing us resists depth; behind one face is only another; for all its seeming three-dimensionality, the Janus head is nothing but masks.

Despite its apparent flippancy, Solanio's mock raises a question about the nature of human nature that ultimately the play will have a hard time answering. Evacuated of their depth and meaning, what Shylock later refers to as human 'affections' or 'passions' – the inclinations or aversions that shape our conduct – reduce to mere physical idiosyncrasies: the quirky, uncontrollable tics that meaninglessly distinguish one man from another. There is little to differentiate affections such as these from the mechanical repetitions of a parrot's voice. Solanio's merrymakers who cannot help but laugh like parrots at a bagpiper, find their Janus-like inversion in the trial scene, in the men Shylock cites who 'when the bagpipe sings I'th'nose, / Cannot contain their urine' (4.1.48–9). For Shylock the example of the bagpipe serves as recalcitrant response to the Duke's plea that the Jew drop his suit: 'We all expect a gentle answer, Jew' (33).[5] The pun on gentle/Gentile, as many have noted, like related quibbling throughout the play on the meaning of 'kind' ('The Hebrew will turn Christian; he grows kind' [1.3.174]), reveals the ways in which Shylock stands for a resistant particularity – for the principle of difference itself. The Duke insists upon this difference at the same time that he appeals to the universal quality of 'human gentleness and love' (4.1.24). Shylock's response is to push still further in the direction of meaningless particularity – a particularity that he identifies with the unruly, unreasoning flesh itself: 'for affection, / Mistress of passion, sways it [i.e. passion] to the mood / Of what it likes or loathes' (4.1.48–51).[6] Where the Duke hopes for depth and reason, Shylock insists instead on mask-like superficiality, confirming the Christians' sense that he is an obdurate shell of a man, 'void and empty/From any dram of mercy' (4.1.3–4).[7] And ultimately, as figure for the cruel superficiality of the flesh, Shylock does contrast with a gentle Gentile depth – but as we shall see, in the process he also reveals the necessarily two-faced nature of Christian mercy.

Of course, for Nevill Coghill writing in 1949, the quality of mercy in the play is hardly strained at all.

> It will, of course, be argued that it is painful for Shylock to swallow his pride, abjure his *racial faith*, and receive baptism. But then Christianity is painful. Its centre is crucifixion, nor has it ever been held to be equally easy for all natures to embrace . . . But from Anthonio's point of view, Shylock has at least been given his chance of eternal joy, and it is he, Anthonio, that has

given it to him. Mercy has triumphed over justice, even if the way of mercy is a hard way.

(Coghill 1950: 23, emphasis added)

We should not be surprised that Coghill's strict separation of 'race feeling' and theological doctrine collapses when he discusses the play's climax and refers to Shylock's 'racial faith' – nor should we be surprised that Coghill's notion of a 'hard mercy' seems to echo the *scharffe barmhertzigkeit*, the sharp or harsh mercy that Luther recommends against the Jews in his late writings (a 'mercy' that includes forced labor; burning synagogues, homes and schools; forbidding rabbis to teach; stealing Jews' cash and precious metals, and prohibiting usury).[8] After all, for Coghill it is the possibility of conversion that should mark the dividing line between a theological and a racial definition of the Jew – and yet there is something about Shylock's forced conversion, coming as it does in the wake of a scene that has sought to 'out-Jew the Jew', that seems to trouble this dichotomy, calling into the question the firm boundary Coghill envisions between the Elizabethans and we moderns, just as Luther's sharp mercy confuses any sharp distinction between a modern eliminationist perspective and a pre-modern conversionist one.

Significantly, the conversion is one of the few plot elements of the trial scene that is entirely Shakespeare's own; while, for instance, Portia's distinction between flesh and blood is a regular feature of the flesh-bond plot, none of the known versions of the story involve the usurer's conversion. Why does Shylock's conversion become important for Shakespeare? And why is it that, as Coghill claims at least, of the various conditions Shylock must meet in order for his life to be spared, it is the forced conversion 'that seems to modern ears so harshly vindictive' (Coghill 1950: 22)? Why is it there, at the very moment that the play effaces the distinction between Jew and Christian in the name of the triumph of faith over flesh, that modern readers have most suspected the play's Christians of *bad* faith?

The problem begins, I think, with an often-overlooked or misread moment of dialogue.

> *Portia:*   Of a strange nature is the suit you follow,
>            Yet in such rule that the Venetian law
>            Cannot impugn you as you do proceed.
>            . . .

> Do you confess the bond?
>
> *Antonio:*   I do.
>
> *Portia:*   Then must the Jew be merciful.
>
> *Shylock:*   On what compulsion must I? Tell me that.
>
> *Portia:*   The quality of mercy is not strained.

$$(4.1.177-9)$$

Even admirers of the play as Christian allegory tend to view Portia throughout this scene, and especially at moments like this one, as a master tactician, skillfully maneuvering Shylock into an ever more rigid statement of the literalism and legalism for which he stands. Portia is 'totally in control' of a situation 'she has engineered' writes Lawrence Danson (1978: 62); her 'final tactic' is to demonstrate to Shylock the untenability of a legalistic viewpoint (Lewalski 1962: 341). The image of Portia as consummate strategist – as *lawyer* even – working in the name of mercy, offers an emblem of the bad faith so many modern readers have discerned in the play. Allegorical readers like Coghill, however, have argued that these 'tricks' are not part of Portia's character but rather 'devices' that serve to forward the symbolic movement of the plot (cf. Coghill 1950: 21–2). Both views are inadequate, however, failing to take into account the seriousness of Portia's commitment to the Law as such. The law of Venice cannot impugn Shylock since his suit is completely in order. Nor does Antonio contest the bond; there, too, all is 'in rule' with Shylock's suit. 'Then must the Jew be merciful.' The line is often read as a casual remark (revealed later on as canny strategy): since there is no legal remedy that can save Antonio's life, the only recourse is an appeal to mercy. But Shylock's response reveals, I think, the genuine dilemma Portia has no choice but to confront: 'On what compulsion must I? Tell me that.'

Mercy presents a problem – indeed, the central problem – within a doctrine of justification by faith alone. Mercy is the grace that imputes righteousness where none has been deserved; it is that love, that faith that gives itself for nothing in return. As such, as Portia tells us, mercy is by definition unconstrained and free. It cannot be compelled and retain its character as mercy; it is, as Shylock recognizes, the very antithesis of 'must' – the very opposite of the Law, bearing out the truth of Luther's formulation: 'No work of law is done gladly and willingly; it is all forced and compelled.' While the work of Law is strained and grudging, revealing our disobedience as much as it reveals our compliance, mercy is liberal and free. 'It droppeth as the gentle rain from heaven/Upon the place beneath'. We cannot earn God's mercy any more than we can grant mercy to others on command. As the Law's antithesis, mercy is also anti-thetical to good works; mercy, like faith, cannot consist in an action that we perform, but rather is the result of God's action within us. But if mercy gives itself for nothing, how can we ensure its presence in our lives? We cannot earn it, we cannot perform it. How then can we be sure that our own deeds are selfless and forgiving – and (it amounts to the same question) how can we be sure that we are ourselves freely forgiven? How can we ensure, in other words, that we are saved?

Portia encapsulates the logic of the problem, as well as the dramatic structure of the trial scene, in the famous climax of her speech:

> Therefore, Jew,
> Though justice be thy plea, consider this:
> That in the course of justice none of us
> Should see salvation. We do pray for mercy,
> And that same prayer doth teach us all to render
> The deeds of mercy.
>
> (4.1.192–5)

If mercy cannot be compelled, Portia suggests, it can somehow be taught. Or, to put it more precisely, the *necessity* of mercy can be taught. Or, to put it even more precisely, the consideration that our works will never save us yields the realization that we rely on God's good graces alone. And *that* humbling realization is itself, Portia seems to suggest, a kind of grace that teaches us mercy. A *kind* of grace, yet not the enabling thing itself: the distance from teaching to action is, as Portia herself has already noted, not so quickly traversed. 'If to do were as easy as to know what were good to do,' Portia tells Nerissa in their very first scene, 'chapels had been churches, and poor men's cottages princes' palaces' (1.2.11–13). There are no shortcuts here, no direct routes either to salvation or to that liberal spirit of grace Portia seeks to embody in Belmont: 'I stand for sacrifice,' she tells Bassanio (3.2.57). There are no short-cuts because there is no real response to Shylock's question: 'On what compulsion must I?' To get to mercy, Portia, like the Venetians stymied by their own legal precedent, must stumble first over the course of justice.

In sum, Portia's office in the courtroom is to perform the very office of the Law, serving not only as a 'Daniel' (as Shylock first calls her), but as the lawgiver Moses himself, who unveils the Law not by treating the flesh as a veil, or the letter as an allegory, but instead by focusing ever more intently upon the flesh and the letter *as such*. Like the laws of Moses, bewildering further in their number and complexity, the Law proliferates wildly in Portia's hands, branching out in every direction, its reach ever more extensive, its satisfaction ever more patently impossible – and it does so in order to compel that which cannot be compelled. Thus, with each new, exfoliating reading of the 'flesh' nominated in the bond, Portia uncovers a new law:

> Tarry a little. There is something else.
> This bond doth give thee here no jot of blood.
> . . .
> Take thou thy pound of flesh.
> But in the cutting it, if thou dost shed
> One drop of Christian blood, thy lands and goods
> Are by the laws of Venice confiscate
> Unto the state of Venice.
>
> (4.1.303–7)

> Shed thou no blood, nor cut thou less nor more
> But just a pound of flesh. If thou tak'st more
> Or less than a just pound . . .
> Thou diest, and all thy goods are confiscate.
>
> (4.1.320–7)

> Tarry, Jew.
> The law hath yet another hold on you.
> It is enacted in the laws of Venice,
> If it be proved against an alien
> That by direct or indirect attempts
> He seek the life of any citizen,
> The party 'gainst the which he doth contrive
> Shall seize one half his goods; the other half
> Comes to the privy coffer of the state,
> And the offender's life lies in the mercy
> Of the Duke only, 'gainst all other voice –
>
> (4.1.341–51)

As the definition of 'flesh' becomes fractally more complex, the Law widens its net, tightens its hold, until there can be no escape from justice: 'Thou shalt have justice more than thou desir'st' (4.1.312). And, at the moment of the Law's tightest, broadest hold and the flesh's greatest complexity, when it has become entirely impossible to delimit the flesh, to cut it away like a veil, since now it denotes 'life' itself – at that very moment, mercy reappears. 'Down, therefore, and beg mercy of the Duke' (4.1.358). The Law has performed its office, constraining Shylock to forgo justice in the name of Christian charity. 'Such blindness', Luther writes, 'must be . . . compelled and forced by the law to seek something beyond the law and its own ability, namely, the grace of God promised in the Christ who was to come' (Luther 1955–76: 35: 244). So does Shylock receive the answer to his question about compulsion: the Law itself compels him to seek mercy – and it does so *mercilessly*.

Yet, of course, Shylock never does beg mercy; he is pardoned before he asks for pardon, and offers scarcely any reaction to the hard mercy of his conversion. But it does not matter, since neither the conversion nor the Duke's or Antonio's mercy seem, in the final analysis, to be designed for the benefit of Shylock. It is, after all, the Christians who have a stake in the problem of mercy, for both their personal and their political salvation. It is they who can benefit from the way Shylock's defeat serves at its point of highest intensity to elicit the 'mercy of the Duke', thereby demonstrating the correlation of 'temporal power' (4.1.185) with divine grace. And it is they who, for their own peace of mind, will want to reconcile the tensions between presumption and despair, Law and Gospel, flesh and spirit, and ultimately between Jews and Christians. But in the Janus-headed world that Luther helps create, instead of the allegorical resolution of opposites, we find a constantly flipping coin. The Christians in this play cannot resolve the question of their own faith without performing the office of the Law; they need Shylock in order to stage the possibility of mercy. And yet, it is precisely this sense of staginess that engenders the suspicion that their faith is, in truth, *bad* faith. The more Portia tries to compel mercy through demonstrating the failure of justice, the more the whole set-up risks seeming rigged – the 'mercy' that finally appears bearing no more authority or credibility than the ever-expanding readings of Shylock's bond and Venetian law. At issue here is just another version of Luther's particular brand of spiritual distress: if the truth is only founded on the recognition of a lie, it is thus itself always vulnerable to a further unveiling.

In the end, such Janus-like ambivalences render the difference between Jew and Christian undecidable, much as the flesh itself becomes impossible to define in clearly delimited terms. But rather than enable a new era of religious tolerance, such ambivalence seems only to render the Jew infinitely more dangerous because infinitely more slippery. And it is ultimately as the figure for a Christian bad faith that this slippery Jew becomes the alibi for a law that is ever-expanding and a mercy that is growing ever more sharp.

## Acknowledgements

I am grateful to my fellow seminarians at the 1999 Shakespeare Association of America session on 'The boundaries of modernity' for their insightful comments on an earlier version of this chapter. I also owe a special debt of gratitude to Brian Manning Delaney, Karen Ford, and George Rowe, whose intellectual support and guidance I could not do without, and to Richard Halpern, whose provocative essay, 'The Jewish question: Shakespeare and anti-Semitism', and whose thoughtful feedback at the SAA, have proved invaluable to my research.

## Notes

1 The 1949 lecture, 'The basis of Shakespearian comedy', was printed in *Essays and Studies 1950*. Coghill's argument proved enormously popular, especially with the following generation of *Merchant* critics. Barbara K. Lewalski (1962) cites Coghill's essay as the inspiration behind her own allegorical interpretation of the play in her important essay, 'Biblical allusion and allegory in The Merchant of Venice'. Similarly, Lawrence Danson (1978) mentions a special indebtedness to Coghill's essay – citing, indeed, the very passage I have quoted above.

2 Thanks to Hugh Grady for encouraging this connection. I use the term 'genealogy' here in a loosely Foucauldian/Nietzschean sense:

> If interpretation were the slow exposure of the meaning hidden in an origin, then only metaphysics could interpret the development of humanity. But if interpretation is the violent or surreptitious appropriation of a system of rules, which in itself has no essential meaning . . . then the development of humanity is a series of interpretations. The role of genealogy is to record its history.
>
> (Foucault 1984: 86)

In complex ways that go beyond the scope of this chapter, Foucault's 'genealogy' serves precisely to demystify the kind of 'origin' Christianity assigns to Judaism.

3  See the final chapter of my forthcoming study, *Reading Shakespeare's Will: The Theology of Figure from Augustine to the Sonnets.*

4  As quoted and translated by Bainton (1950: 169). For Bainton, Luther's focus upon a God who works by contraries, damning where he means to save, reveals the 'medieval' cast of the reformer's thought. What Bainton seems to miss, however, is how Luther's sense of a necessary ambivalence at the heart of Christian life utterly transforms a medieval understanding of the relationship between flesh and spirit.

5  See e.g. Greenblatt (1978: 295–6) for a discussion of the bagpipe speech as exemplifying the ways in which Shylock 'seems to embody the abstract principle of difference itself.' To a certain extent, Greenblatt qualifies his earlier discussion of Jews in Shakespeare's England, in his review of Shapiro (1996) (see Greenblatt 1996). Halpern (1997: 213) discusses the question of racial difference and the 'Hath not a Jew eyes?' speech.

6  Shylock will give no reason for his obstinacy, except to cite the same obstinate particularity with which he, as Jew, is identified. Yet of course, for Shylock it is this particularity of the flesh that Jews and Christians most share in common; his 'Hath not a Jew eyes?' speech suggests that the universality to which the Duke appeals may, in the final analysis, be conceivable only through the flesh. If Shylock speaks for the Jews' particular, fleshly resistance to a language of Christian 'kindness' or universalism, he does so only by transforming the predicament of the flesh into a new universal.

7  Halpern (1997: 193ff) discusses such superficiality, and its relation to depth, in terms of Marx's critique of the special fetishism of the money-form.

8  Luther discusses harsh mercy in the most widely-quoted passage from his longest and most virulent treatise against the Jews: the 1543 'On the Jews and their lies' (written just two years before his death). See Luther 1955–76: 47: 268 ff. As Shapiro (1996: 23 n. 27) points out, this 1971 volume of *Luther's Works* offers the first complete English translation of the polemic – although there is evidence that the Elizabethans had indirect knowledge of Luther's anti-Semitic writings. The German text, 'Von den Juden und ihren Lügen,' and in particular the passage on harsh mercy, can be found in Luther (1883–1919: 53: 522).

# 8

# Jewish invader and the soul of state
## *The Merchant of Venice* and science fiction movies
### ERIC S. MALLIN

### Racist inscription

*Independence Day* (directed by Roland Emmerich, Twentieth Century Fox, 1996), a movie about evil space invaders threatening to destroy the world, features two heroes from the American social and historical margins: an African American and a Jew. Through courage and cunning, the two figures – fighter pilot Captain Stephen Hiller and scientist David Levinson – conduct the crucial attack on the aliens that liberates Earth from the threat of utter destruction. The blunt if subtextual 'message' is that racial harmony is salvific, for Black and Jew triumph together and save all humankind. The suggestion of the *universal* protective virtue of this harmonic force, however, is somewhat compromised by the attributes of the aliens themselves: the physically powerful, implacably hostile, and technologically superior invaders embody traditional racist fantasies of Black and Jew.

Further problematizing the 'feel-good' plot, the heroes are themselves profoundly tied to monstrous, alien stereotypes linking them with the invaders. For instance, the brainy scientist is the only earthling to realize that the aliens have been broadcasting a countdown-to-destruction signal; thus the Jew alone can understand the Other. Levinson implants a computer virus in the alien 'mother ship' to break down its defense systems, an idea he gets from suffering his own common cold; Jews are physically weak but intellectually strong (Gilman 1996). Thus Jew and alien connect at the level of the symbolic body through the viral medium (Rogin 1998: 65). And Hiller, the African American fighter pilot, responds with force and anger – not reason or rationality – to the invaders. Blacks are physically strong, intellectually weak. One of the film's more calculated productions of stereotype occurs when Hiller has successfully out-maneuvered the attacking entities and captured one that has crash landed in the desert. Here he comically protests in monologue to the comatose creature that he hauls in his parachute across the scorching sands:

> You know, this was supposed to be my weekend off. But noooo. You got me out here draggin' your heavy ass through the burnin' desert, wit' your dreadlocks stickin' out the back of my parachute. You' got to come down here wit' a' attitude, actin' all big 'n' bad. [*Pauses; looks furious.*] And what the *hell* is that smell?

Morphology marks the alien's racist inscription: the 'dreadlocks' to which Hiller refers are actually tentacles. As Jonathan Freedman has claimed, drawing on Sander Gilman's (1996) work, 'In anti-Semitic discourse of the later nineteenth and early twentieth centuries, the Jew's monstrosity is performed by the transformation of the hand . . . into bat wings, vampire talons, spider legs, or octopus tentacles' (Freedman 1998: 94). He refers here specifically to representations of Jews, but insofar as science fiction aliens enfold the immense paranoid history of alterity and its relations, Captain Hiller drags a vessel of labile prejudices. What is more, the powerful objection to the alien's aroma historically codes racist responses (Taussig 1993: 66), which might have something to do with why Hiller greatly exaggerates his own black English discourse throughout the speech. Here we see the historical target of prejudice turning the terms of some African Americans' physical and social difference (heavy ass, dreadlocks, big bad attitude) against an even less welcomed 'race' or presence.

The unassailable wit of this scene depends on the rage of one alien – attractive, honored, even heroic – at the transgression of another, a transgression he understands *in terms of his own stereotype.* Hiller's ascribing his own 'big 'n' bad' attitude (which the movie has well established by this point) to the invader further augments the connection between the two figures. The space invaders in

*Independence Day* are not encoded Blacks because they are hostile and powerful, not Jews because they are tentacled and smart; they are the mutant conflation of such prior racist representations. The sympathetic heroes overcome, to universal acclaim, a version of what they replicate. They defend against self-caricature.

'Speaking broadly,' Judith Williamson says,

> the whole point about most of the ideologies manifested in mass cultural 'texts' is that they are dominant or hegemonic ideologies, and are therefore likely to be intimately connected with that very class which is furthest from 'the masses'. The function of most ideologies is to contain difference or antagonism, and the most effective way to do this . . . is to *set up* difference.
>
> (J. Williamson 1986: 100, original italics)

I would like to expand on this insight with reference not only to mass culture and space invader movies, but also to an unlikely analogue text: Shakespeare's *The Merchant of Venice*. The play sets up – and, in typical Shakespearean fashion, repeatedly undermines – the perception of difference in order to question some ideological operations that are threatened under the shadow of similarity or undifferentiation. *Merchant* skews parallels into convergences, the best-known instance being the mirror relationship of the two central antagonists, Shylock and Antonio. Their radical difference, so passionately asserted by Antonio and his friends, does not make itself readily apparent to Portia ('Which is the merchant here, and which the Jew?' she improbably asks) or to the Stationers' Register recorder ('a booke of the Marchaunt of Venyce or otherwise called the Iewe of Venyce').[1]

I am not attempting to show an organic textual connection between these films and the play so much as an organic *ideological* one. In attempting to set up difference, that absolute demarcation between repulsive alien and exquisite human, the space invader film and *The Merchant of Venice* produce *complicated likeness*, a tacit acknowledgment (or an uncontrolled truth) of the bad faith furnished by racialist distinctions. I shall claim that Shakespeare's play has a crafty functional similarity to the alien invasion film, and I adduce two recent examples of the genre to make the point: *Independence Day*, and Paul Verhoeven's *Starship Troopers* (TriStar Pictures, 1997). Reading contemporary science fiction movies side-by-side with this play, even in the absence of intertextual reference, can help anatomize the ideology of representing the marginal figure – the 'alien' – as a force for unification and defense of the state which marshals its powers against that figure. The ironies of unification on the poisoned ground of collective hatred cluster thick in *The Merchant of Venice*. But such ironies should lead us to consider the source of ideological discord, and *Independence Day*, like the far more complicated Verhoeven film, can help modern readers detect the operations of prejudice in popular culture, even in Renaissance popular culture. My argument will be grafted onto one of Horkheimer and Adorno's choice insights about anti-Semitism – they call it 'self-hatred, the bad conscience of the parasite' (Horkheimer and Adorno [1972] 1997: 176) – as I read these entertainments in the light of rationalized prejudice. If the contemporary Hollywood sci-fi film can insinuate a justification for the destruction of the racialized other in the monstrous form of an alien, certainly *The Merchant of Venice* could do so with its insistently captious, asocial Jew. However, Shakespeare's play mounts a more conflicted ideological operation than does the space invader film: while *Merchant's* plot endorses prejudice and the cultural demolition of the Other, its image and symbol structure undercuts its racist protagonists and the urgency of their argument.

The three texts share a formal arrangement that points to a thematic disposition: the Beautiful defends turf or self against the incursions of the Ugly. While this pitched struggle of forms is especially clear in *Starship Troopers*, it amounts only to an interpretive ruse. That is, the texts feature the Beautiful as a misdirection, a snare for audiences who would identify it (or its cognates, the Blessed or Fortunate) with the Good. For even as the handsome Captain Hiller sees, however subconsciously, in the dangerous invader some form and pressure of his own reflection, so the Christians in *The Merchant of Venice* see in Shylock a dislocated self-image from which they recoil, but which proves extremely difficult to efface.

What ties *Independence Day* and *Starship Troopers* to *The Merchant of Venice* is not merely their use of the 'heroic' characters' youth and beauty as a drug to induce narcissistic audience identification (Modleski 1986b: 161). These texts reveal, through their disposition of the alien, a mental structure – a dynamic of reception and audience response – that produces a habit of moral recoil and rationalization *in lieu of* identification. In Venice, I shall argue, the Jew figures metonymically: he is *not* the completely unknown or unknowable, or even the distantly comparable, but rather, the too familiar, the co-extensive. Violence comes to Shylock not as the society's attempt to enforce difference so much as its bid to avert identification. Like Shakespeare's play, the science fiction films allow the audience to *misrecognize* its own image, willfully and relievedly, insofar as the alien bears no physical likeness to the human. Such a maneuver paradoxically bolsters the racist dynamic, which founds itself upon the necessity of dehumanizing its object. By definition, nothing could be less human than an alien. Or, Shakespeare shows us, more human either.

## Christian Shylock

Many readers and audiences have long seen that the ethical difference between the (allegedly good) Christians and the (supposedly bad) Jew in *The Merchant of Venice* is repeatedly undermined by the very characters who proclaim it. Plot, too, subverts difference. Insofar as Shylock sponsors Bassanio on his romantic quest, the Jew works as an integral part of the Christian community by providing the necessary economic conditions for romance. Antonio voices this irony in terms of *sameness*: 'This Hebrew will turn Christian; he grows kind' (1.3.173–4). Antonio sees all generosity, kindness, or 'natural' behavior as self-reflective. But Shylock's considerable cultural and characterological differences should not be trifled with, and should not be fully suppressed any more than they should be thickheadedly asserted. 'To be sure,' Stephen Greenblatt has written, Shylock 'appeals at moments to his sameness . . . and this sameness runs like a dark current through the play, intimating secret bonds that no one, not even the audience, can fully acknowledge' (Greenblatt 1990: 43). But if, as Greenblatt suggests, Shakespeare compels the audience to turn these intimations into alienations, into 'reassuring perceptions of difference' (1990: 43), the fact remains that the Christians can never quite pry themselves loose from Shylock's grip on their collective psyche. Even in punitively forcing him to convert, Antonio perfectly figures Shylock's dogged inseparability, his irresistible *incorporation* into their world.

What, then, truly is 'alien' about the Jew? It is far from obvious, for instance, that Shylock, despite his implication in the capitalistic economy of Venice, actually functions adequately *as* a capitalist once the play begins, particularly since his bond with Antonio deliberately refuses the exchange or profit motive (S. Wilson 1995: 110–11; Cohen 1995: 74–5). If any attribute would alienate the Jew in Venice, this would be it. In fact, Shylock at least twice shows that money means comparatively little to him – compared, that is, to how it 'means' for the Christians (Goddard 1951: 81–116; Girard 1991: 243–53). First and most significantly this occurs when he accepts the bond for a pound of flesh on the possible but far from certain forfeit of three thousand ducats; and second, when we hear that he would not have traded Leah's turquoise ring 'for a wilderness of monkeys' (3.1.102).

One way to understand this trait is to say that for Shylock, things are incommensurable. We sense that throughout the play, the Christians have a looser notion of commodities and exchanges, and that for them, nothing – not life, love, nor the body – is without its substitute or price (Shell 1982). Shylock never could have exposed himself to Portia's hairsplitting in the trial scene if he had not fundamentally *already* failed as a capitalist; his demand for Antonio's Christian flesh as compensation for the loss of Jessica, his flesh and blood, to Christians is, in more than one way, 'a losing suit'. His refusal of the financial transaction – first by accepting an interest-free loan, next by rejecting the monetary settlement of the debt in court – must, more than anything, make him wholly unintelligible to the Venetians, must mark him as outside of the system of values that animates their commercial universe. On the surface, the attacks on Shylock as dog, cur, Pythagorean thing seem to arise from his unquenched bloodthirstiness, his desire for murder. Perhaps, however, these epithets – foundationally racist for the Renaissance (Boehrer 1999: 164–8) – derive first from *economic*, then moral unintelligibility, as Shylock surmises: 'Is it possible / A cur can lend three thousand ducats?' Not a bit – and thus the Jew becomes, to Gratiano and other Venetians, 'the most impenetrable cur' (3.3.18), the 'indistinguishable', unknowable, psychic alien. Notions of race, of otherness breed mainly from epistemological deficit; and knowledge, in this culture, pivots on the understanding of money.

And yet, where Shylock's bond may have evoked an alienated (because unprofitable) relation to the culture, his attempted *collection* of the bond, his insistence on having its forfeiture terms fulfilled, ought to be perfectly intelligible to the assembled Venetians. For, as he amply demonstrates, his choice of cashing the bond means spending his money on a worthless commodity. Now at first, this seems merely a perversity, even though he cleverly used the unprofitable nature of the deal to get Antonio and Bassanio to commit to it in the first place: 'what should I gain / By the exaction of the forfeiture? / A pound of man's flesh taken from a man / Is not so estimable, profitable neither, / As flesh of muttons, beeves, or goats' (1.3.159–63). By claiming that he extends this friendship to Antonio to 'buy his favour', Shylock frames the bond in terms uncannily emulative of the Christians' own relationships: such a transaction, the sale of friendship, precisely defines Antonio and Bassanio's typical exchanges. Buying favour, it seems, has recognizable value; the merchant can grasp this idea. The contract is sealed.

But when the bond comes due, the idea of purchasing favour has long been abandoned, and Shylock's complete lack of profit (in cash or influence) makes his act seem monstrously arbitrary – even, to some critics, 'madness' – and wholly inhuman. Yet the arbitrariness is entirely the point. He secures this point early in the trial scene when he says to the Duke:

> You'll ask me why I rather choose to have
> A weight of carrion flesh than to receive
> Three thousand ducats. I'll not answer that,
> But say it is my humour. Is it answered?
> What if my house be troubled with a rat,
> And I be pleased to give ten thousand ducats
> To have it baned? What, are you answered yet?
>
> (4.1.39–45)

Rather than make him seem incomprehensibly foreign, however, Shylock's words here evoke the *essential* grounds of the capitalist ethos, and thus the very soul of Christian extravagance. Shylock, perhaps for the first time, gives up precise accounts, balances, and tabulations. Instead, he asserts his right to spend his money however he sees fit. This desire sounds simple enough, but it is utterly uncharacteristic of him – it is, we might say, an indulgence. It is, in fact, the mirage glimpsed through the mists of Belmont: the promise of conspicuous, superfluous consumption of enormous store. Shylock's deed here converges and conjoins with Bassanio's dream (maybe even to the extent of killing off the troubling creditor): the dream of squandering resources as he pleases.

At the precise moment, then, of Shylock's greatest adversarial position against the Christians, his intransigent courtroom refusal of exchange or profit, he also most intensely embodies their deepest desires and most extensively voices their group plutocratic fantasy: to spend money without concern of profit, to follow a losing suit and not mind the loss. The basic assumption of the critic who takes the Christians to task is that they are fundamentally and deceptively greedy, and wish only to maximize gains, which indeed they accomplish by eventually finagling Shylock's holdings for their own 'use' while keeping expenses to a minimum (Engle 1993: 96–7). But the real wish of people who clamor after lucre is to not have to do so, to be liberated from the profit motive by achieving an infinite stockpile; and the index of such wealth comes in the day-to-day practice of disregarding expenditures. Thus Bassanio, whose unregulated spending first summons Shylock's crafty largesse, best represents the play's fiscal unconscious, the wish to spend without tally – and in a lovely plot irony, Shylock himself embodies the dual cost of such desire: first by replicating it, then by being punished for it.

Christians in Venice express a longing for riches that coin the stars, that rise above grubby transaction or account: 'Look how the floor of heaven / Is thick inlaid with patens of bright gold' (5.1.57–8), Lorenzo rhapsodizes. I believe that in other circumstances, Shylock's refusal of up to 36,000 ducats would turn him into a hero in the unacknowledged depths of the collective Venetian psyche, as it would indicate a financial reserve nearly past belief.[2] But they cannot stand to see their desires add up to *this*. Shylock performs what could only be the subject of great wonder and envy to the Christians: after asserting that profit holds no meaning for him, he agrees to pay well beyond market value for a commodity that has, literally, no use. But he also lays bare the implications of their fantasies: transforming flesh to commodity, the capitalist dream drains life of value. Shylock becomes the difference that never sufficiently exists, the appalling externalization of identical cultural desire. To the Christians, who understand mainly the eye-for-an-eye of trade and exchange, Shylock refuses fair and generous recompense *because he can*, and extravagantly enforces an unprofitable contract *because he wants to*. Nothing could be more perverse, less attractive, and better fitted to the Christians' ideological imaginary.

### Alien/nation

If Shylock does express the unspoken longing of Christian economic relations, he becomes the vanishing point, not the proof, of difference. In *The Merchant of Venice*, Jews and Christians live in the nightmare of one another's idea. Antonio and Shylock undergo parallel symbolic castrations; Christians become notorious usurers with the Jew's property; Portia, in response to Shylock's refusal to mitigate the contract, demolishes him by using his own strategy of punctilious literalism to spring Antonio from the contractual cage. The Christians, it seems, cannot stop imitating the Jew. Thus they behave in accordance with Horkheimer and Adorno's reading of the anti-Semitic 'mimetic impulse which can never be completely destroyed' ([1972] 1997: 183–4). Certainly the idea also applies to Antonio's parodic *imitatio Cristi* – even the merchant's most heroic, self-sacrificial moments are imitative of a Jew – but more important, the mimesis of Shylock is inaccurate as an imitation. Horkheimer and Adorno deduce what the Christians of Venice never acknowledge, that 'antisemitism is based on a false projection. It is the counterpart of true mimesis . . . Mimesis imitates the environment, but false projection makes the environment like itself' (1997: 187). As this maxim suggests, prejudicial mimesis throws both the projector and image on to a perceptual curve: no hostile imitation could fail to distort. The Venetians ascribe to Shylock the animality and demonism that haunt their own 'bad conscience'.

Slavoj Žižek provides a logical formula to explain the mimetic substrate: 'The proper answer to anti-Semitism is therefore not "Jews are really not like that" but "the anti-Semitic idea of Jew has nothing to do with Jews; the ideological figure of a Jew is a way to stitch up the inconsistency of our own ideological system"' (Žižek 1994: 326). If mimesis does help scratch the racist itch, the Christians in the play might be seen to stage, amplify, exorcise in their distorted construction of Shylock something about themselves that they find irresistibly disturbing, an ideological 'inconsistency' they have unconsciously avoided. Alongside the picture Shylock presents as the embodiment of their most profligate fantasies, a related source of their troubled mimesis is surely their practice of slavery as an integral part of the capitalist ethos; the *common trade or sale of living flesh for money* problematizes their exclamations of horror at Shylock's claiming the corporal penalty on his contract.[3] For, as the Jew famously points out, the Christians have among them 'many a purchas'd slave', whom they badly mistreat because, as he says, 'you bought them' (4.1.89–92). In cursing Shylock's purchase of one of their own, they demonize what they cannot confess: simply, the hideously exploitive assumptions of ownership undergirding capitalistic acquisition; complexly, all the exclusions and hierarchies that structure their society and filter the access to favour and status. Even before he carves any flesh, Shylock hits a nerve: the Jew's bond exposes immense ethical problems in Venetian social structure.

At this juncture we may turn to glimpse the light from contemporary cinema. Verhoeven's *Starship Troopers* tells the futuristic story of a young, not too bright, but terribly handsome army recruit named Johnny Rico, who enlists with his friends as something of a high-school graduation lark. Before that point we see him briefly in school, where he pays insufficient attention to the classroom work: he is too busy flirting with his girlfriend, the beautiful Carmine Ibanez. As he makes goo-goo eyes at Carmine in class, the teacher recounts the history that the students learned this year; they have learned, he says, 'about the failure of democracy, when the social scientists brought our world to the brink of chaos', about how 'the veterans . . . took control, and imposed the civility that has lasted for generations since.' Because of Johnny's frisky classroom inattention, we too may fail to notice that the instructor is delivering a history of the current fascist state, and that 'the civility' under which the society lives euphemizes, *mutatis mutandis*, martial totalitarianism. But just as the dominant cultural assumptions and motives in *Merchant* must be invisible to those who maintain them, so too this understated scene of indoctrination presents history as reasonable and necessary truth, the required underpinning to Johnny's subsequent unthinking participation in war. For 'the veterans' in Earth's future have obviously established a world where the highest values are militaristic: where force is a political good, sacrifice in service of the state is the supreme privilege. Convenient, then, that just as he is about to quit basic training, Johnny's home town of Buenos Aires is destroyed by an asteroid 'launched', we are given to understand, by the creatures of Klendathu, a planetary system several million miles from Earth.

The Klendathans are arachnids – the humans call them 'bugs' – and their motives for waging war (if they have indeed done so) are never made clear. This murkiness figures significantly in the film's meanings, for the humans' eagerness to invade so as to defend the world must be, like the Christians' retaliation against Shylock, the result of both a perceived attack and a philosophical (and aesthetic) architecture. As they embark on full-scale ground warfare with the arachnid aliens, who are indeed repulsive and terrifying – enormously powerful, huge, dismembering insects who kill with pincers and razor-sharp jaws – it is hard to imagine that the humans could be at fault in the war. We see only an occasional demurrer, such as a news reporter who ventures to ask the troops if the 'bugs' were not just defending territory on which humans had encroached. At this, Rico grabs the microphone and shouts at the camera, 'Well, I'm from Buenos Aires and I say: kill them all! Yeah!' This hardly works as a counter-argument, but it works well as an anatomy of militarism: prior losses justify mindless aggression.

As does ideology. When Shylock rationalizes his desire for Antonio's flesh with the excuse 'An oath, an oath! I have an oath in heaven. /Shall I lay perjury upon my soul? / No, not for Venice' (4.1.223–5), we can see him making an awful religious appeal to revenge, different in degree if not kind from the Christians' religious appeal to profit. The Duke in particular, expecting 'a gentle answer, Jew' (4.1.33), urges Shylock to clear Antonio's debt: the Duke hopes Shylock 'wilt not only loose the forfeiture, / But, touched with human gentleness and love, / Forgive a moiety of the principal . . .' (4.1.23–5). But of course this vision of financial mercy dissolves as soon as Shylock falls under the decree of law. When Antonio is asked by Portia 'what mercy can you render him', Gratiano, that vexing figure, interjects: 'A halter, *gratis*. Nothing else, for God's sake' (4.1.374). Shakespeare cunningly puts the savage revenge wish in the mouth of a character whose name translates 'Grace', who offers to hang Shylock gratis – w*ith grace*, that is. The analogy I wish to draw here is between the vengeful motivations framed in religious terms on both sides in Shakespeare's trial scene, and the fascistic ethos masquerading as educational doctrine, necessary 'civility', and unifying ideology in *Starship Troopers*. For both texts imagine a world organized around not only defense, but also *defensiveness*. To return to Žižek's notion of anti-Semitism as a patch over ideological inconsistency, the alien invader film can also be understood as a genre of nationalistic *apologia*, however ironically set out. And the Venetian attitude towards Shylock must likewise be seen as both retaliatory and, especially, defensive or self-protective.

For exposing the Christians' ideological rifts around their precious and recondite idol of capital, the Jew must be expelled. But it is also crucial that Shylock's violent condensation of Christian extravagance comes about only in a constricted form, the Jew's *legal* subversion of the state, his holding it accountable for his bond and for the Christians' own practices and fantasies. Shylock's revenge is conducted along the lines of a legitimate transaction, subject to precedent, modification, or judicial rejection, and the formality of his attempted bodily assault on Antonio makes it at once horribly coldblooded and oddly routine: despite the extraordinary nature of the court case, it is part of accepted civic procedure. With and without Portia's legal fictions, the state admits that Shylock has a case, and must be heard. Thus it happens that the Jew's claim subtends a wider angle than merely personal animus: his attack on Antonio becomes inextricably an assault against the state, which causes racist and mimetic codes to converge against him. As Kwame Anthony Appiah avers about eighteenth- and nineteenth-century writing, 'the nation is the key middle term in understanding the relations between the concept of race and the idea of literature' (Appiah 1990: 282). Notions of race are indeed often inextricable from doctrines of nationhood and their representation, and Shylock occupies a curious point on any literary map of national identity: as an infidel but integral member of the economic structure of society, he is still regarded as a resident exile and symbolic stranger. He lives as a distinct but unmoored presence in Venice, a city which is practically its own nation,[4] and he profits and suffers massively from his outsider status. He has no nation except the spiritual, and therefore in a sense no race; but his rootlessness marks his danger to Venice, which as we shall see *produces* him as an alien.

Plot in *The Merchant of Venice* follows a specific vector on the graph of racialist thought: it charts the ways in which prejudice can mobilize defense of the state, the republic. Here is the point of contact between the play and science fiction movies: the defining of 'alien' as that which pesters the communal and ideological habitat. Both our science fiction films are structured around invasion plots: either the human world is invaded, which is to say, nearly obliterated (*Independence Day*); or the humans righteously invade a planet as retaliation for a perceived hostile assault on their homes by extraterrestrial life forms (*Starship Troopers*). The aliens in these films magnify and fetishize the threat that Shylock represents.

Obviously, defensive armaments in *The Merchant of Venice* do not consist of bombs or guns. Instead, the nationalist impulse to defend economic and ideological networks against perceived attack calls upon the machinery of the law and civil procedure (Balibar 1994: 192–204; see also Balibar and Wallerstein 1991) – ironically invoked by Shylock as the main weapon *against* the state. For the Jewish invader leaves no doubt that the system of justice, the operational premises of Venice and modern mercantile society, are all at stake in his trial:

> *Shylock:*                                         by our holy Sabbath I have sworn
> To have the due and forfeit of my bond.
> If you deny it, let the danger light
> Upon your charter and your city's freedom.
>
> (4.1.35–8)

Shylock links the legitimacy of his claim to his otherness and the rights that bestows upon him; the repeated possessives matter here. He swears by 'our' Sabbath – he cannot mean that of the combined Judeo-Christian community – though Shylock's claim more importantly rests on the modifier 'your'. He knows of the city's business practices and exploits the law to claim legitimacy. As Antonio had earlier said, 'For the commodity that strangers have / With us in Venice, if it be denied, / Will much impeach the justice of the state' (3.3.27–9), his word *commodity* interestingly comprising a range of meanings that include free trade, worthiness, value, and something like 'widely acknowledged legal standing'. The city's profit is connected, universal; it 'consisteth of all nations' (3.3.31). But the trumpeted universalism of Venice comes seriously into question when Portia penetrates the loophole Shylock has given her:

> *Portia:*                                     Take thou thy pound of flesh.
> But in the cutting it, if thou dost shed
> One drop of Christian blood, thy lands and goods
> Are by the laws of Venice confiscate
> Unto the state of Venice.
>
> (4.1.303–7)

The entire anti-Semitic track of the play has brought us to this moment of monolithic, impenetrable statism. Portia clamps the ideological vise: if Shylock sheds *Christian* blood, what he thought was his private property ('thy pound of flesh') will cost him immensely, causing all his other property to revert to the state of Venice, by the laws of Venice, stipulated in the court of Venice. Portia becomes, much more so than the Duke, the voice of state, drowning out the play's earlier claims of valuing the commerce of outsiders as if they were part of a universal community. What the trial secures is the assertion of the Jew as unarguable outsider.

But the crucial moment of the play's demolition of Shylock, its central maneuver of national defense, has yet to come. Portia's

devastating, rights-depriving redefinition or her de-citizenizing of
Shylock proceeds, with further appeal to the name of the city-state:

> It is enacted in the laws of Venice,
> If it be proved against an alien
> That by direct or indirect attempts
> He seek the life of any citizen,
> The party 'gainst the which he doth contrive
> Shall seize one half his goods . . .
> In which predicament I say thou stand'st,
> For it appears by manifest proceeding
> That indirectly, and directly too,
> Thou hast contrived against the very life
> Of the defendant . . .
>
> (4.1.343–56)

The 'predicament' Portia specifies seems to be that, having refused
'some surgeon . . . / To stop [Antonio's] wounds, lest he do bleed to
death' (4.1.253–4), Shylock can be accused of attempted murder.[5]
But in fact, the more serious predicament, appearing 'by manifest
proceeding', is that Shylock has been identified – interpreted by the
court – as an 'alien'. The name seems to carry a more severe and
derogatory valence than 'stranger', and it makes all the difference
to his fate, for the false judge's pronouncement implies that an
attempted murder by a citizen would, incredibly, have made a
world of legal difference. Using the law as simultaneously the state's
best weapon and shield, Portia focuses her institutional death ray
on Shylock, bringing him the name 'alien' and the legal demise
attending it (Whigham 1979: 110; Auden 1963: 229). The Jew's
christening, so to speak, conflates state and sectarian wrath against
him.[6] By setting Shylock firmly outside the protection of the law
with a single word, Portia's performative *coup pour l'état* underscores
his ideological as well as practical vulnerability to the state's devices
of torture, dissimulation, and mercy – which all curiously have the
same dominating effect.[7] Portia, in other words, exorcises the alien
from the soul of state.

   In the trial scene, Portia explodes Venice's shell of universalism –
or at least, the city's supposed transcendent valuation of international commerce – to expose its defensive racist and isolationist
embattlements.[8] Certainly the play troubles any question of nationalism even as it troubles ideas of race, particularly in light of the

indistinction between Venice and England, Belmont and Elizabeth's court (Prosser 1992; Marcus 1988). Nationalist rhetoric floats ambiguously in Portia's acerbic commentary on her suitors (commentary that insults most of Europe); in Shylock's references to his 'sacred nation', which must always be, for a diasporic Jew, sad and ironic; and especially in the courtroom, with Portia's construction of Shylock as irreducibly 'alien' to the place he lives and works.

It is no accident that the law's major hold on Shylock, his proclaimed 'alien' status, dovetails with Portia's hostility towards the play's other Others, especially Morocco and 'all of his complexion'. The language and psychology of racism work wonders for bolstering state defense: racism is not only a mimetic production but also a mimetic purge. Portia's gratuitous, comic snottiness about her suitors heralds not only her many other forms of cruelty but specifically her political rationale for demolishing Shylock: to establish more firmly the boundaries of state, an unanticipated function of her role inside the borders of the marriage plot. Thus the Venetian courtroom works as an ideological state apparatus and also as a way of letting Portia cleanse herself of those unwanted suitors to whom she may however be attracted,[9] punishing them retroactively, through the Jew, for their impertinent attempts on the inner circle of her sexual society. But Shylock's main threat is not to the psyche or, notably, to the erotic self; it is to the group consciousness. Frank Whigham sharply describes the action of the play in terms of class invasion (Whigham 1979: 112), and Shylock's assault against Venetian high privilege can be seen as another form of this incursion. For he challenges not only class boundaries, but also the sacred state ideal of hierarchy itself.

The xenophobic structures of *The Merchant of Venice*, like those of *Starship Troopers* and *Independence Day*, can be excavated with the help of Etienne Balibar's important insight that racism and nationalism must be understood dialectically. He writes that 'racism is not an "expression" of nationalism, but . . . *a supplement internal to nationalism*, always in excess of it, but always indispensable to its constitution and yet always still insufficient to achieve its project' (Balibar and Wallerstein 1991: 54). Such a reading can partly illuminate the racist impulses and critiques in contemporary science fiction, where the defeat of the space creatures must be managed either by resident aliens (Blacks and Jews) or beautiful fascist warriors with whom we must conflictedly identify, all of whom fight to the death for the defense of the state. Even in the postmodern

age, as much as the cultural dominant would like to see the alien as
Other, some troubling miscegenations and mimetic entanglements
do crop up; racism proves 'still insufficient to achieve [the] project'
of national defense because the exclusory categories it needs to
establish are so unruly. Which is the merchant here?

## Complicated similarity

Ruining the Jew, Portia performs important cultural work for
Shakespeare's audience: she destroys the dark image inside the glow-
ing light of Christian self-regard. But she is not allowed to do so
until Shylock has bedimmed his tormentors' self-flattering picture.
Shylock is, to some extent, 'a strategem for projecting what [the
Venetians] must needs recognize as evil in themselves onto an alien
Other' (Fiedler 1991: 28), but he is also a genuine deconstructor of
their comfortable, simplistic opposition of virtue versus wickedness.
This role is most evident in the rationale he offers for cutting
Antonio. He defines his purchased right to kill as *essential* capitalism,
the utter freedom from moral and ethical constraints: 'What if my
house be troubled with a rat, / And I be pleased to give ten thousand
ducats / To have it baned?' (4.1.43–5). This is not only the dream of
capitalist extravagance that I described earlier; it is a brutal,
pragmatic truth. Shylock exposes and partakes of the metaphorical
and potentially literal bankruptcy of such an ideology, and neces-
sitates anxious-sounding declarations of moral superiority from the
Venetians.

Shakespeare's audience members may have had trouble imagin-
ing that such an alien could embody their closely held economic
and moral contradictions. But the same process of representational
identification and displacement occurs in contemporary science
fiction films. The formal difference from Shakespeare's concerns
seems to be that the movies subdue attempts at ideological analysis,
but on closer inspection, they may not succeed. In *Independence Day*
and *Starship Troopers*, the alien forces are explicitly and irremediably
inhuman. So neither film threatens or challenges the *definitional* or
taxonomic boundaries of *homo sapiens*, just as neither one stages any
sort of infiltration of human life by alien that would signify a
merging of the human and interplanetary Other. But each film
presents a *single* moment of telepathic contact between a captive
alien and interrogating earthlings, as if to hint at and scurry away
from exactly the possibility that aliens configure: difference is *not*

irremediable, and thus it must be carefully maintained under conditions of surveillance, imprisonment and imminent torture or
death. These moments of alien autopsy or experimentation 'set up
difference', in J. Williamson's words (1986: 100), but they also
reflect back upon us our own implacable hostility and imperialist,
epistemological urges. In *Independence Day*, the alien that Hiller cap-
tures and drags through the desert eventually speaks through the
corpse of a scientist it has strangled, and telepathically threatens
the U.S. President; but an army officer quickly shoots it dead to end
the infiltration threat. Even to have aliens speaking through human
corpses, however, suggests an uncomfortable phylogenetic overlap,
implying that the creatures are in some sense human images however death-laden and distorted, an idea already present in the
invaders' nuclear-style weapons of mass destruction (Rogin 1998).
And in *Starship Troopers*, the Earth soldiers capture a 'brain bug',
the ruler and cerebral cortex of the arachnid operations. The film
shows the hideous experimentation to which this creature will be
subjected by some of the particularly fascistic protagonists (or
'military scientists'), one of whom, reading the creature's thoughts,
triumphantly pronounces it 'afraid'.[10] The claim is met with wild
cheers from the assembled troops – relieved at victory, perhaps
discomfited by similarity. So aliens have unanticipated emotional
resemblances to people and historical crises, and some of these
resemblances are, predictably, critiques.

The arthropods in *Starship Troopers*, for instance, do not resemble
us; we resemble them. Similarities are manipulated cinematically,
such as in long-shot framings of human troops pouring into ships or
swarming over hills; they look remarkably insect-like. Other evocative analogies appear in the Verhoeven film when we see army
officers who have been wounded or dismembered by fighting the
adversary: their prosthetic, mechanized arms or limbs make them
iron-plated, buglike. Encounters with the alien are debilitating or
dehumanizing (fatal, dismembering, or otherwise transformative);
but perhaps they show merely how awful and unrecognizable
*humanity* becomes in certain contexts. For the waves of arachnid
troops suggest, wonderfully, the drone-worker organization and
moral content of *all* human military action: as one reviewer wrote,
'human beings become something resembling insects themselves in
a militaristic totalitarian state, and the irony of humans being as
cavalierly treated as bugs are by people is not ignored by the film-
makers' (McCarthy 1997: 98).

Because the aliens in *Starship Troopers* almost entirely lack accessible interiority, they can be killed or exterminated without ethical restraint. They thus reveal more about human history than alien future; they present perfectly, if somewhat obliquely, as subjects of ethnic violence (K. Williamson 1997: 18). For the troopers resemble not only the Nazis; they also open a flow of other historical cross-currents when they have something like a hoe-down following a successful campaign against the enemy. With the southern anthem 'Dixie' playing in the background, their victorious moment recalls the history of slavery and racial turmoil that pocks the American past.[11]

Such historical agon is plainly recollected in the struggle with the aliens: the tagline of the movie, spoken by an officer under attack, is 'the only good bug is a dead bug', a remembrance of the genocidal motto of the Indian wars in North America and in Hollywood's representations.[12] These signals operate subliminally but with unmistakable force. Race, domination, and oppression are the barely submerged topics of the film, the complexity of which resides in the simplest trick of mass-culture: an audience will usually identify with the beautiful, the winners, no matter how morally or intellectually vapid.[13] Verhoeven's movie reproduces a Shakespearean method by complicating the nexus of ideological alliance and audience identification. The cyborg-gorgeous, multiracial starship warriors even dress like Nazi soldiers (Maslin 1997). But these attractive humans remind us of fascist storm troopers, in both dress and comportment, only after it is too late – after we realize that the ugly arachnids whom they defeat (and are soon to torture) are at least in part historical inscriptions of Jews. We have accepted the invitation to identify with the perpetrators of historical horrors before we know it, because the 'heroes' are so familiar, so physically lovely, so intent on avenging the attack on Earth and everything we hold dear, and so on. And this identification plays, *Merchant-of-Venice*-style, into the film's polyvalent, encoded racism. Shakespeare sets the same ethical trap: the ugly or strange couldn't possibly have any legitimate claims, and comedy beckons when the beautiful are victorious. The alien in *Starship Troopers* becomes the disturbing image of Nazi *or* American victimage, swarming and sneaky Jews or potent Blacks or even Japanese, depending on which war we choose as the appropriate subject of allegory. The juvenescent militia who savage the aliens must be excused, because the soldiers at least look like (an ideal version of) us. Here is grim postmodern parody of Second World War racist and nationalist propaganda – or it is merely a new context for that propaganda, which makes it seem parodic.[14]

Even the movie's pivotal event, the destruction of Buenos Aires by an asteroid from a belt near Klendathu, is problematic. Earth's presumption that this asteroid hit is an act of interplanetary war, a 'bug meteor' supposedly directed by 'bug plasma', does not logically pan out. Nothing else in the movie suggests that the creatures have such a technology; and the humans' retaliatory campaign seems instead a mass-unification effort to cope with a natural event, the random destruction of millions. For in the history of virulent oppression, the 'natural' does not function as a mitigating category of understanding – witness the countless pogroms that pullulated in the medieval era against Jews because of the bubonic plague – and so the asteroid offers a pretext for the discharge of state violence, compensatory for governmental failure to keep citizens safe from disaster.[15] Even in *Independence Day*, where the fact of the alien invasion cannot be disputed or chalked up to accident, the astral Other still projects historical, ideological need. For the attack unites America and all the world behind the unpopular U.S. President, a (doveish) Gulf-War veteran, whose recent experience as a fighter-pilot in that unconscionable campaign is played again, this time from the morally preferable underdog position. Thus the aliens occupy the symbolic place of the U.S. in its most recent war: a dauntingly powerful invader wreaking incendiary havoc. The movie, however, needs to excuse America's questionable past involvement by correcting history and translating Americans into scrappy go-getters, defeating – well, their evil, culpable selves, on the symbolic historical grid. As Rogin says about the film, 'Where history fails, science fiction steps in' (Rogin 1998: 26). In this inscription, the aliens' much-superior weaponry, like that of the United States in the Gulf War, cannot secure an easy victory; and in both fictional and historical cases, with America deemed triumphant, the winners are left with quite a mess to tidy up when the fight is over. (One wonders if Saddam Hussein's reported ecoterrorism in Kuwait is worse than the presence of immense crippled spaceships littering the planet after the alien invasion is quelled in *Independence Day*.)

What counted as 'alien' in the English Renaissance, and what space invaders metaphorize in contemporary mass culture, may not, surprisingly, differ all that much. Following Žižek's lead, we can argue that the extraterrestrial alien, a displaced construction or representation of the racist and jingoistic impulse, lives approximately where Shylock does: in the fracture zone of ideologies and beliefs. The inhuman represents what society cannot *psychically* colonize. In Shylock's case, that is the recognition of hollow, profligate desires at the cultural core, especially those leading to capitalist freedoms which loosen and dissolve moral bonds. But the Jew also means, for Christians, the guilt of unethical but pivotal practices such as slavery and other forms of oppression; he means, too, the sense that glittery privilege surely does not drop as the gentle rain, but is purchased, even at the price of considerable, unacknowledged human suffering.

An enlightened crowd of theatergoers which recoils at Shylock's forced conversion might feel amused, excited, or detached at the sight of people rejoicing in victory over dead space creatures, because *those* aliens are so 'inhuman'. But this inhumanity precisely translates the normal, the stock disengagement required of racist and anti-Semitic assaults; it is the perceived monstrosity of the Other that liberates objectification and murder. If *Independence Day* and *Starship Troopers* seem to be militaristic mass culture fluff, they can nonetheless be viewed ideologically, as guides to historical and national or indoctri-national processes. Because the battles they depict put world rather than nation at stake, their racist subtext is masked by the apocalyptic rhetoric of absolute necessity. The hideously costly victories won by the movies' 'humans' (as worthy of quotation marks as the 'Christians' in *The Merchant of Venice*) conceal the films' darker knowledge: that racism animates nationalism and indeed, the nation; that unity depends on a common enemy.

## Blood

The physical monstrosity of the alien is the great relief (and trick) of space invader movies: the formal properties of difference, of inhuman morphology, imply a reassuring gulf between human and alien. One of the crucial cinematic tools of such reassurance is blood. When Johnny Rico battles an especially hard-to-kill arachnid on Klendathu, the creature's death is heralded by a splattering of its sulphurous hemic fluid all over the pretty hero. The ghastly fluorescence of this anatomical matter justifies any violence against such phylogenetically removed life forms. And the autopsy scene in *Independence Day* likewise marks the outer-space creature as wholly other and thus properly subject to whatever fate humans choose for it; the alien's gluey, smegmatic 'blood' especially warns of the creature's danger and impurity and its alterity. Imagine how profoundly disturbing it would be if, in attacking an alien, the human hero were to sever an antenna or tentacle and discover a rich crimson river flowing out of the wound.

Representation of blood orients texts in ideology. Just so, Shylock loses his rights because he is named an 'alien', but he loses his suit because of that supremely important substance. It is uniquely significant that Shylock's case unravels because he is blocked from access to blood. I quote again from Portia's winning moment:

> Portia:   This bond doth give thee here no jot of blood.
> The words expressly are 'a pound of flesh'.
> Take then thy bond. Take thou thy pound of flesh.
> But in the cutting it, if thou dost shed
> One drop of Christian blood, thy lands and goods
> Are by the laws of Venice confiscate
> Unto the state of Venice.
>
> (4.1.301–7)

This juridical move carries such symbolic aptness that Shylock can barely bring himself to protest it. Not because of the unassailability of her reasoning (which is legally porous at best), but because the Jew has *always* been subject to the exclusions reified in her decree; the interdiction merely establishes the normal, the expected outcome: his blocked access to privilege. Whether we take 'blood' to mean Christ's sacrificial blessing from which Shylock is permanently distant, or aristocratic lineage which he cannot, as a stranger, ever meaningfully claim, or merely a general metaphor for transcendent or aesthetic animation of the dead material flesh, Shylock's exclusion from blood absolutely figures his position on the social and spiritual margins.

And Portia's dismantling of the bond forces this exclusion to be figured as fully racialized, biological: *of course* she would claim that the Jew should not have access to, as she astonishingly calls it, 'one drop of Christian blood'.[16] In this way she can finally contradict Morocco's earlier assertion that there is no significant difference between the blood of an infidel black man and that of a right-appearing Venetian (2.1.6–7). Portia's triumphant moment must also be especially satisfying for the Christians because of Shylock's earlier argument that blood signifies his belonging in the community – 'if you prick us, do we not bleed?' (3.1.54) – even though he used this argument to rationalize revenge, not specifically to claim membership. But the most shocking and, in a way, ideologically radical thing about Portia's specification of the blood Shylock cannot have is that it produces the *Christians* as *differentially constituting a privileged race*. Since they have had some trouble until this moment pinpointing Shylock as a racial Other, or categorically distinguishing him, this expedient of blood is a happy one for them. It compensates for and even glosses Salerio's earlier incoherent rant to the Jew that Shylock's daughter actually belongs to a separate race: 'There is more difference between thy flesh and hers than between jet and ivory; more between your bloods than there is between red wine and Rhenish' (3.1.33–5). His metaphor dangles over the precipice of bloody literalism – unless, that is, Jessica's conversion really does give her entry into a new race, not merely a new creed. If the Christians are biologically distinguishable as a race, then the Jew's difference, so hard to locate with precision, will finally *a fortiori* stand out.

Shylock makes an unusual if culturally foundational alien, entwined and congruent as he is with the Christians' own fantasies and ethical debilities. It takes sustained labor for the Venetians to deny him his rights and to avert their own identification with him; his alien-ation is essential to the proper function of their state. But for that to occur convincingly, Portia must establish the Jew as *ontologically* (not merely stylistically or doctrinally) separate, so that he and his kind may remain distinguishable from the natural-born Christians. And Shylock's bloodless bond gives her the chance to do so, to triumph over complicated similarity by decisively removing the now truly alien Jew. But as a Bernard Malamud character discovered, it is 'a wonderful thing' that 'there are Jews everywhere' (Malamud 1950: 53); for Shakespeare may have implanted an alien where Portia least suspects it.

When Shylock realizes what the still-concealed Portia has in store for him, he becomes a version not of Antonio, or Morocco, or any of the play's defeated Others. Strangely, he becomes most like Bassanio, for whom the bond was first generated. Shylock, like Bassanio, receives repeated assurances of having won ('lawfully by this the Jew may claim / A pound of flesh'; 'A pound of that same merchant's flesh is thine', etc.), and yet he surprisingly loses, being tightly bound and without full use of property in the end. And the case can be made that Bassanio, whose alienation from Portia begins when he recounts publicly that 'all the wealth I had / Ran in my veins' (3.2.253–4), secures an apparent triumph that leads to bondage: marriage will, for him, signify economic, erotic, and psychological restriction, managed under Portia's justifiable surveillance (Fiedler 1972). In other words, both the Jew and Bassanio can be read as the ground on which Portia figures her personal triumphs. Unlikely as a parallel between the Venetian gentleman and the Jewish moneylender might seem, it has been nominally established throughout the play. For of all the characters in Venice, Portia's true love could have reminded us from the beginning of Shylock in one important way: he bears the name of a well-known Jewish-Italian family in Renaissance England, the Bassanos of Venice.[17] The Bassanos were musicians and luthiers originally brought to England to improve the quality of music in Henry VIII's court. An historian of Jewish names lists 'Bassan and Bassani (from Bassano in northern Italy)' as 'surviving Sephardic family names . . . derived from places of origin' (Kaganoff 1977: 14). Portia, as it happens, may have a harder time expelling the alien than she thought. For she finds herself with a bankrupt prodigal who never does swear to keep her ring – a Jew for a husband.

## Acknowledgements

I would like to thank Hugh Grady, R. W. LaBrum, Sonia Lipitz, Michael Rogin, Hilary M. Schor, and Frank Whigham for their help at various stages of this chapter.

## Notes

1  As cited in Brown (1955: xi). See Girard (1991) for the most comprehensive treatment of the theme of difference and differentiation in the play.
2  He says 'If every ducat in six thousand ducats / Were in six parts, and every part a ducat, / I would not draw them, I would have my bond' (4.1.84–6). Interestingly enough, this is the exact upper-limit sum that Portia suggests paying Shylock when she first hears about the bond: 'What, no more? / Pay him six thousand and deface the bond. / Double six thousand, and then treble that, / Before a friend of this description / Shall lose a hair thorough Bassanio's fault' (3.2.297–301). The coincidence of what Portia would conceivably offer and what Shylock would flatly refuse suggests yet another covert, psychic overlap between Jew and Christians.

3 Marc Shell's (1982) brilliant essay on the play gives the most convincing and evenhanded account of the Christians' intricate hypocrisy, extending even to the notion of marriage as a similar kind of purchase of flesh (see esp. pp. 64–8).

4 See McPherson (1990), Boose (1994), Shapiro (1996), and Maus (1997b) for useful commentary on this aspect of Shylock's civic estrangement.

5 There are two profound curiosities about these lines. First, Portia's request for a surgeon reveals that she thinks Antonio could conceivably *survive* the cut (unless, as Hilary M. Schor suggests to me, she is merely luring Shylock into the trap of admitting attempted murder; on this possibility see also Moody 1991: 84). But if *Portia herself* admits that the merchant could survive the knife, then she has no basis to claim, as she does presently, that Shylock *necessarily* means to kill Antonio – that is, since she asks for a surgeon she at least allows for the possibility that Shylock *might not* mean the wound to be fatal, and so her subsequent reading of his homicidal intentions must remain in the area of a reading, not a fact, as she treats it. More subversively still, Portia the judge openly admits, in saying 'lest he do bleed to death', that flesh *must* contain blood – and thus her risible legal fiction that the bond does not automatically entitle Shylock to the blood in flesh ought to be, at the least, subject to challenge. Of course, her fiction has more important symbolic than literal implications, as I shall discuss at the end of this chapter.

6 In the *OED*, 'alien' denotes 'one separated or excluded from the citizenship and privileges of a nation' (s.b. B.4), and the relevant cited quotations are all *biblical* instances of a person who has become estranged from the divine covenant.

7 In Laurence Olivier's interpretation, Shylock crumples at the line 'if it be proved against an alien', as if to convey: 'yes, I knew it would come down to this'. See *The Merchant of Venice* (dir. John Sichel, LIVE Entertainments Inc. 1973).

8 Balibar (1994) details some compelling if counterintuitive overlaps between racism and universalism, to wit: 'no definition of the human species, or simply the human – something which is so crucial for universalism, or universalism as humanism – has ever been proposed which would not imply a latent hierarchy' (Balibar 1994: 197). One of the telling moments in *Merchant* in which, as Balibar (1994: 198) says, 'you cannot find a clear-cut *line of demarcation* between universalism and racism' comes in the famous 'quality of mercy' speech. Portia's ideologically loaded attempt to argue for a universal value of heavenly virtue on earth clearly reviles Judaism for its supposed dedication to 'justice': for, 'Jew', she emphasizes, 'in the course of justice none of us / Should see salvation' (4.1.192-5).

9 I shall extend this suggestion at the very end of the chapter. For now let me offer that the possibility exists, later to bloom in *Othello*, that the Venetian maiden is drawn to the Prince of Morocco. Critics have long thought that Portia unquestionably gives hints to Bassanio during the casket test about the lead casket. But just before she sends Morocco off to the test, she says: 'After dinner / Your *hazard* shall be made' (2.1.44).

Though hardly as obvious a hint as providing an accompanying rhyme, Portia may well be subconsciously whispering 'hazard, remember to hazard' in the ear of her champion; the motto on the lead casket is 'Who chooseth me must give and hazard all he hath'.

10  The 'brain bug' further figures Jews as the victimized subject of the Nazi-coded starship warriors – mainly because of historical paranoia and caricature about high Jewish intelligence (Gilman 1991: 128–49; 1996).

11  The racial overtones of the scene are briefly muffled by a politically correct feint: as 'Dixie' plays, a white heroine dances with a fellow black male soldier. But presently the hero, excessively Aryan-looking Johnny Rico, cuts in and, within a few minutes of screen time, has sex with the woman (whom he has been avoiding until now). Thus he saves her from the clutches of the Other – as if the anthem had its own subliminal effect. I owe the observation about 'Dixie' to Rebecca W. LaBrum.

12  Compare Rogin's (1987: 50) discussion of the Indian's meaning in repressive American political history: 'Indians were the first people to stand in American history as emblems of disorder, civilized breakdown, and alien control . . . The violent conquest of Indians legitimized violence against other alien groups, making coexistence appear to be unnecessary'.

13  On this point Richard Halpern's (1997) essay helpfully explicates the parallel allure of the Christians, and their opulent, sensual world, for an audience of *The Merchant of Venice*: 'The theatrical imaginary, which anti-theatrical writers of the early modern period depict as a subversive force, here works in the service of orthodoxy, cementing solidarity with the gentile characters and overpowering Shylock's dissonant tones' (Halpern 1997: 217).

14  Verhoeven cites, as part of the film's relevant background, his witnessing the German bombing of Rotterdam, which at the time 'stood as history's most devastating single air offensive'. But contributing to his movie's (and experience's) ideological complication might be the fact that both 'the English and Americans, but mostly the English, were continuously bombing the area to destroy [the German V-1 rocket] launching pads' (K. Williamson 1997: 18). Contrastively, Emmerich, a German, may be less conflicted about the underlying ideological strategies of *Independence Day*: 'It's politically incorrect to use any nationality for bad guys . . . Aliens are the best movie villains since Nazis' (quoted in Rogin 1998: 15). For more on the cinematic alien, see Kuhn (1990).

15  All we see in the film of arachnid 'technology' is, significantly, an extension of their natural or bodily abilities, even though the film is explicit about how intelligent they are. The plasma 'rockets' they fire at the incoming human ships are biochemical explosives launched from the hind ends of enormous squatting bugs, aiming upwards – so it seems exceedingly unlikely that the arachnids could redirect an asteroid with such precision over light-year distances. We also discover that the arachnids learn about the Earthling invasion by sucking the brains out of human army officers. So even their intelligence-gathering is a bodily process, not the result of superior technology *per se*. Verhoeven makes the creatures smart so their persecution and torture by his Nazi-like

heroes can be justified and can carry historical echoes. But I think there is little evidence for the arachnids' military aggression.

16 On the prohibited blood as symbolic of 'the love the Christians deny [Shylock], the essential life of the spirit', see Moody (1991: 85); for the suggestion that the blood Shylock cannot have signifies his exclusion from the aristocratic realm, I am indebted to Hewitt S. Thayer. See also Boose (1994: 39–42) on Shylock's cultural rather than biological interpellation, and Halpern (1997: 213) on the Christians' spiritual rather than physical differences from Shylock.

17 See also Shapiro (1996: 249–50) and this passage about Bassano from Shylock's biographer John Gross (1992): 'The name, so close to Bassanio, suggests tantalizing Shakespearean possibilities; so does the fact that one of the family, Emilia Bassano – after her marriage, Emilia Lanier – has been identified by A.L. Rowse with the Dark Lady of the Sonnets' (Gross 1992: 34–5). As Gross points out, Lanier (or Lanyer), author of *Salve Deus Rex Judaeorum* (1611), has no trouble blaming the Jews for the Crucifixion.

# 9

# Shakespeare and the end of history
## Period as brand name
### DOUGLAS BRUSTER

As I write this, the current telephone book in Austin, Texas lists more than a dozen 'Renaissance' businesses – firms, that is, that call themselves 'Renaissance ___'. These include a women's hospital, a hotel, a builder, a glass company, and a pest control service (this last perhaps an ironic match for a word that promises rebirth). In this context, 'Renaissance' is an all-purpose modifier that seems to assure us of the quality of services rendered. A business using 'Renaissance' in its name – for instance, 'Renaissance Stone Design' – shares a family resemblance with 'Prestige Roofing', 'Deluxe Carpet Cleaners', 'Classic Pizza', and 'Elite Electrolysis and Waxing', all listed in the same telephone book.

The modifiers of these businesses ('Prestige', 'Deluxe', 'Renaissance', etc.) are at once interchangeable and vital. For, however empty of meaning, however effortlessly contrived, and however poorly they describe the business in question, they are central to these firms' identities, and testimony that presumption remains the largest asset of contemporary business. We could say that these names succeed not in spite of, but because of their indecorum; as claims made against an account that society never balances, what they advertise is less any quality of service than the freedom to boast.

The word 'Renaissance' has always been more claim than reality. And although its prevalence in business and in academic writing may suggest that it has always been with us, 'Renaissance' as a period label is of relatively recent origin. Its use in relation to *English* history and literature is more recent still. While we instinctively think of Shakespeare as a writer of the Renaissance, we could say that he became a Renaissance author not through taking up a pen in the late 1580s or early 1590s, or even when writing the major tragedies of the early 1600s. Instead, Shakespeare became an author of the English Renaissance primarily in the 1920s, when it first became common to speak of an 'English Renaissance' at all.

However recent this term, the tenure of Shakespeare as a 'Renaissance' playwright has lately come under pressure from other ways of placing him in history. It is becoming more common, for instance, to call Shakespeare and his contemporaries 'early modern' authors, a label which emphasizes those things about this period of English history and its culture that survived to define the 'modern'. If 'English Renaissance' has a deceptively short lineage, 'early modern England' is even newer as a term to describe and define a historical period. Used by English historians since the early 1960s, it was taken up by literary critics only since the mid-1980s. Although it lacks the glamor of 'Renaissance', 'early modern' has its own implications, ones which bear examination.

Knowing something about when and why 'Renaissance' and 'early modern' came into use puts us in a better position to understand their role in the field, and correspondingly, the field itself. More than an academic exercise, an inquiry of this nature shows us, first, that 'periods' themselves have periods – that is, that terms invented to describe the past come into use, and experience their greatest popularity, in identifiable segments of time. Through its interest in the weight of these keywords as they fall into discourse, such an examination also helps to define the status of value and belief in current criticism of Shakespeare.

This, then, is the subject of the remarks that follow: the names we give to the era of Shakespeare and his contemporaries, the genesis of those names, their influence on the way we interpret the past, and their significance for understanding the 'Shakespeare' we live with. My argument here is that, as used in literary criticism today, 'Renaissance' and 'early modern' imply more than they actually say. Neither term is based on a well-considered account of what a period is, or its defining contours and boundaries. They are more typically extensions of the naming practice seen in the examples of 'Renaissance' businesses found in any telephone directory: labels which seek to suggest qualities in objects, practices, persons, and times that do not obviously possess them.

## An American 'English Renaissance'

Those who write on the literature and history of the 1500s and 1600s have at their command a range of terms for defining the time which relates to their object of interest. Among these are numerical markers: someone may write, for instance, of the sixteenth- or seventeenth-century lyric, or of pamphlets of the 1590s or 1620s. The seeming objectivity of these descriptors is given a personal thickness in such terms as Henrician, Elizabethan, Jacobean, and Caroline, and a larger, familial import in such terms as Tudor and Stuart. These share something with century and decade labels in that, while adding personality to the mix, they offer fairly uncontroversial chronological boundaries. Other terms that involve events include 'Reformation' and 'post-Reformation', 'pre-Civil War' and 'pre-Restoration'.

The most popular terms for discussing the era indicated by this range of labels, however, are 'Renaissance' and 'early modern'. Chances are good that any new book or essay relating to this era will use one of these two terms. It is just as likely, though, that few of these books or essays will explain why they use the terms they do, or explore the implications of using them. We should start, therefore, by looking at when these terms initially appeared.

The term 'Renaissance' first came into use during the nineteenth century. Most readers are familiar with its appearance in Jacob Burckhardt's (1965) landmark *The Civilization of the Renaissance in Italy*, published in 1860 (Kerrigan and Braden). It was advanced before this, however, by Jules Michelet in 1855, in the seventh volume of his *Histoire de France*, titled *La Renaissance* (Ferguson, 173 ff.). Although Michelet framed the 'Renaissance' as a European phenomenon, throughout the latter half of the nineteenth century the term and concept were increasingly used in relation to Italy and, to a lesser extent, France. Historians and critics were reluctant to speak of an 'English Renaissance' because England lacked a rich history in the plastic arts of painting and sculpture, because it lagged behind much of Europe in architecture, and because its literature – the mode of cultural expression for which later commentary would most credit England – was seen as having reached maturity only late in the sixteenth century, well after the Continental Renaissance was held to have occurred.

Ironically, two French scholars, Hippolyte Taine and J. J. Jusserand, appear to be first to write of the 'English Renaissance': Taine in *Histoire de la littérature anglaise* (1863–4) and Jusserand in *Histoire littéraire du peuple anglaise* (1894, 1904). Scattered uses of this phrase cropped up thereafter. In 1895, for instance, Mandell Creighton, Lord Bishop of Peterborough, published his Rede Lecture (delivered earlier that year), titled 'The Early Renaissance in England'. Perhaps under the pressure of the Continental Renaissance's earlier date, Creighton tries, in this lecture, to show a *fifteenth*-century Renaissance in England, one that centered on court poetry and the revival of learning. However, Anglo-American critics generally avoided this usage as it pertained to any century of English history. As late as 1920, for instance, Hyder Rollins could publish *Old English Ballads, 1553–1625*, a title that would seem anachronistic in several ways only a decade later.

These last two instances, centering as they do on titles, call for a brief discussion. The remarks that follow rely heavily on titles of books and essays to identify trends in the use of 'Renaissance' and 'early modern'. It is important to note, therefore, that the titles of works often diverge from the nomenclature of the arguments they advertise. Indeed, in several essays and books discussed here, critics use one term in a title and another, or others, in the body of their works. For instance, in the first sentence of his 1936 article, 'Symbolic color in the literature of the English Renaissance', Don Cameron Allen intoned: 'The indebtedness of the so-called Renaissance to the Middle Ages increases with every new investigation of their relationships; and one is often led to wonder if the term "Renaissance" is not a misnomer and if one would not be right, if one referred to this period as "the later Middle Ages"' (Allen 1936: 81). There are many possible reasons for the kind of divergence seen in this instance, from a critic's dissatisfaction with a term, a natural tendency toward synonyms, and the 'house style' of a particular journal or monograph series, to an attempt to capitalize on current fashion or public taste. These last may explain Allen's title: whatever scruples he had concerning the term, they did not prevent him from going on to publish five influential books with the word 'Renaissance' in their titles.

Beginning in the early 1920s, 'English Renaissance' was increasingly adopted as a period term.[1] For instance, in an article in *Studies in Philology*, Thornton S. Graves (1920) employs 'Elizabethan' and 'pre-Restoration' interchangeably, but not 'Renaissance'; two years later, however, he is contributing a review essay (soon to become a regular feature in that journal) titled 'Recent literature of the English Renaissance' (Graves 1922a). Later in the same number Graves (1922b) also published an essay which uses 'Elizabethan' in the general sense, but does not use 'Renaissance'. Similarly, where Louis B. Wright would use the term 'pre-Restoration' and 'Elizabethan' interchangeably in an article issued in 1928, three years later he would publish two essays in *Studies in Philology* using the phrase 'English Renaissance' in their titles, most likely at the journal's request (Wright 1931a, 1931b). Wright's most influential publication, in fact, would be titled *Middle-Class Culture in Elizabethan England* (1935), in the preface to which he wrote: 'For want of a better term, I have followed the conventional practice of using the word "Elizabethan" to describe the period beginning with the accession of Elizabeth and ending with the Puritan Revolution in the 1640's' (Wright 1935: viii).

Use of 'English Renaissance' became more common as the 1920s progressed – and not only in *Studies in Philology*. By 1929, and throughout the 1930s, scholars would use this term with unmistakable boldness. We see this in such works as J. William Hebel and Hoyt H. Hudson's influential anthology, *Poetry of the English Renaissance* (1929); Martha Hale Shackford's *Plutarch in Renaissance England* (1929); Lily B. Campbell's 'Theories of Revenge in Renaissance England' (1930/31); George T. Buckley's *Atheism in the English Renaissance* (1932); Israel Baroway's 'The Bible as Poetry in the English Renaissance' (1933); and H. O. White's *Plagiarism and Imitation during the English Renaissance* (1935). The phrase 'English Renaissance' had become routine in scholarship by the mid-1930s. Since that time, of course, it has obtained what appears to be permanent acceptance in the titles of such publications as *English Literary Renaissance* and *Renaissance Drama*, the latter of which focuses on, though is not exclusively devoted to, English plays of sixteenth and seventeenth centuries.

As we have seen from its use in commerce, the word 'Renaissance' suggests a quality that such descriptors as 'sixteenth-century', 'Reformation', and even 'Elizabethan' do not. Like an attractive box or embellished label, 'Renaissance' adds prestige to things, scholarship included. This embellishment was also occurring outside the pages of academic writing in the first half of the twentieth century. At the same time that the idea of an 'English Renaissance' was being solidified in scholarly usage, Americans were hard at work constructing the prestigious myth of the English Renaissance in imaginative works. Of course, 'Renaissance' texts and figures had long been a staple of both English and American culture; Shakespeare's plays, in particular, have been important to American culture for almost as long as it has existed (Bristol 1989). But in the 1920s and 1930s, a broad and intensive interest in literature of the sixteenth and seventeenth centuries constituted a kind of 'double renaissance': an efflorescence, in relation to England, of a period concept (that of the Renaissance) that was itself held to signify the renewal or rebirth of earlier ideas, forms, texts, and energy. The English Renaissance we know is largely an American invention, and coalesced during the 1920s and 1930s.

During this time, Americans called the English Renaissance into being through a culture-wide pattern of invocation. The 'English Renaissance' made its formal debut between the world wars in the titles of literary works that quoted or otherwise alluded to Renaissance works, in revivals of that era's plays, in books and films set in Elizabethan times, in radio programs centering on the stories of that period, and in institutions and scholarly works devoted to its literary heritage. Related to the modernist tendency to quote resonant literary passages in its poetry – the obvious example being *The Waste Land* with its dense weave of references – this pattern of invocation involved a focus on prestigious individuals and texts from sixteenth- and seventeenth-century England.

America in the 1920s and 1930s fostered what Joan Shelly Rubin (1992) has called the 'making of middlebrow culture'. Middlebrow culture originated in an impulse to enlighten an interested citizenry by means of 'improving' works. This led to the diffusion of popularized literature and ideas, in such formats and agencies as the Book of the Month Club, in radio programs and discussion groups, in colleges' extension programs in the humanities, and in publication series dedicated to the intellectual betterment of the average reader. The 'English Renaissance' fashioned at this juncture of American history, then, unfolded in an environment peopled by authors, publishers, and producers striving to make otherwise elite works available to general audiences.

This phenomenon left its mark in many places. For instance, such titles as *Look Homeward, Angel*, *The Sound and the Fury*, and *For Whom the Bell Tolls* – only a few of the many works of this period to quote English Renaissance texts in this manner – packaged their narratives as 'high' art, as literature to be taken seriously, by invoking already canonical texts. During this period there was also an intensive interest in the English Renaissance as a source of filmed 'costume dramas'. These included not only the well-known adaptations of Shakespeare in *A Midsummer Night's Dream* (Warners, 1935) and *Romeo and Juliet* (MGM, 1936), but also such films as *The Private Life of Henry VIII* (London Film Production, 1933), *Mary of Scotland* (RKO, 1936), and *The Private Lives of Elizabeth and Essex* (Warners, 1939), which took the stories of English history (however loosely adapted) as their source.

Behind this interest in the English Renaissance appears to have been a desire to legitimize modern letters, and American culture, by casting them as the rightful inheritors of English forerunners. As Hugh Grady and Richard Halpern have pointed out, invocations of Shakespeare were central to both artistic and critical modernism during the first half of the twentieth century. Sometimes these invocations implied a 'parallel lives' theme worthy of Plutarch, a formation by which American efforts were joined to English precedents in an attempt to bridge time and geography.

Perhaps nowhere was this tendency so explicit as in a series of textbooks published by Noble and Noble, beginning in the 1930s. This series, called *Comparative Classics*, paired 'modern' works by Eugene O'Neill, Maxwell Anderson, and others, with 'classic' works, meaning those from the classical era, and from the English Renaissance. Among other texts, Milton's 'Minor Poems' were published with modern descriptive verse, *Macbeth* with O'Neill's *The Emperor Jones*, *Romeo and Juliet* with Rostand's *Cyrano De Bergerac*, and *Hamlet* with both Euripides' *Electra* and O'Neill's *Beyond the Horizon*.

If Eliot's patterns of quotation in *The Waste Land* implicitly ask readers to compare the modern present with the past, a past that Eliot often represents through the English Renaissance, Noble's *Comparative Classics* series turns this request into a schoolroom exercise. Appended to the twinned plays *Julius Caesar* and Anderson's *Elizabeth the Queen*, for example, is a collection of questions, positions, and topics that teachers can put to their students. These include the following:

Point out three things in *Julius Caesar* that were made necessary by stage limitations.

Show two ways in which *Elizabeth the Queen* is more free.

Compare the two plays as to the historical truth of the principal characters, Elizabeth and Caesar.

Compare Anderson's Fool with any of Shakespeare's Fools. Who supplies the place in *Julius Caesar*?

'What Private Griefs' – A Comparison of the Plotters: – Brutus and Cassius vs. Cecil and Raleigh.

(Shakespeare 1935: 291–3)

The edition is careful to insist that students note the differences between Renaissance and modern plays. But in the end the 'comparative' principle and format of the series undermine the historicist impulse, proving that we compare things that we believe essentially alike.

At work in this series, and in the larger movement it represented, was not an unqualified admiration of masterpieces across the ages, regardless of their time of composition. Instead, it was an attempt to join the modern present with certain resonant moments in literary and cultural history: Classical Greece, and the European – especially, the English – Renaissance. Throughout the 1920s and 1930s, American artists and scholars worked to solidify apparent links connecting these special eras in Western history, with America somehow the logical descendant of these elevated cultures. We see this in the foundation of institutions dedicated to the study of earlier literatures and history, such as the Folger Shakespeare Library and the Huntington Library. The cornerstone of the Folger was laid in 1930, and the Huntington published its first *Bulletin* in 1931. Scholars would use these libraries, and draw on some of the ideology they represented, to construct not only an 'English Renaissance' but an American one as well.

The term 'American Renaissance' is a familiar one by now. Coined in F. O. Matthiessen's famous study, *American Renaissance: Art and Expression in the Age of Emerson and Whitman* (1941), it refers to the flowering of American letters in the mid-nineteenth century, in the works of such authors as Melville, Hawthorne, Emerson, and Whitman. Matthiessen's book continues to be one of the most influential studies of American literature; in the wake of the book's influence, the 'Renaissance' he describes can, like the 'English Renaissance', seem self-evident. But because this 'American Renaissance' is, as a term and concept, so clearly attributable to a single person, Matthiessen's idea has been criticized for its role in the formation of an elitist canon of American literature (Avallone 1997). What his critics have not acknowledged, however, is that Matthiessen's 'American Renaissance' followed, and can be seen as a product of, the 'English Renaissance' which was being constructed in America by many scholars and artists during the 1920s and 1930s. Matthiessen's graduate work, as well as his first book, concerned 'Elizabethan' literature. In fact, the title of this 1931 book, *Translation: An Elizabethan Art*, speaks to Matthiessen's interest in the way one culture can 'translate' the energies of another.

The constructive power of the 'English Renaissance' also appears to have made itself felt in the scholarship of Willard Thorp, a Princeton University professor of English. His doctoral thesis of 1926 was *The Triumph of Realism in Elizabethan Drama, 1588–1612* (Thorp 1928). During the 1930s and 1940s, Thorp's interest in literary 'realism' was shifted from the Elizabethan era to that of Matthiessen's 'American Renaissance'. Like Matthiessen, Thorp's scholarship figured importantly in setting up the canon of American literature. Thorp published (in 1938) *Representative Selections* of Melville's writings, and (in 1947) edited *Moby-Dick* for Oxford University Press. Trained as scholars of what was increasingly called 'English Renaissance' literature, Thorp and Matthiessen both contributed to a scholarly movement which translated an English Renaissance into an American one.

## Early modern

Recently, the phrase 'early modern' has begun to replace 'Renaissance' in literary criticism relating to England. Seemingly a simple phrase, 'early modern' betrays some of its complexity even in the understated tension between its components: 'early', which takes time in one direction, and 'modern', which leads it in another. This tension remains an integral part of what 'early modern' is, and does, in the study of Shakespeare and his contemporaries. Like a hand with index finger extended, 'early modern' points back in time with one finger while three others aim squarely at the here and now.

Since its adoption by the field, 'early modern' has performed a variety of functions. It serves, variously, as a slogan by which one may advertise the newest critical wares – in the words of Heather Dubrow, it remains a 'badge, a ready way for scholars practicing contemporary modes of criticism to distinguish themselves from their predecessors and recognize one another' (Dubrow 1994: 1026); as an assertion about a larger sequence of history that – owing to the specific frame implied by the word 'early' – is rarely demonstrated in the pages of criticism unconcerned with modernity as a whole; and, in its capacity as an assertion seldom proved, as an antidote for fears about presentism and anachronism.

When did 'early modern' first come into use? To answer this, we need to examine the genesis of the 'modern' period in historiography. In a sensitive discussion of periodization relating to the sixteenth and seventeenth centuries, Margreta de Grazia (1997) looks to Hegel's *Philosophy of History* as a text central to the setting-up of the 'modern' in historical consciousness (1997: 10–11). De Grazia outlines the 'decisive break', for Hegel, occasioned by the fifteenth century, and made irrevocable by the Reformation, Martin Luther, and Protestantism's transfer of spiritual authority from institution to individual. Following Hegel, such figures as Marx, Michelet, and Burckhardt helped establish the idea of an epochal divide, an idea centering on 'their identification of the emergent period with heightened consciousness' (de Grazia 1997: 12).

While historians had always been willing to write about broad eras, with the *Annales* school in the twentieth century came a new explicitness, both in theory and practice, of what it means to conceive history in terms of such expansive time frames. The historians affiliated with the journal *Annales* often embraced what Fernand Braudel (1958) famously called *la longue durée*. As opposed to the histories which unfolded out of political events or the efforts of powerful individuals, Braudel was interested in larger subjects, and larger units of time. His research would involve, for instance, not only Spain, or Italy, but 'the Mediterranean and the Mediterranean world' (Braudel 1949); we see a similar scope in the translated title of *Civilization and Capitalism, 15th–18th Century* (Braudel 1981–4). Widely credited (along with others of the *Annales* group) for revolutionizing the study of history, Braudel was explicit about his debts to Marx, whose genius, Braudel held, 'lies in the fact that he was the first to construct true social models, on the basis of a historical *longue durée*' (quoted in Burke 1990: 50).

By 1957, the example of the *longue durée* began to make itself felt across the channel in one of the leading historical journals, *History* (*Journal of the Historical Association*). In its February number that year, *History* began dividing its book reviews by means of period categories. These categories included 'Medieval', 'Early Modern', and 'Later Modern'. Significantly, the books reviewed in the 'Early Modern' section in 1957 all employed older nomenclature, and generally concentrated on the influence of political figures in history. Among the books reviewed were Cyril Falls's *Mountjoy: Elizabethan General* (1955), Conyers Read's *Mr. Secretary Cecil and Queen Elizabeth* (1955), D. H. Wilson's *James VI and I* (1955), R. T. Petersson's *Sir Kenelm Digby* (1956), and J. W. F. Hill's *Tudor and Stuart Lincoln* (1956).

It would not be until the mid-1960s that, bolstered by the examples of broad periodization at use in the work of the *Annales* group, younger historians concerned with the social history of sixteenth- and seventeenth-century England began referring to 'early modern England' in the titles of their scholarship. An important event in this chronology was the 1965 Past and Present Annual Conference, which focused on 'Social Mobility'. Two papers from this conference were published in the April 1966 number of *Past and Present*: Lawrence Stone's 'Social mobility in England, 1500–1700', which uses 'early modern' in the body of its argument, but not in its title; and Alan Everitt's 'Social mobility in early modern England', which uses this period label in its title but not in its argument. The provisional nature of 'early modern' here is apparent not only from its tentative use, but also from the fact that, two years earlier, in his *Past and Present* article 'The educational revolution in England, 1560–1640', Stone (1964: 41) had spoken of his task as being that of 'the historian of a pre-nineteenth-century society'. Only a decade later, this would seem an occasion for which use of the phrase 'early modern' was not only appropriate, but nearly obligatory.

We might note that Stone and Everitt take great pains to justify their nomenclature, explaining exactly what (to their minds) was 'modern' about 'early modern England'. For Everitt, social changes which merit our attention included 'the dramatic effects of the enclosure movement, the rise in prices, the dissolution of the monasteries, the progress of commercial farming, the expansion of London, the development of transport, the increase of population, and the catastrophe of the Civil War' (Everitt 1966: 72–3). Interested more in social class than in agriculture, Stone sees English society as experiencing a 'seismic upheaval of unprecedented magnitude', one which led to the transformation of the 'status hierarchy' of the sixteenth century to the 'loose competitive status agglomerations to which we are accustomed today' (Stone 1966: 17). To Stone, England was 'early modern' from the following events and

conditions: the price revolution, changes in land ownership, urbani-
zation, increasing specialization, a growing bureaucracy, greater
physical movement of people, increased litigation, expansion of
educational opportunity, and greater commercial activity. Both
Everitt and Stone are careful to point out that the 'modernity' they
describe was neither uniform nor pervasive; it was, instead, an
unevenly emergent aspect of social life.

The notion of 'early modern England' had so caught on with a
subsequent generation of historians that by the middle and late
1970s it would appear in the titles of such studies as Keith Thomas's
*Rule and Misrule in the Schools of Early Modern England* (1976), Joan
Thirsk's *Economic Policy and Projects: The Development of a Consumer
Society in Early Modern England* (1978), and J. A. Sharpe's *Defamation
and Sexual Slander in Early Modern England* (1980). To my knowledge,
the first work of literary criticism to employ the phrase 'early
modern England' in its title was Annabel Patterson's *Censorship and
Interpretation: The Conditions of Writing and Reading in Early Modern
England* (1984). Because her study has made an important contribution to the field, and because it appears to have led others to speak
of 'early modern England' in their criticism, Patterson's understanding of 'early modern' merits scrutiny here.

One thing to notice about Patterson's title is its authoritative
resonance. Its subtitle, in particular, seems confident and objective –
almost as though representing a genre of inquiry separate from
literary criticism. In this, it followed the clinical title of Barbara
Lewalski's *Protestant Poetics and the Seventeenth-Century Religious Lyric*
(1979), which may be said to read like the cover of a policy briefing.
The intentional sobriety of this latter title was pointed out by
William Kerrigan and Gordon Braden (1989), who argue that it
marks the beginning of a 'revolution in critical fashion': 'In place of
"Christian" we find the sectarian precision of "Protestant", and in
place of "humanism" with its strong epochal ring, we find the timeless "poetics". Instead of the evocative "Renaissance", we have the
flatly denotative "Seventeenth-Century", with which nobody will
bother to quarrel' (Kerrigan and Braden 1989: x). As we will see,
the 'revolution' which Kerrigan and Braden hold Lewalksi to have
spurred was continued by Patterson (1984), whose usage of 'early
modern' would be widely adopted by literary critics.

Patterson's main objective in *Censorship and Interpretation*, as she
states in her introduction, is

to break down the barriers between academic discourse and 'real'
issues, by recovering for inspection and inquiry that stage in
European culture when all the major European powers were
themselves emergent nations, engaged in a struggle for self-
definition as well as for physical territory, and when, in consequence, freedom of expression not only was not taken for granted,
but was a major subject of political and intellectual concern.

(Patterson 1984: 3)

This sentence is both a summary of the book's topic and an
apologia for the term 'early modern'. Referring to the latter as a
'stage', Patterson (1984) quickly gains the benefit of a develop-
mental narrative. Indeed, in its very style this sentence reveals the
microprocessor-like speed associated with the function of 'early
modern' in literary criticism. That is, it couples with incredible
quickness two things at a great distance from one another. This sentence proposes, for instance, a highly specific project – 'inspection
and inquiry' into history through a set of sixteenth-, seventeenth-,
and eighteenth-century literary texts – as a solution to a general,
present-day problem, 'the barriers between academic discourse and
"real" issues'. In doing so, it races past us a set of undemonstrated
claims, offering them as fact: 'that stage in European culture when
all . . . and when, in consequence . . . a major subject'. Like 'early
modern' itself, the syntax of this long sentence is stretched taut to
cover a variety of times and topics.

In contrast to those of the historians examined in preceding para-
graphs, Patterson's definition of the 'early modern' is a thin one; it
centers on the idea of the nation-state, and, in particular, the
nation-state's relation to freedom of expression. Perhaps because of
literary criticism's traditional pursuit of single themes, this thinness
is almost always part of its uses of 'early modern'. Connecting the
theme of freedom of expression in the twentieth century with analogous formations in sixteenth- and seventeenth-century English texts,
Patterson's argument sees the past as both prologue to the present,
and also much like it. As did the 'parallel cultures' myth of the English
Renaissance earlier in the twentieth century, Patterson's early
modern paradigm gives readers of old books the comfort of feeling at
home in the past by allowing them to see it as a version of the present.

It would take four years from her book's appearance for the field
to adopt Patterson's usage. The year 1988 was the turning point, in
fact. Before this, for example, such critics as Stephen Greenblatt

and Jean Howard had used the word 'Renaissance' in relation to English literature of the sixteenth and seventeenth centuries: we can see this in Greenblatt's *Renaissance Self-Fashioning* (1980), and (as editor) *Representing the English Renaissance* (1988b), and Howard's 'The new historicism in Renaissance studies' (1986). During and after 1988, however, both critics would use the phrase 'early modern' in their titles: Greenblatt in *Learning to Curse: Essays in Early Modern Culture* (1990), and Howard in 'Crossdressing, the theater, and gender struggle in early modern England' (1988). Howard's first sentence in this article ('How many people crossdressed in Renaissance England?') uses the older period term, as does the body of the article itself. But in her next book, in 1994, she would adopt the newer descriptor in both her title, *The Stage and Social Struggle in Early Modern England*, and her text.

'Early modern' gained such acceptance in literary criticism by the early 1990s that significant discussion of the term itself began to occur. In 1992, Leah Marcus began an essay on the subject by asking 'What manner of beast is early modern studies?' (Marcus 1992: 41), before contrasting the latter with 'Renaissance' studies in the first full-fledged examination of the two terms. The following year, Frances Dolan (1993) would publish in *PMLA* an article concerning 'The face-painting debate in early modern England', which occasioned a series of letters to that journal's 'Forum'. Like Marcus's essay, this brief exchange highlighted key tensions between competing models of history and interpretation, models broadly associated with 'Renaissance' and 'early modern'.

This 'early modern' exchange began in 1994 when Crystal Dowling wrote to challenge Dolan's employment of 'early modern', arguing that Dolan's use of the phrase worked to hide the historical divergence of her evidence. As Dowling (1994) pointed out, 'all the attacks on face painting that Dolan quotes range from 1583 to 1616 whereas all the defenses come from 1660 and 1665' (Dowling 1994: 119). Dolan (1994a: 120) replied that this term was 'more helpful in enabling me to attend to similarities in gender constructions from the late sixteenth century to the end of the seventeenth', and welcomed 'the sweeping view permitted by the category "early modern"'. Later that year, Dubrow (1994) contributed to the same venue a thoughtful meditation on problems arising from the newly popular 'early modern'. These problems included, to Dubrow, the tendency of 'early modern' to keep the Middle Ages an 'Other' (a problem also, she pointed out, with 'Renaissance' as a period term), its tendency to overemphasize the reach of capitalism, to underemphasize regional differences, and, largely, to neglect religion.

Dolan's reply to Dubrow expanded on her earlier answer, and contains four observations that have special relevance here:

> I think it is significant that many scholars . . . use a range of periodizations, adopting whichever one best suits the project at hand . . .
>
> . . . instead of a new consensus (*early modern*, for instance) replacing an old (*Renaissance*), the possibilities are proliferating.
>
> This multiplicity and the concomitant necessity of choosing mean that it is necessary to reflect constantly on periodization.
>
> . . . juggling is always involved in creating (rather than discovering or describing) periods and their literatures.
>
> (Dolan 1994b: 1026–7)

Much of what Dolan says here is uncontroversial. Most critics (including myself) do use 'a range of periodizations' in their work, and such terminology has indeed proliferated. What makes these remarks relevant is that, for the most part, they represent mainstream thinking about how we write criticism. And it is in this typicality that we see the major difficulties that spring from 'early modern'.

We could begin by noticing the instrumentality of the term. As spelled out in Dolan's (1994b) reply, 'early modern' is, like other period terms, a tool rather than a truth. Offering too casually the view that periods are created rather than discovered or described – as though, for instance, Reformation England were merely a creation of A. G. Dickens in 1964 – Dolan puts critics in a wholly rhetorical world, and the world of the past wholly in the rhetoric of critics. Much of her position, in fact, offers a consumerist celebration of choice; we might recognize in her phrase 'the possibilities are proliferating' a genre of advertising which eagerly promises abundance without consequence. And where Dolan suggests that 'this multiplicity and the concomitant necessity of choosing mean that it is necessary to reflect constantly on periodization', we can sense a claim that is true only if circular. Expansion of choice, in itself, does not mean reflection on the objects chosen. On the contrary, a good argument could be made that the multiplicity which Dolan embraces means that critics will reflect *less* frequently, and *less* deeply, on the issue of historical and literary periods.

In her confusion of selection with reflection, Dolan foregrounds the way criticism has become detached from belief. Noticeably absent from her remarks is any sense that one term could be truer than another, or even that a critic could *believe* this to be the case. Where period designations are concerned, we are left as enlightened agnostics: all the labels are constructs; none is perfect; each has its proper time and place. While the refusal to commit is often held to be an intellectual virtue, it is also, in its supple instrumentality, a potential concession to the lure of opportunity. When belief gives way to occasionalist use of language, for instance, what we write about literature is in peril of being seen as an empty gesture toward the elusive rewards of the academic market. 'Early modern' risks, in this sense, being seen as part of a critic's professional wardrobe: a fashionable item with which to accessorize one's ensemble of words, an ambitious phrase that draws on the power of appearance.

'Early modern' often seems produced as much by the social formations of the present as by those of the past. That the designation frequently speaks to the professional lives of those who use it has been addressed by Michael Dobson (1996), who, in a characteristically insightful review of four recent critical studies, discerned 'an important shift in perceptions of Shakespeare's position within his culture, and indeed of that culture's priorities':

> Rather than being first and foremost a Stratford bourgeois pre-
> occupied with dowries and second-best beds, the Bard who
> emerges from these studies is an assiduously networking pro-
> fessional, and one, furthermore, whose courtly aspirations and
> connections aren't to be taken lightly. Consequently, the Eliza-
> bethan England these books persuasively depict is far closer in
> spirit to the Rialto and its serious money than to Windsor and its
> merry wives. Its literary and political circles are peopled by
> upstarts and would-be cosmopolitans, marketing their humanist
> skills across patronage networks which, structurally hostile to
> the domestic, operate in a dangerously ambiguous space some-
> where between the professional, the amicable and the erotic.
> In this culture favours are reciprocated in cash, in books or in
> kind; rival factions exchange information among themselves by
> letter and in closets; while sycophants and sexually available

apprentices rub shoulders and scratch backs with confidential secretaries and common players. It is a culture preoccupied with status and with clothes, in which an internally inconsistent patriarchy is always under threat but always in place: a culture, nonetheless, in which certain outstanding women, partly or wholly cross-dressed à la Portia, can achieve a sexily masculine success. It is a culture, in short, which bears striking resemblances to the one that developed in the Eighties around the annual conference of the Shakespeare Association of America.

(Dobson 1996: 24)

The sting at the end of this paragraph is a deserved one. Although it is not shocking to see critics creating a Shakespeare in their own image, it is surprising to see how little consciousness there is, in criticism, of that very reflexiveness. Given the term's sober, somewhat Marxist origins in the writings of British social historians, for instance, it is ironic that 'early modern' has become a popular brand name among American Shakespeareans. But such an irony extends past the fact of its adoption, and into the details of its usage.

As we have seen from its use in Patterson's *Censorship and Interpretation*, 'early modern' is less a replacement of 'Renaissance' than its structural equivalent. If 'Renaissance' connotes value through the trappings of aristocratic culture, 'early modern' offers up the self-serious attitude of the technology age. It is bathed in the gleaming light of the computer monitor – one difference between 'Renaissance' and 'early modern' essays being that many of the former were written in longhand, or on typewriters, whereas most of the latter have been written on computers. The difference is indeed cosmetic, and importantly so. As Marjorie Garber (1998) has suggested, the greatest aesthetic change in contemporary editions of Shakespeare – the switch from Roman to Arabic numerals as markers of acts and scenes (by which, for instance, I.ii becomes 1.2) – derived from the example of Marvin Spevack's *Harvard Concordance to Shakespeare* (1973), which used Arabic numerals in its entries, and thus encouraged subsequent scholars to give their references to Shakespeare's texts in the same manner. In this way, changes in technology have encouraged changes in the look of contemporary editions of Shakespeare's texts. Inasmuch as the latter reinforce our sense of an 'early modern' Shakespeare, we have modern technology and the sensibilities it encourages (rather than Shakespeare) to thank for the modern appearance of his texts.

Another of the ironies surrounding 'early modern' involves its relation to issues of social class. Often credited with helping us pay attention to subordinated groups in history, 'early modern' seems at times to advertise historically emergent, privileged habits and interests on the American coasts. While it may be unfair to hold 'early modern' to be a term of the California freeway, the New York subway, and the analyst's couch, a term through which the culture of the British isles in the sixteenth and seventeenth centuries is inflected through ways of life on Manhattan island in the twentieth and twenty-first, it is clearly a designation which confesses an interest in the past's contemporary utility.

## The last Shakespeare in history

There are two unspoken truths about 'early modern' as used in literary criticism relating to England. Both are worth stating here, not only because they have gone unsaid, but also because they figure centrally in the question of period labels that this chapter has explored.

The first is that what most makes this literature 'early modern' is not any of the things that critics normally offer in defense of the term. Not, that is, a new interest in questions of nationality, subjectivity, race, exploration, or gender. That these things are as 'new' as is often claimed is a point of debate: medievalists can fairly describe the same as important features of many of the texts they study. Instead, what makes the works of Shakespeare, Sidney, Nashe, Jonson, Wroth, and Donne 'early modern' is a thing so integral to our criticism that we rarely talk about it: the English language. English literature of the sixteenth and seventeenth centuries can be called 'early modern' because the English language had entered its modern state. As Baugh and Cable remind us,

> we attain in this period to something in the nature of a standard, something moreover that is recognizably 'modern.' The effect of the Great Vowel Shift was to bring the pronunciation within measurable distance of that which prevails today. The influence of the printing press and the efforts of spelling reformers had resulted in a form of written English that offers little difficulty to the modern reader.
>
> (Baugh and Cable 1978: 250)

This modernization of written and spoken English is what allows us to label texts from the sixteenth and seventeenth centuries 'early modern'. Because they give us less 'difficulty' than the works of Chaucer, Langland, Gower, and the Pearl Poet, they seem chronological neighbors in a way that the writings of these earlier authors do not. We should observe that the first uses of 'early modern' in relation to England came not from historians or literary critics but from philologists. In this regard, we could note Arvid Gabrielson's 'Early Modern English . . .' in the 1930 number of *Studia Neophilologica*, and E. J. Dobson's 'Early Modern Standard English' in the *Transactions of the Philological Society* in 1955. 'Early modern English' thus preceded and enabled 'early modern England'.

The reason Shakespeareans almost never discuss language in this context is that doing so means giving away the game, confronting the fact that what we do depends less on our commitment to various ideas and causes than it does on a book of such incredible articulation that it might be dubbed the speech manual of modern culture. I am referring, of course, to the First Folio. This 1623 text brings us to the second unspoken truth about 'early modern' studies relating to England: they would not exist without this great work of early modern English. 'Shakespeare' – by which I mean Shakespeare's writings, and the host of associations those writings have generated over the centuries – is the center from which countless studies of 'early modern' texts and phenomena take their being. However scientifically these projects are described, they would have far fewer readers were it not for Shakespeare's well-spoken plays and poems, and the hold the latter have had upon our culture. Although 'The Age of Shakespeare' sounds trite as a designation, in signaling who pays the piper of our academic tune it is perhaps more honest than 'early modern', which is honest (about its presentism) in only an unconscious way.

It is to Shakespeare's language – more specifically, to the articulation of his plays and poems – that we must look in order to understand the importance of periodization trends relating to the sixteenth and seventeenth centuries. 'Shakespeare' has become something like the mouthpiece of Western culture in English, an eloquent representative of the age of speech in a society of the spectacle. As we become increasingly swayed by the power of the visual, Shakespeare stands out to us like an uncanny reminder of a faculty we have already lost. He does so in an ever more singular fashion, as though his works hold a monopoly of well-spoken English. No longer a supremely gifted writer working in a time and place remarkably rich in literary talent, he is instead a figure in whom the precedents of his craft and the efforts of his contemporaries have been collapsed.

Such condensation of status and value has produced a 'Shakespeare industry' both inside and outside the academy. However justified the attention generated through the operations of this industry, it has worked to change the way we write about Shakespeare's works. An interest in Shakespeare that leads us to ignore the achievement of his contemporaries, for instance, is regrettable. And where 'early modern' is sometimes held to be a corrective to this tendency – by democratizing our objects of study – in casting the traces of Shakespeare's time as harbingers to our own, this period concept has effectively done the opposite. Gradually erasing any associations of his era ('Tudor', 'Elizabethan'), and replacing them with first an aristocratic ('Renaissance'), then a quasi-scientific label ('early modern'), we have accelerated the process by which a man has become his words, and those words have become, in turn, valuable, and even value itself.

This estrangement is a necessary step in the commodification of his eloquence: Shakespeare has become, through our period labels, the costume in which we have most recently cloaked the vitality of his language. We say 'early modern Shakespeare', then, as though it is merely one more Shakespeare in an infinite sequence. But it is precisely this admission of sequence – a sequence without content, only difference – which testifies to the end of Shakespearean history. Absolved of any integrity of relation to a particular time or place, these sequential Shakespeares signify only in relation to each other, and only by declining to mean. The 'ever new' Shakespeare is, in this perpetual newness and constant circulation within the commercial and educational institutions of our culture, always the same.

## Acknowledgements

I am grateful to Mark Thornton Burnett, Michelle Girard, Hugh Grady, and Eric Mallin for reading earlier drafts of this chapter, and for their helpful comments.

## Note

1  I have discussed twentieth-century constructions of the English Renaissance in the final chapter of *Quoting Shakespeare*. Part of this section
summarizes material examined at more length there.

# 10

# The Hamlet formerly known as Prince

## LINDA CHARNES

The Whine of 99: Everyone's getting rich but me!
(cover legend, *Newsweek*, 5 July 1999)

The last decade of the millennium saw a *Hamlet* boom unmatched since the onset of American mass media. The prince who in Shakespeare's play literally ends up nowhere (dying in a state that is neither quite Denmark nor Norway) now walks everywhere among us, a ghost in mass culture, from light comedies or adventure movies like *L.A. Story* and *Last Action Hero* to venues as ambitious as Branagh's bombastic 1996 film version.[1] The play has always been a rich reserve of Shakespearean sound bites and clichés. But this alone does not tell us much about why *Hamlet* in particular has enjoyed such a startling re-emergence into popular prominence. The same figure whose failure to inherit and refusal to take the throne in Denmark lead to the death of his state has somehow become (perhaps on the basis of this refusal) the unofficial legislator of late-twentieth-century democratic man – the man who would, and would not, be king. What Bartleby the Scrivener was to the man in the gray flannel suit, Hamlet has become to the Range-Rover set.

But what can middle-class Americans possibly have in common with this Prince? The dictum (by now long familiar in high school classrooms) that Hamlet is the Everyman of the human condition, caught between desire and duty, conscience and cowardice, religion and revenge, passion and reason, has grown hoarfrost. If we look at Hamlet's actual political status in the play, no one could be less an Everyman: first, Hamlet – as sole heir of a royal father – is a Prince; second, he is at the center of all the other characters' attentions. Everyone in this play is obsessed with taking Hamlet's pulse; in this regard at the very least, he is even more king than the king.

Despite all this, Hamlet insists on removing himself from events that he is nevertheless at the center of.[2] Thus we might say that Hamlet's simultaneous lack of political interest and self-righteous aggrievement have created a cultural Wormhole, whisking him out of Shakespeare's era and dropping him squarely into our own. Middle-class Americans can be said to share Hamlet's general dissatisfaction, nervous boredom, and self-righteousness. We have, however, something that Hamlet seems to lack – an aggressive sense of entitlement to ever more of whatever is available. Why is it that we who are not heirs apparent keep demanding more royalties and privileges while Hamlet – a Prince – evinces no desire for what he is literally entitled to? In a play in which everyone else knows exactly what they want (except Ophelia, whose desires are sacrificed to the agendas of father, brother and king; even Gertrude wants everyone just to get along), whether it is sex, status, money, land, or authority, Hamlet will have none of it and becomes during the course of the play a nation unto himself. In the cultural milieu of late Elizabethan England, in a play which is resolutely patriarchal, monarchical, and nationalistic, this is (to say the least) an untenable position for Hamlet to take. Veering between grandiosity and abjection, Hamlet will neither suffer to be governed nor assume the responsibility of governing others.

Patriarchy, monarchy, and nation: these are the ideological and political foundations of Shakespearean England. They are also the dominant (although by no means only) arbitrageurs of desire, designating what men of standing are expected to want and thereby imposing what's supposed to be – ideologically at least – a shared basis for masculine identity. But they are no longer the touchstones of Our America. At least not the first two. Monarchy has been abolished for over two hundred years; the overt resolutions of patriarchy have been shaken (if not stirred); and even American nationalism has grown less vocal and more splintered in the face of a growing multi-ethnic society and foreign and economic policies many citizens cannot agree on. The prerogatives of patriarchy and monarchy have become increasingly subsumed into and even transmogrified by the operations of an ideologically democratic nation. They have not, however, vanished.

We are not a monarchy – we are a democracy; Hamlet cannot be us. We do not stand to inherit entire nations from our fathers, even if we are their namesakes. Our entitlements are considerably more amorphous than those Hamlet can and should lay claim to. And yet throughout the course of the play Hamlet will claim nothing except to have that within which passes show (1.2.85).[3] This invisible 'that' Hamlet refers to has been the source of considerable confusion and speculation in critical analyses of the play as well as in mass cultural film versions. Most literate Americans realize when they hear the name Hamlet that something important is being invoked: and yet no one (including Shakespeare scholars such as myself) knows exactly what that might be. If nothing else, we know that Hamlet stands for Big Ideas, especially ideas that rebel against corruption of some kind. Mention Hamlet to the average middle-class American and certain things spring to mind: romance, high culture, adolescence, high school English, failed exams, revenge, procrastination, and other vague themes related and unrelated. What does not seem apparent is an awareness that Hamlet is a Prince who should, by the time the play begins, be a King. How is it that this rather important fact seems to have gone missing in the popular imaginary?[4]

The general take on Hamlet has always focused, in a negative way, on his indecision and inability to take direct action. And yet, as a society our own primary way of dealing with unacceptable political circumstances is exactly the same as Hamlet's – rationalized delay. A less popular method, but one increasingly resorted to, is to disrupt or stop the production of whatever contributes to the reproduction and continuation of that circumstance – the call-in-sick strategy. However unproductive such strategies may appear to be, they are not lacking in agency. In *Hamlet*, delay and disruption frisk like twinned lambs under the shadow of a failure of paternal and political will. In American culture, they provide a stanch against a political will that twists in the wind, ruled by multinational capital and cyber-stock, sovereigns (King and Prince respectively) that generate overwhelming financial expectations among ordinary Americans while eliminating any sense of a shared cultural or political legacy.

When the pop musician Prince Rogers Nelson decided to abandon his stage name Prince (replacing it with an unpronounceable glyph), he stated to the world that the title by which we knew him no longer denoted him truly. While this gesture resulted only in a more annoying name (the Artist-Formerly-Known-as-Prince), it is not the first time a Prince has disavowed his title. Like the Artist, Prince Hamlet can neither inhabit nor escape a title that trails him like an embarrassing odor. Along with Prince Hal of the Henriad, Hamlet bears two paternal signifiers – royal and patrimonial. But while Hal may be called many things during his sojourn in Eastcheap, he is never not a Prince, never not understood to be a future King. Here, then, are the two most paradigmatic sons in the Shakespearean corpus – Hal, who cannot not be a King, and Hamlet, who cannot be one. Both are set up to repay debts they never promised (*I Henry IV* 1.3.187); both struggle with the after-effects of paternal errors in judgment; both turn to clownish surrogate fathers (Falstaff and Yorick, respectively); and both face doubles who show them how they should be doing their jobs (Hotspur and Fortinbras). Hal and Hamlet represent a dilemma that clearly obsessed Shakespeare and that is: what exactly is the nature and function of a proper patrimony? What are the require-ments of leaving a legacy? What are fathers supposed to pass down to their sons, and what are sons expected to give in return? And what happens when entitlement – political, legal, or affective – ceases to be a motivating factor for individual agency?[5]

Patrimony consists of two structures: the first nominal or patrony-mic, and the second (equally laden with symbolism) biological. A father must designate his heir and dispose of his monies accordingly in his last will and testament. There are, after all, testes in the etymology of testimony: they share the same Latin root, *testis* – which means to bear witness. They also share the root *testa*, which means both the skin or coating of a seed, and that by which the exis-tence, quality, or genuineness of anything is or may be determined, a means of trial. To testiculate is to encase or join together elements within a sac or enclosure; to testificate is to certify a fact in docu-mented form (cf. *OED*, 3269–3270, *passim*).[6] It is no mere metaphor that a testament is a document wherein a father's will and his goods conjoin, forming a legal coating (figuratively speaking) over his seed. This is the same conflation of meaning crudely familiar in references to the family jewels, and so on. But the implications of this hybridized legal term, in which the morphology of a male body part is implemented in juridical form, demonstrate that in

Shakespeare's culture (as in our own), there is no biology that is not also politically symbolic.

That this was understood in early modern England was clear in the passage of perpetual entail laws in 1557, which designated that even fathers themselves are subordinated to the rules of patrimony. Just as a royal son is expected, barring dementia or incapacity, to succeed his father, so too must a father properly transmit his testament to his son. In this way, patrimony functions as a prosthesis: a legal structure grafted onto a living body, technically and ideologically inalienable from that body. In early modern culture time must be understood biosymbolically as the matriculation of the social relationship from the body of the father to that of his issue. Organized by patrilinear successive monarchy, the passage of political time is inseparable from biological time: the father's body *is* the political calendar. To say this is not to naturalize the way in which patriarchy works; only to point out that in such a culture, the legal disposition of the father's place, position, property, and name, is expected to flow in the same direction as his semen. The money shot is not a concept invented by the pornography industry; patrimony in its original conception is the linkage between testes and testament.[7]

Throughout Shakespeare's plays there are many offspring whose stances toward their fathers can best be phrased as 'show me the money'.[8] And in the tragedies, as well as many of the comedies, conflicts are usually engendered by paternal (and/or royal) failure to properly testificate or testiculate. Shakespeare's concern with the deformations of paternal and political legacy also runs through both history tetralogies. Despite, however, all its acute tensions between fathers and sons, the Henriad represents a triumphant recuperation of patrimonial logic under the conditions of extreme ideological and economic restructuring extant in Shakespeare's England. From *Richard II*, in which the sublime object of royal ideology is presumably – and mistakenly – embodied solely in the Monarch, to *Henry V*, in which every Englishman becomes a shareholder in the sublime corporation of England as represented by King Harry's crown, the law of patrimonial reproduction survives its symbolic transformations. The redistribution of sublime Matter, which Shakespeare takes all four plays of the second tetralogy to accomplish, ensures (temporarily at least) that anyone who attacks the monarchy attacks as well the body of the corporate shareholders, for whom the monarch is now less the embodiment than the guarantor. Patrimony in the Henriad is rendered functional again by Hal's construction of a hybrid paternity that grafts his father's body human onto Richard's body sublime – masterfully creating a legacy that can be legitimized precisely by being disconnected to any one particular father. Hal's homage to the usurped sun king (the royal reburial and paid mourner's rites) renders him the symbolic offspring of Richard II (and therefore entitled to inherit something directly from Richard), even while the play makes it clear that he is Henry's biological son. In this way, King Harry manages to protect and even promote patrimonial legitimacy by decentralizing its location, making every Tom, Dick, or Francis a brother to himself and thereby a symbolic son to Henry IV.

Of course this recuperation is not without fissures. As Lisa Jardine (1996) has written about the Henriad, there is a straight contradiction between lineage and conquest, and in the formation of national identity there is an inevitable tension between royal marriage (in which two partners come from different nations, and may effect a cross-national territorial merger) and the passing on of the crown by lineal descent (Jardine 1996: 10). The tenuous nature of the legal claims Henry V makes on France are fudged, as Jardine puts it, by his successful courtship of the French Princess Catherine. Thus the Henriad secures patrimony at the expense of a doubt about the general possibility of effecting such lineal transactions without the weakening intercession of women (Jardine 1996: 10). Patrimonial entail may be protected by marriage, but patrilineal purity is inevitably diluted by sexual reproduction.

In *Hamlet*, a particular father is very much the issue and phobia about the corrupting 'seepage' of women into the pure 'stock' of the father is everywhere apparent. If patrimony requires the begetting of heirs, Hamlet will not do it. For Hamlet, all children are women's children and therefore tainted by corruption. As Janet Adelman (1992) has argued, 'the structure of *Hamlet* . . . is marked by the struggle . . . to free the masculine identity of both father and son from its origin in the contaminated maternal body' (Adelman 1992: 7–24 *passim*). This struggle – so evident in *Hamlet* and indeed as Adelman's work has shown, in many of Shakespeare's plays – also defines one of the key goals of the testamentary process more generally. Patrimony, properly understood, is designed to suppress maternal origin and substitute the paternal will as the site of plenitude for both cultural and material capital. However, Hamlet's refusal of reproduction is more than just a misogynist repudiation of women since, as I have argued elsewhere, women are for Hamlet the identified symptom of much more threatening realization (Charnes 1997). Encrypted within Hamlet's refusal to reproduce is an awareness that he is always-already the reproduced, that his fate is to serve as back-up to a father who will not, to borrow Marjorie Garber's memorable phrase, give up the ghost (Garber 1987: 124).

King Hamlet continues to govern from beyond the grave and seems oblivious to Hamlet's political rights as royal heir. There have of course been long-standing critical debates about whether or not Hamlet's Denmark is an elective monarchy, since the status of the actual Danish Constitution (as implemented by the group of aristocratic landowners known as the Rigsråd) included a proviso for a monarch to be elected (Hibbard 1987: 37). Whether or not Shakespeare would have known about the Danish Constitution is to some degree moot; even if he had, Danish history reveals that by 1448 the Oldenberg dynasty began with Christian I (Sohmer 1996: 21) and, apart from civil skirmishes provoked by Catholic bishops and nobles out of fear of encroaching Lutheranism, the throne remained in the hands of Oldenberg heirs. In 1536 Christian III took the throne, which then went to Christian's son Frederick in 1559. In 1588 Frederick's son Christian IV succeeded and reigned until 1648 (Sohmer 1996: 21). During Shakespeare's entire lifetime, then, Denmark was a de facto successive monarchy, since the Rigsråd always elected the King's oldest son. Consequently it is not necessarily contradictory that Shakespeare would mention election in a play that so clearly stacks the deck for succession – a play entitled *The Tragedy of Hamlet: Prince of Denmark*.

It is, however, strange – since references to election are few and fleeting in the play, notably at 5.2, when Hamlet refers to Claudius as 'He that hath killed my king and whored my mother, / Popped in between the election and my hopes' (5.2.66–7); and at the end of the scene when Hamlet, dying, prophecy(s)'the election lights / On Fortinbras'(5.2.297–8). In both instances these references are conspicuously jarring. First, everyone in the play behaves as if Hamlet's right to succeed his father were a given; presumably, therefore, he would not have needed the election in any way other than, perhaps, as a formality. Second, Fortinbras hardly needs the election either, since his army has occupied Denmark by main force. Perhaps Shakespeare knew that even though Denmark had an electoral provision in its Constitution, it was no longer operative. If this is the case, raising the question of election in the play serves only to further emphasize the shadowiness of the legacy King Hamlet has bequeathed the prince.

But what exactly is Hamlet's patrimony? What has the dead King willed to his only son? As Richard Wilson informs us, by the middle of the sixteenth century, 'an older grid of inheritance with its lateral network of social affiliations and obligations was abandoned for a new documentary and legal system of transmission, focused on selected lineal descendants' (Wilson 1993: 187). Even if an 'afflicted testator' wished to disinherit his immediate lineal successors, freedom of testation

> was circumscribed by the tradition that when a man died leaving wife and issue, only one-third of his estate was devisable by will, while a third went to his wife as dower and the other to his children. Entitlement of heirs was further safeguarded by canons of descent which ruled that inheritance was patrilinear, an heir could never be disinherited.
>
> (Wilson 1993: 188)

Certainly an heir could not be disinherited if the first born, or sole issue, were a son.

Despite the clarity of expectation entail was designed to guarantee, nowhere in *Hamlet* is there any explicit mention of the dead King's will.[9] But while a King might literally die intestate, a King cannot effectually die intestate, for the entire royal structure is built on direct linear succession of property, authority, and monies. Even if we were to speculate about the divisions of King Hamlet's personal estate upon his death in terms of the necessary third being allotted to wife and issue, it is hardly likely that the old king would have used his freedom of testation to bequeath the remaining third to Claudius. If as the ghost rails, Claudius 'won to his shameful lust/ the will of my most seeming-virtuous queen', that would still leave him with only a third of a claim to the kingdom (Gertrude's will or portion) – with Hamlet being by default the two-thirds shareholder, more than enough upon which to base a claim to the throne. As Eric Mallin has argued, 'as much as [Hamlet] denies his stature, however, it remains obvious to the other characters' (1996: 111), and especially to Laertes, who warns Ophelia not to set her sights above her station as Hamlet is subject to his birth (1.3.18). But if his 'will is not his own', as Laertes puts it, it is not because his choice must 'be circumscribed / Unto the voice and yielding of that body /

Whereof he is the head.' It is because his father has not left a will; and despite Hamlet's obvious legal right to do so, this son will not step forward to claim any legacy that has not been specifically articulated by his father.

What is most surprising about Hamlet's unassuming stance is how unsurprising it becomes as the play progresses. Despite the over-determination of being a paternal namesake, there is an almost complete lack of identification between Hamlet and his father. In his first soliloquy, he compares Claudius to the King and finds him 'no more like my father / Than I to Hercule' (1.2.152–3), a comparison which suggests that Claudius's lack of resemblance to his father can be measured in terms of his own. Thus Hamlet seems to have identity without identification, strangely situating himself outside of the reflective filiations of politics, friendship (with the exception of Horatio), and love. He retains only the name and none of the addition of a king. As Mallin (1996: 112) nicely puts it, 'something weird has happened to the procedure, not just the outcome, of the succession'.

When Laertes refers to the body of which Hamlet is the head, he speaks of Denmark, the King's sublime body, and by extension his subjects. But the body of Denmark seems to have undergone a strange entropy, its exact boundaries becoming amorphous and semi-permeable. There is already a de facto divorce between the body and head of state, and it was first effected not by Claudius but by King Hamlet himself, before the play even begins. When Marcellus asks his fellow sentinels

> Why this same strict and most observant watch
> So nightly toils the subject of the land
> And why such daily cast of brazen cannon
> And foreign mart for implements of war
>
> (1.1.74–7)

Horatio answers that 'King Hamlet, long ago pricked on by a most emulate pride' (1.1.86), staked a major portion of his kingdom on a wager with King Fortinbras of Norway. Both fathers were prepared capriciously to gamble away their sons' patrimonies, thereby breaking the laws of entail that in Shakespeare's day bind fathers as well as sons. That King Hamlet won the wager would lead, one might think, to this story being trumpeted to general acclaim. Instead, Horatio tells Bernardo how the whisper goes, suggesting something shameful in the enterprise. After all, the outcome of the wager might have gone the other way. King Hamlet may not have broken the letter of entail, but he broke its spirit, treating his kingdom as if it were his private property and acting as if he had (or would have) no sons to whom he might one day have to answer. While one hesitates to speculate about young Hamlet's childhood, his father's cavalier disregard for his offspring's political future seems to have registered in the Prince. When Hamlet tells Horatio that he does not hold his life at a pin's fee, he reveals that although he has a title, he does not have what a title is meant to convey: a sense of entitlement.

For Hamlet to take the throne upon his father's death would be to proclaim himself heir and go after what is rightfully his, despite his father's will, or lack thereof. After all, young Fortinbras is doing so, sharking up 'a list of landless resolutes and aiming to recover of us by strong hand / And terms compulsory those foresaid lands / So by his father lost' (1.1.104–7). Frequently noticed is the fact that Fortinbras is in a political situation analogous to Hamlet's: his uncle Norway now sits on his father's throne. But Fortinbras refuses to accept 'the same covenant / and carriage of the article designed' (95–7) by his father and King Hamlet. The elliptical way in which the sealed compact was struck (as described by Horatio, who provides the only narrative we get about the event) suggests that Denmark and Norway were not technically at war prior to the carriage of the article designed but rather that the conditions of war were pricked on by the fathers' emulate pride.

When the Ghost describes the details of his murder and Claudius's guilt, he should urge Hamlet to proclaim himself the lawful heir of Denmark, reclaim his throne from a foul usurper, and prosecute him for fratricide, regicide, usurpation, and unlawful marriage. But this would not be in keeping with what Horatio describes as the Ghost's extravagant and erring spirit (1.1.159). After all, such a revenge would be LEGAL, and would protect the future of the state, as well as permit the Prince to proceed as if he were, in fact, the Prince of Denmark. But what has Hamlet's father to do with laws, either of nature, or of culture? Instead, the ghost's only will is to revenge and remember him. A legal proceeding against Claudius would take into account the crime committed against the son as well as against the father, for in patrimonial culture there is no crime against the latter that does not affect the former. Irrespective of undecideable debates about Denmark's actual status as an elective Monarchy, for an Elizabethan audience, as Jardine (1966: 39) points out, Claudius's marriage to Gertrude 'historically . . . is . . . unlawful . . . and . . . it deprives Hamlet of his lawful succession'. Given that Hamlet clearly registers the offense done to his father that, according to Ecclesiastical law, makes the marriage unlawful, he could legitimately step forward, declare the marriage invalid and Claudius a usurper – especially since, according to Jardine (1996: 45), 'the offense is against Hamlet; the offending party is Claudius.'

The procedure of patriarchal succession must be based on the unquestioned blood linkage between father and son. We are never given to know how long Claudius has skulked about the court at Elsinore or what his role was prior to the King's murder. Nowhere is there a fully convincing explanation of why Gertrude agrees to her admittedly over-hasty marriage (2.2.57) and why 'no one utters a peep of protest about Claudius's ascent' (Mallin 1996: 113). Unless we accept Hamlet's view of Gertrude's nymphomania (which I cannot endorse since we never see Gertrude acting even remotely lubriciously), his failure to challenge the succession, coupled with Gertrude's inexplicable willingness to see her son bypassed, raises the possibility that Claudius could be Hamlet's biological father (something more than hinted at in Branagh's 1996 film, in which Branagh's Hamlet was made closely to resemble Derek Jacobi's Claudius). At the very least, this would go a long way toward explaining why the dead King left no provision for Hamlet and does not insist that he claim the throne.

One need not, however, argue that Claudius must be Hamlet's real father, only that Hamlet's paternity is a question raised in many ways throughout the play.[10] Veiled disavowals of paternity are detectable in the way the Ghost never addresses Hamlet directly as son, but rather resorts to a grammar of indirection, calling Hamlet 'thou noble youth'. His references to himself as 'thy father's spirit' are usually couched in syllogism: 'if thou hast nature in thee' (1.5.81) and 'if thou didst ever thy dear father love' (1.5.23). It is less interesting to try to make a case for Claudius's paternity than to say that the space created by the doubt is filled with a series of *paternity tests* in which both the nature and culture of the ties between fathers and sons are strained to the limits of credibility.

Even if the play showcases Fortinbras as an exemplar of the son's right and expectation directly to succeed his father, can we hold him up as the model son? While he is preparing to reclaim his birthright, he is also explicitly going against his father's will. His actions clearly show that all bets are off between dead fathers – and that a compact between fathers cannot be honored at the expense of the covenant that binds fathers and sons. Fortinbras makes no claims beyond the recovery of those lands that were by his father lost, demonstrating that he well understands both the spirit and the letter of perpetual entail. To this extent Fortinbras is a model of the path Hamlet might take. But if everyone in the play turns a blind eye to the explicitly political nature of Claudius's crime, it is because Hamlet himself does; and in so doing, he performs the symptom-ology of the 'questionable shape' of his true patrimonial legacy, which is: *remember me, revenge me, but do not replace me.*

A problem, since to be a Prince is to be a future King. If the possi-bility for the latter is annulled, the former is emptied of substance – an only son and first-born royal heir cannot be a once and future Prince. The designations King and Prince have meaning only in the relation of linear succession; without such a framework, the only part of the father's title that carries forward to the son is the patronym Hamlet. In this scenario, the political inheritance that should derive from biological reproduction has been replaced by the mere repetition of the patronym; and the very concept of patri-mony is suborned, since reproducing the name, without the addition of a king, takes the testes out of testament.

We have a word for this, in postmodern culture: we call it cloning. As Baudrillard (1993) has argued, cloning is

> The dream, then, of an eternal twinning as replacement for sexual procreation, with its link to death. A cellular dream of scissi-parity – the purest form of parenthood in that it allows us at last to dispense with the other and go directly from one to the same.
>
> (Baudrillard 1993: 114)

When the Ghost enjoins Hamlet to 'remember me', the effect is not ideological interpellation but rather scissipation – the process of being cut, divided or split. The ghost's command reveals a pro-foundly disturbing fantasy at the heart of patrimonial culture, one that can even be seen in Shakespeare's own final revisions to his last will and testament: a fantasy of keeping one's essence pure, without the contamination of Otherness, a dream of exercising in perpetuity one's undivided will by eradicating the difference that literally conceives and constitutes succession. To be a first-born son under primogeniture is one thing; to bear the father's name is a doubly derivative legacy that leaves little room for any kind of autonomy. The result in *Hamlet* is not a fantasy of self-genesis, since as Baudrillard points out,

> such phantasies always involve the figures of the mother and the father – sexed parental figures whom the subject may indeed yearn to eliminate, the better to usurp their positions, but this in no sense implies contesting the symbolic structure of procreation: if you become your own child, you are still the child of someone. Cloning, on the other hand, radically eliminates not only the mother, but also the father, for it eliminates the interaction between his genes and the mother's, the imbrication of the parent's difference, and above all, the joint act of procreation.
>
> (Baudrillard 1993: 114–15)

Bound by his father to enact his will without succeeding him, Hamlet becomes a scissoid replicant – a creature meant to go perpetually from the one to the same. Remember me means just that – remember only me, while the maternal body is effaced from the replicant relation. The King's sublime body – here manifest in his command-ment – cannot 'Live / within the book and volume of [Hamlet's] brain / unmixed with baser matter', unless the son agrees to be the father's clone.

What would the stakes of such an agreement be? No less than the dissolution of the subject, since identical duplication ends the division that constitutes him (Baudrillard 1993: 115). As Baudrillard evocatively puts it, cloning eradicates the mirror stage,

> the timeless narcissistic dream of the subject's projection into an ideal alter ego – for the projection too works by means of an image – the image in the mirror, in which the subject becomes alienated in order to rediscover himself . . . Nothing of all this is left with cloning. No more mediations – no more images: an individual product on a conveyer belt is in no sense a reflection of the next (albeit identical) product in line. The one is never a mirage, whether ideal or mortal, of the other: they can only accumulate.
>
> (Baudrillard 1993: 115)

They can only accumulate, a series of identical products on conveyer belts. Is this not in effect what the Ghost is asking of his son? That he act without either reflection or differentiation? The distinction that should constitute Hamlet as subject is precisely the one his father will not recognize. And since successive monarchy (and to some extent all patrimony) depends upon a patriarchal fantasy of cloning – that sons will be the 'True Originall Copies' of their fathers – Hamlet's implied lack of resemblance to his father visually raises the specter of adultery, thereby forcing Gertrude and the joint act of procreation back into the picture, a sure-fire way to puncture the fantasy of maternal erasure at the center of patriarchal will power.[11]

In *Hamlet* the time is out of joint because the elaborate political and social mechanism of filiation is broken even while it is obsessively insisted upon at the level of the signifier. This is the remarkable fact of plot that Claudius, perhaps the most successful straw man in literary history, obscures: that the throne of Denmark was imperiled initially by King Hamlet himself; that Hamlet's displacement from the throne was first practiced, however fantasmatically, by his own father; that the first crime we hear about in the play was the enactment, through the wager with Fortinbras, of a *symbolic filicide*. The way the play invokes, and then induces us to forget, how the whisper went occludes the failure of entailment on both ends: the fathers' refusal to will entailed property to sons and the sons' refusal to provide heirs. Rife with unclaimed patrimonies, *Hamlet* stages the ways in which the patrimonial fantasy of eternal twinning is incommensurable with the fact of flesh and blood heirs. Thus it reveals a parody of differentiation at the heart of patriarchal culture and the subsequent fragility of a political inheritance rooted in primogeniture.

In its representation of a bankrupt paternal legacy, Hamlet's Denmark is closer in many ways to the spirit of contemporary America than it is to Shakespearean England. For all that has been written about Hamlet as forerunner of the modern subject, his fate more closely resembles that of the Replicants in Ridley Scott's 1989 film *Blade Runner*: to be driven by memories of a familial relationship that the play suggests never existed. Scott's Replicants (cyborgs who are human in every way but biological origin) are haunted by a vague sense that their memories of childhood and family life are as fabricated as they are, even as they cling to these memories as evidence that they exist as real human beings. The most heartbreaking moments in the film occur when these creatures discover that their memories are not their own but rather have been down-loaded into their mental technology by their scientist creator. Even

a presumably postmodernist – if not post-humanist – vision such as
*Blade Runner* presents harbors a deeply humanistic yearning insofar
as it underscores the necessity of narrative memory in the creation
and maintenance of subjectivity. Even Replicants need to be able
to tell stories about themselves that they can believe in.

Similarly, Hamlet's pledge of allegiance to the Ghost's command-
ment paradoxically constitutes the very memories he can now
claim to have sacrificed for his father:

> Remember thee?
> Ay, thou poor ghost, while memory holds a seat
> In this distracted globe. Remember thee?
> Yea, from the table of my memory
> I'll wipe away all trivial fond records,
> All saws of books, all forms, all pressures past,
> That youth and observation copied there,
> And thy commandment all alone shall live
> Within the book and volume of my brain
> Unmixed with baser matter.
>
> (1.5.95–104)

In the gesture of renouncing his own history (whatever that may
have been) Hamlet retroactively ratifies 'all pressures past', 'all
trivial fond records'; in their place he downloads his father's history,
his father's heavily edited memories, his father's sexual jealousy of
Gertrude and Claudius. Like the Replicants, however, just because
Hamlet's memories are not his own does not mean he is not nostalgic. Hamlet may look and act nothing like his father, but he can at
least attempt to evince the *prosthetic subjectivity* that his father expects
of his fantasy clone.

After all, one does not need a new story to produce a clone: the
only history that matters is the donor's. The real promised end of
cloning is that it enables reproduction without the messy and unpredictable interference of other narratives. By neither generating nor
requiring new bio-allegiances or kinship networks, cloning makes
the passage of political time irrelevant, if not redundant. Unlike
cloning, sexual reproduction always generates a new story – the
participation of women, the creation of new bloodlines and genetic
configurations (with all the accidents of change and lack of resemblances therein), new filiations, and the potential, consequently, for
a changing politics. The postmodern paradigm par excellence of

over-determined patrimony, cloning appears in fantasy form in Shakespeare's corpus and, I would add, in the history of patriarchal culture more generally, long before twentieth-century medical technology was able to say Hello, Dolly.

Perhaps this is why plot is so famously hamstrung in *Hamlet*. Shakespeare does attempt to represent a timeless human nature – and in an alarmingly literal way: not because its themes are universally true in all cultures for all time, but because the play ferrets out the refusal, deeply encoded in the very notion of patrimonial legacy, to permit sons (or daughters) to supersede – or even abandon altogether – their fathers' wills of what the future should be. This kind of timelessness resists new narratives and thereby disallows the revolutions of history that inevitably occur when one generation ushers in the next. Shakespeare's *Hamlet* does stand the test of time, insofar as in the pathological narcissism of its fathers we see a vision of the future: the ability to worship at the shrine of self offered by our own DNA – the choice, now almost technically possible, to become our own offspring. What could be more over-determined than genetic cloning, a process that guarantees the eternal return of the same? Had this prospect been available to the Ghost in *Hamlet*, there is little doubt that he would have availed himself of it.

In *Hamlet* Shakespeare reveals the structural narcissism at the heart of primogeniture and by extension linear royal descent. In doing so, he suggests – deliberately or not – that the process of inheriting a throne is fundamentally anti-political. A politics by definition negotiates contestatory claims and positions rather than a static situation in which all power relations are given. It is no accident, therefore, that in *Hamlet*, adultery – and not the Ghost – becomes the identified specter. Adultery re-introduces contestatory sexual politics within a marriage, threatening the static biological arrangements that marriage is supposed to guarantee along with the property relations established thereby. The most frightening thing perhaps about the specter of adultery in *Hamlet*, and in early modern culture generally, may be the way in which its threat of dubious paternity holds the mirror of biological nature up against the fantasy of juridical cloning effected by primogeniture and thus the legal subsumption of women's identities to those of fathers and husbands.

The two Hamlets' fixation on Gertrude's sexuality ultimately obscures for both father and son a political situation of far greater import: the survival of Denmark itself. *Hamlet* is a play about a nation sidetracked to death by the 'rank sweat of an enseam'd bed' (3.4.85). This alone makes it the poster play for American politics in the late twentieth century, with its last great political scandal of the millennium: the impeachment of President William Jefferson Clinton. Independent Counsel Kenneth Starr began with the task of investigating one possible crime – the Whitewater real estate swindle – only to lead us into a quagmire of sexual and familial betrayal. As Laura Kipnis (1998) wryly observes, 'even if *Time* [Magazine] hadn't designated Bill Clinton Libido in Chief, you'd have to have been in a coma this decade not to notice that politician adultery is occupying an inordinate amount of the nation's attention' (Kipnis 1998: 314). In this instance *Time* is not out of joint: rather, it exemplifies the extent to which we have ceased to function as political citizens and instead become – like Hamlet, whether we want to or not – a nation of sexual detective-revengers.

Our obsession with sexual fidelity as 'a protective talisman' (Kipnis 1998: 315) of political character and stability differs little from Hamlet's. The main difference is in the nature of our idealism about the fathers of our Nation. We do not subscribe (not consciously at least) to the medieval political theology of the King's two bodies. We do not believe that our highest officials – whether Supreme Court Justices or Presidents – partake of this second, divine body that makes their flesh more exalted than our own. Nevertheless, we continue to act as if we do, replicating the *Hamlet*-scenario and continuing to insist that our Leaders be Hyperions to our Satyrs.

But no matter how many crimes our social detectives uncover about our best and brightest, the cynicism they leave in their wake is more than compensated for by the thrill, the *frisson*, of discovering that we are still closet idealists; that we are capable of feeling something – anything – intensely about our Leaders and therefore about ourselves. We feel most betrayed not by any particular act our Leaders may have committed, but by the way they puncture our dual American (and Hamletian!) fetishes of transcendence and innocence. It would be a mistake, however, to dismiss all this as an example of American Puritanism, or the hypocrisy of a culture that wallows in sexual prurience. We speculate about politicians' sex lives not because we really want to find them guilty but because as long as we are suspicious, as psychoanalyst Adam Phillips has put it, it makes us believe that 'there is something to know, and something that is worth knowing' (cited in Kipnis 1998: 316). In Phillips' view,

> Adultery is . . . at heart a drama about change. It's a way of trying to invent a world, and a way of knowing something about what we may want: by definition, then, a political form.
>
> (Kipnis 1998: 314)

As we have seen, in *Hamlet* adultery is the only political form; political stability, succession and even national survival all dissolve in the wake of King Hamlet's voracious sexual narcissism and the legacy it bequeaths the Prince.

Shakespeare's fascination with the violent coercion of identity exacted by paternal legacy vexes his entire corpus, which is full of children who cannot, or will not, be like their fathers. For all the devastation this tension generates, Shakespeare shows us time and again that such dissemblance is the only route to political change.[12] *Hamlet* offers no recuperable models of paternal sublimity, nothing with which to reconstitute the foundation of the royal state. In his refusal to take up the crown, a wife, the state, and father offspring, Hamlet breaks the continuity of production that would enable the dream of patriarchal inevitability to continue. He can only, with his dying voice, give Denmark away to Fortinbras, the most perfect clone in the Shakespearean corpus.

*Hamlet* is a play for contemporary America, with its deep uncertainty about what kinds of stories to tell about our public figures (and by extension, ourselves) and what kind of government we can affectively subscribe to. Are we an elective, or a successive, democracy? What difference does or should it make if a presidential candidate is or is not a presidential son and namesake? When beating the Bushes for successors, what difference does a W make? In spite of ourselves, and in keeping with our British colonial heritage, we seem to be a democracy that craves monarchs. The death of John F. Kennedy Junior in a plane crash in July 1999 brought these longings to the surface of our national rhetoric. 'America's Crown Prince Drowns', headlines proclaimed, as if his political inheritance were inscribed in his name. We were besieged with images of John-John playing at his father's feet under the presidential desk, and famously, saluting the presidential casket, as if these images provided the ocular proof of his political entitlement. No matter how much the adult JFK Jr. stated his disinclination toward politics (and especially the presidency), we thrust his greatness upon him posthumously, speaking of his tragic legacy and 'how lightly he wore his royalty' (Alter 1999: 50), as if there were some special Providence in the fall of this sparrow. As tragic as his untimely death was, it revealed more than anything how deeply runs our sentimental desire to find the stamp of the father in the form of the son.

Phantom monarchy lives on not only in how we want to behold our magistrates but also in the way we nurse our own sense of entitlement to what were once the prerogatives of royalty: life, liberty and the pursuit of happiness, with the latter increasingly defined as wealth. Even as we demand our riches, we refuse to be held responsible for how the political system is actually run. To this extent Hamlet can certainly be regarded as a postmodern Everyman; or at least as a model of what the new American cyber-dream tells us we can all be – a virtual Prince. If the allure of cloning is the endless perpetuation of self, and the lure of the global stock market is the effortless perpetuation of wealth, what kind of legacy will we be able to offer history? The postmillenial Hamlet is already with us – and if we listen carefully we may hear him philosophize, with the same degree of angst that used to be reserved for murdered fathers, thus:

> To buy, or not to buy – that is the question:
> Whether 'tis nobler in the mind to suffer
> The slings and arrows of outrageous fortune,
> Or to take stock against a sea of troubles,
> And by investing end them? To buy, to sell,
> And by selling to say we end the heartache
> And the thousand natural shocks
> That markets are heir to – 'tis a consummation
> Devoutly to be wished: to hold, to trade,
> To trade, perchance to regret – Ay, there's the rub
> For in regret what dreams may come,
> When we have shuffled off this blue-chip stock
> Must give us pause. There's the respect,
> That makes calamity of so long a life.

Finis

## Acknowledgements

Earlier versions and sections of this chapter were presented at the
Shakespeare Association of America Conference, Cleveland, April

1998; and at the Folger Public Lecture in Honor of Shakespeare's
Birthday, Washington D.C., April 1998. I am very grateful to Peter
Stallybrass and Susan Gubar for their valuable input and critical
responses to this material.

## Notes

1 There are far more references to *Hamlet* in all forms of contemporary
  media than I could possibly list here. I shall mention two of the more
  banal appearances, such as the Wendy's commercial in which Dave
  Thomas, wearing a codpiece, does the 'To be or not to be' speech; and
  the scene at the end of the film *The Big Lebowski*, where John Goodman's
  character says 'Good night, sweet prince, and flights of angels sing thee
  to thy rest' while sprinkling the ashes of his cremated bowling buddy
  into the wind. My favorite *Hamlet* citing occurs in a tire commercial, in
  which two books are presented to the viewer: a copy of Shakespeare's
  *Hamlet* and a pamphlet entitled *Tire Tips*. The voiceover says: 'One of
  these offers you timeless wisdom you can use every day of your life. The
  other is a play'.
2 This quotation is from Bradley Greenberg's unpublished essay 'The
  Princes Orgulous', to which I was a respondent in the Problem Plays
  seminar at the 1999 Shakespeare Association of America.
3 All references to the play are from the Norton Shakespeare (Greenblatt
  1997).
4 During my sojourn as a Seminar Director at the Folger Shakespeare
  Library in spring of 1998, I had occasion to travel by train in and
  around the Washington D.C. area. Since, to my knowledge, no official
  survey exists of what people think about *Hamlet*, I polled a captive audience of fellow Amtrak travelers about what – if anything – came to
  their minds when I mentioned *Hamlet*. Terrorizing people in several
  cars, I recorded the following: roughly one-third said that they had no
  special associations at all with the name; others said that *Hamlet* made
  them think of romance, England, death, drama, Shakespeare, flunking
  high school English, poor test scores, Central Park, Kenneth Branagh
  holding a skull, and men in tights. The one person who said anything at
  all about plot said 'Isn't Hamlet the guy who killed his father?' Not a
  single person said anything about Hamlet being a Prince, or the heir to
  a throne. While this poll is admittedly unscientific, I did speak to
  people across a range of ages, genders, ethnicities, races, and even
  nationalities. One person I queried turned out to be a fellow Shakespeare
  scholar. He declined to comment.

5  Since this chapter deals with *Hamlet*, I make only limited references to the Henriad. A more extensive discussion of legacy in *Hamlet* and the Henriad is the topic of my book manuscript *Shakespearean Outposts*.

6  These definitions are excerpted from longer entries in *The Compact Edition of the Oxford English Dictionary* (1971: see pp. 3269–70 *passim*).

7  Linda Williams (1989: 106) analyzes commodity culture, sexual pleasure, and phallic subjectivity as they interpenetrate in the hard-core porno's money shot. The money shot is the moment of male ejaculation, captured on film, in which the release of semen is visible to the spectator. According to Williams, the money shot is a fetish in both the Marxian and Freudian senses: in combining money and sexual pleasure – those simultaneously valuable and dirty things – the money shot most perfectly embodies the profound alienation of contemporary consumer society (Williams 1989: 107). This may be so, but I would argue that the conflation of semen and money is certainly not the product of contemporary alienation – it has a long juridical history, encoded in patriarchal property and sexual relations.

8  This phrase was immortalized by Cuba Gooding Jr's character – the professional football player – in the 1997 film *Jerry McGuire*.

9  In his chapter on 'The Political Hamlet', Mallin (1996) notes that the Ghost of King Hamlet tells the heir apparent many things in their first interview, but the political status of the youth goes conspicuously unmentioned; both royal Hamlets seem concerned about things other than the legalities of the succession. The Ghost never protests young Hamlet's loss of position, only his own. Nor does Hamlet himself, for most of the play, lament his pre-emption from rule (Mallin 1996: 111). Mallin speculates that Hamlet's disinterest in his political inheritance is disingenuous: since avenging someone else's murder presumably requires a lack of self-interest, Hamlet could not also actively pursue the crown, since that would decidedly be an example of the reverse. Throughout this chapter, Mallin elegantly weaves the thematics of Elizabethan succession anxieties with the problems of theatrical genre and the demands of scripting a tragedy versus a history.

10  Garber (1987) discusses the way in which the failure of the paternal metaphor is not unrelated to what might be called paternal undecidability, or the undecidability of paternity – the fact, so often commented on in Shakespeare's plays, that the father is always a suppositional father (Garber 1987: 132–3). In Garber's view, confronted with an over plus, a superfluity of fathers (psychoanalytic readers all comment on the splitting of the father into Claudius, Polonius, even old Fortinbras and old Norway), Hamlet finds both too many fathers and too few (Garber 1987: 133). In Charnes (1997) I have argued that Hamlet's paralysis – and that of contemporary mass culture as well – is triggered by a glimpse of what Slavoj Žižek calls the obscene, or anal father, the site of rotting corruption that is the dark underbelly of presumably disinterested Law. In this chapter, however, I am looking beyond the failure of the paternal metaphor toward the structural instability of the fantasy that enables the production of political history: the fantasy of eternal twinning in offspring.

11  Shakespeare knows how to imply resemblance between fathers and sons.
    Recall *1 Henry IV,* in which Falstaff, play-acting King Henry IV,
    addresses his mad wag son Hal:

> That thou art my son I have partly thy mother's word, partly
> my own opinion, but chiefly a villainous trick of thine eye,
> and a foolish hanging of thy nether lip, that doth warrant me
>
> (2.5.367–70)

12  No body of work represents this principle more completely than the
    Henriad, in which a son who plans to inherit the throne must do what-
    ever it takes not to resemble a usurper father. In *Henry V,* King Harry
    commits affective parricide, turning his father into a kind of ghost. And
    within the historical logic of the second tetralogy, this exchange works
    quite nicely. But Hamlet offers no such strategy; faced with a real
    ghost who insists that Hamlet remember him, Hamlet can only fade
    away, O, O, O, O!

# References

Abrams, M. H. (1953) *The Mirror and the Lamp: Romantic Theory and the Critical Tradition*, New York: Oxford University Press.

Adelman, J. (1992) *Suffocating Mothers: Fantasies of Maternal Origin in Shakespeare's Plays, 'Hamlet' to 'Tempest'*, London: Routledge.

Adorno, T. W. (1977) '"The actuality of philosophy"', *Telos* 31: 120–33.

—— (1978) *Minima Moralia: Reflections from Damaged Life*, trans. E. F. N. Jephcott, London: Verso.

—— (1984) *Aesthetic Theory*, trans. C. Lenhardt, London: Routledge and Kegan Paul.

—— (1990) *Negative Dialectics*, trans. E. B. Ashton, London: Routledge.

—— (1991) *The Culture Industry*, ed. J. M. Bernstein, London: Routledge.

—— (1993/4) 'On tradition', *Telos* 94: 75–82.

Aers, D. (1992) 'A whisper in the ear of early modernists; or, reflections on literary critics writing the "history of the subject"', in D. Aers (ed.) *Culture and History 1350–1600*, Detroit, MI: Wayne State University Press.

Allen, D. C. (1936) 'Symbolic color in the literature of the English Renaissance', *Philological Quarterly* 15: 81–92.

Alter, J. (1999) 'Huddling against history', *Newsweek*, 26 July: 50–3.

Anderson, P. (1998) *The Origins of Postmodernity*, London: Verso.

Anon. (1620) *Hic Mulier*, excerpted in K. U. Henderson and B. F. McManus (1985) *Half Humankind*, Urbana, IL: University of Illinois Press.

Anon. (1909) 'On worthy Master Shakespeare and his poems', in *Mr. William Shakespeares Comedies, Histories, & Tragedies*, 2nd edn, rpt, London: Methuen.

Appiah, K. A. (1990) 'Race', in F. Lentricchia and T. McLaughlin (eds) *Critical Terms for Literary Study*, Chicago: University of Chicago Press.

Ariès, P. (1989) 'Introduction' to *A History of Private Life: iii, Passions of the Renaissance* ed. R. Chartier, trans. A. Goldhammar, Cambridge, MA: Harvard University Press.

Auden, W. H. (1968) *The Dyer's Hand*, New York: Vintage.

Avallone, C. (1997) 'What American Renaissance? The gendered genealogy of a critical discourse', *PMLA* 112: 1102–20.

Bainton, R. (1950) *Here I Stand: A Life of Martin Luther*, New York: New
American Library.

Balibar, E. (1994) *Masses, Classes, and Ideas: Studies on Politics and Philosophy
Before and After Marx*, trans. J. Swenson, London: Routledge.

Balibar, E. and Wallerstein, I. (1991) *Race, Nation, Class: Ambiguous Identities*,
New York: Verso.

Barish, J. (1981) *The Antitheatrical Prejudice*, Berkeley, CA: University of
California Press.

Barker, F. (1984) *The Tremulous Private Body*, London: Methuen.

Barker, F. and Hulme, P. (1985) '"Nymphs and reapers heavily vanish":
the discursive con-texts of *The Tempest*', in J. Drakakis (ed.) *Alternative
Shakespeares*, London: Methuen.

Baroway, I. (1933) 'The Bible as poetry in the English Renaissance', *Journal
of English and Germanic Philology* 32: 447–80.

Barthes, R. (1968) *Writing Degree Zero*, trans. Annette Lavers and Colin
Smith, New York: Hill and Wang.

—— (1975) *The Pleasure of the Text*, trans. R. Miller, New York: Hill and
Wang.

Barton, A. (1990) *The Names of Comedy*, Toronto: University of Toronto
Press.

Bates, C. (1992) *The Rhetoric of Courtship in Elizabethan Language and Literature*,
Cambridge: Cambridge University Press.

Baudrillard, J. (1981) *For a Critique of the Political Economy of the Sign*, trans.
C. Levin, St Louis, MO: Telos Press.

—— (1988) *Selected Writings*, ed. M. Poster, Stanford, CA: Stanford University Press.

—— (1993) *The Transparency of Evil: Essays on Extreme Phenomena*, trans.
J. Benedict, London: Verso.

Baugh, A. C. and Cable, T. (1978) *A History of the English Language*, 3rd edn,
Englewood Cliffs, NJ: Prentice-Hall.

Beaumont, F. and Fletcher, J. (1905) *The Works of Francis Beaumont and John
Fletcher*, ed. A. Glover, Cambridge: Cambridge University Press.

Beech, D. and Roberts, J. (1996) 'Spectres of the aesthetic', *New Left Review*
218: 102–27.

Belsey, C. (1980) *Critical Practice*, London: Methuen.

—— (1985a) 'Disrupting sexual difference: meaning and gender in the
comedies', in J. Drakakis (ed.) *Alternative Shakespeares*, London: Methuen.

—— (1985b) *The Subject of Tragedy: Identity and Difference in Renaissance
Drama*, London: Methuen.

Bennett, A. and Royle, N. (1999) *An Introduction to Literature, Criticism and
Theory*, Hemel Hempstead: Prentice Hall Europe.

Berger, Jr, H. (1997) 'What does the Duke know and when does he know it? Carrying the torch in *Measure for Measure*', in H. Berger, *Making Trifles of Terrors: Redistributing Complicities in Shakespeare*, Stanford, CA: Stanford University Press.

Bernstein, J. M. (1991) 'Introduction', in T. Adorno, *The Culture Industry*, London: Routledge.

—— (1992) *The Fate of Art: Aesthetic Alienation from Kant to Derrida and Adorno*, Oxford: Polity Press.

—— (1997) 'Against voluptuous bodies: of satiation without happiness', *New Left Review* 225: 89–104.

Berry, P. (1989) *Of Chastity and Power: Elizabethan Literature and the Unmarried Queen*, London: Routledge.

Bevington, D. (ed.) (1992) *The Complete Works of Shakespeare*, 4th edn, New York: HarperCollins.

Bloom, A. and Jaffa, H. (1964) *Shakespeare's Politics*, Chicago: University of Chicago Press.

Bloom, H. (1999) *Shakespeare: The Invention of the Human*, New York: Penguin Putnam.

Blumenberg, H. (1983) *The Legitimacy of the Modern Age*, trans. R. M. Wallace, Cambridge, MA: MIT Press.

Boehrer, B. (1999) 'Shylock and the rise of the household pet: thinking social exclusion in *The Merchant of Venice*', *Shakespeare Quarterly* 50, 2: 152–70.

Bondanella, P. and Musa, M. (eds and trans) (1979) *The Prince*, in *The Portable Machiavelli*, New York: Penguin.

Boose, L. (1994) '"The getting of a lawful race": racial discourse in early modern England and the unrepresentable black woman', in M. Hendricks and P. Parker (eds) *Women, 'Race', and Writing in the Early Modern Period*, London: Routledge.

Bowie, A. (1990) *Aesthetics and Subjectivity: From Kant to Nietzsche*, Manchester: Manchester University Press.

—— (1992) 'Aesthetic autonomy', in D. Cooper, J. Margolis and C. Sartwell (eds) *A Companion to Aesthetics*, Oxford: Blackwell.

—— (1997a) *From Romanticism to Critical Theory: The Philosophy of German Literary Theory*, London: Routledge.

—— (1997b) 'Confessions of a "new aesthete": a response to the "new philistines"', *New Left Review* 225: 105–26.

Bradley, A. C. (1909) 'Shakespeare's theatre and audience', in *Oxford Lectures on Poetry*, London: Macmillan.

Bradshaw, G. (1987) *Shakespeare's Scepticism*, Ithaca, NY: Cornell University Press.

Braudel, F. (1949) *La Méditerranée et le Monde Méditerranéen à l'époque de Phillippe II*, Paris: Colin.

—— (1958) 'Histoire et sciences sociales: la longue durée', *Annales Economies Sociétés Civilisations* 13, 4: 725–53.

—— (1981–4) *Civilization and Capitalism, 15th–18th Century*, 3 vols, New York: Harper and Row.

Bredbeck, G. (1992) *Sodomy and Interpretation: Marlowe to Milton*, Ithaca, NY: Cornell University Press.

Bristol, M. (1989) *Shakespeare's America, America's Shakespeare*, London: Routledge.

Brooks, C. (1947) *The Well-Wrought Urn*, New York: Harcourt.

Brown, J. R. (ed.) (1955) *Shakespeare: The Merchant of Venice*, London: Methuen.

Bruns, G. L. (1992) *Hermeneutics Ancient and Modern*, New Haven, CT: Yale University Press.

Bruster, D. (1992) *Drama and the Market in the Age of Shakespeare*, Cambridge: Cambridge University Press.

—— (forthcoming) *Quoting Shakespeare: Form and Culture in Early Modern Drama*, Lincoln, NB: University of Nebraska Press.

Buckley, G. T. (1932) *Atheism in the English Renaissance*, Chicago: University of Chicago Press.

Burckhardt, J. (1965) *The Civilization of the Renaissance in Italy*, trans. S. G. C. Middlemore, London: Phaidon Press.

—— (1990) *The Civilization of the Renaissance in Italy*, trans. S. G. C. Middlemore, Harmondsworth: Penguin.

Bürger, P. (1984) *Theory of the Avant-Garde*, trans. M. Shaw, Minneapolis, MN: University of Minnesota Press.

Burke, P. (1985) 'Popular culture in seventeenth-century London', in B. Reay (ed.) *Popular Culture in Seventeenth-Century England*, New York: St Martin's.

—— (1990) *The French Historical Revolution: The 'Annales' School 1929–89*, Stanford, CA: Stanford University Press.

Burnett, M. T. (1997) *Masters and Servants in English Renaissance Drama and Culture: Authority and Obedience*, New York: St Martin's.

Burton, R. (1989–94) *The Anatomy of Melancholy*, 4 vols, Oxford: Clarendon.

Butler, M. (1984) *Theatre and Crisis, 1632–1642*, Cambridge: Cambridge University Press.

Campbell, L. (1930/31) 'Theories of revenge in Renaissance England', *Modern Philology* 28: 281–96.

Cartwright, K. (1991) *Shakespearean Tragedy and its Double: The Rhythms of Audience Response*, University Park, PA: Penn State Press.

Cavell, S. (1987) *Disowning Knowledge in Six Plays of Shakespeare*, Cambridge: Cambridge University Press.

Caygill, H. (1989) *The Art of Judgement*, Oxford: Blackwell.

Cerasano, S. P. (1993) 'Philip Henslowe, Simon Forman, and the theatrical community of the 1590s', *Shakespeare Quarterly* 44: 146–58.

Cerasano, S. P. and Wynne-Davies, M. (1992) ' "From myself, my other self I turned': an introduction', in S. P. Cerasano and M. Wynne-Davies (eds) *Gloriana's Face*, Detroit, MI: Wayne State University Press.

Chambers, E. K. (1923) *The Elizabethan Stage*, 4 vols, Cambridge: Cambridge University Press.

Charnes, L. (1997) 'Dismember me: Shakespeare, paranoia, and the logic of mass culture', *Shakespeare Quarterly* 48, 1: 1–16.

Chettle, H. (1592) *Kind-Hart's Dreame*.

Cicero (1989) *Ad Herennium*, trans. H. Caplan, London: Heinemann.

Cloud, Random (1997) 'What's the Bastard's name?', in G. W. Williams (ed.) *Shakespeare's Speech Headings*, Newark, DE and London: University of Delaware Press.

Coghill, N. (1950) 'The basis of Shakespearian comedy', in *Essays and Studies 1950*, London: J. Murray.

Cohen, W. (1995) '*The Merchant of Venice* and the possibilities of historical criticism', in I. Kamps (ed.) *Materialist Shakespeare: A History*, New York: Verso.

Coleridge, S. T. (1930) *Coleridge's Shakespearean Criticism*, 2 vols, ed. T. M. Raysor, Cambridge, MA: Harvard University Press.

Cook, A. J. (1981) *The Privileged Playgoers of Shakespeare's London: 1576–1642*, Princeton, NJ: Princeton University Press.

Craig, D. H. (ed.) (1990) *Jonsonus Virbius*, in *Ben Jonson: The Critical Heritage, 1599–1798*, London: Routledge.

Crane, M. T. (1993) *Framing Authority: Sayings, Self, and Society in Sixteenth-Century England*, Princeton, NJ: Princeton University Press.

Creighton, M. (1895) 'The Early Renaissance in England', Rede Lecture, delivered in the Senate House on 13 June 1895, Cambridge: Cambridge University Press.

Critchley, S. (1995) 'Black Socrates? Questioning the philosophical tradition', *Radical Philosophy* 69: 17–26.

Danson, L. (1978) *The Harmonies of the Merchant of Venice*, New Haven, CT: Yale University Press.

Danto, A. C. (1986) *The Philosophical Disenfranchisement of Art*, New York: Columbia University Press.

D'Avenant, W. (1964) *Dramatic Works of Sir William Davenant*, New York: Russell and Russell.

Davis, N. Z. (1975) 'Women on top', in *Society and Culture in Early Modern France*, Stanford, CA: Stanford University Press.

de Grazia, M. (1996) 'The ideology of superfluous things: *King Lear* as period piece', in M. de Grazia, M. Quilligan and P. Stallybrass (eds) *Subject and Object in Renaissance Culture*, Cambridge: Cambridge University Press.

—— (1997) 'World pictures, modern periods, and the early stage', in John D. Cox and David Scott Kastan (eds) *A New History of Early English Drama*, New York: Columbia University Press.

de Grazia, M., Quilligan, M. and Stallybrass, P. (1996) 'Introduction', in de Grazia *et al.* (eds) *Subject and Object in Renaissance Culture*, Cambridge: Cambridge University Press.

Dekker, T. (1968) *The Gull's Hornbook* in *Selected Writings*, ed. E. D. Pendry Cambridge, MA: Harvard University Press.

Derrida, J. (1978) 'Freud and the scene of writing', *Writing and Difference*, trans. A. Bass, London: Routledge.

Dews, P. (1987) *Logics of Disintegration: Post-Structuralist Thought and the Claims of Critical Theory*, London: Verso.

—— (1995) *The Limits of Disenchantment: Essays on Contemporary European Philosophy*, London: Verso.

Dobson, E. J. (1955) 'Early modern standard English', *Transactions of the Philological Society* 25–54.

Dobson, M. (1996) 'Cold front in Arden', *London Review of Books* 18, 21: 24–5.

Dolan, F. E. (1993) 'Taking the pencil out of God's hand: art, nature, and the face-painting debate in early modern England', *PMLA* 108: 224–39.

—— (1994a) 'Reply', *PMLA* 109: 120.

—— (1994b) 'Reply', *PMLA* 109: 1026–7.

Dollimore, J. (1989) *Radical Tragedy: Religion, Ideology, and Power in the Drama of Shakespeare and his Contemporaries*, 2nd edn, London: Harvester.

—— (1994) 'Shakespeare understudies: the sodomite, the prostitute, the transvestite and their critics', in J. Dollimore and A. Sinfield (eds) *Political Shakespeare: Essays in Cultural Materialism*, 2nd edn, Ithaca, NY: Cornell University Press.

Doran, S. (1996) *Monarchy and Matrimony: The Courtships of Elizabeth I*, London: Routledge.

Dowling, C. (1994) 'Face painting in early modern England' (letter), *PMLA* 109: 119–20.

Drakakis, J. (ed.) (1985) *Alternative Shakespeares*, London: Methuen.

Dubrow, H. (1994) 'The term *early modern*', *PMLA* 109: 1025–26.

Dusinberre, J. (1994) 'As who liked it?', *Shakespeare Survey* 46: 9–22.

Eccles, M. (ed.) (1980) *A New Variorum Edition of Shakespeare: Measure for Measure*, New York: Modern Languages Association.

Eliot, T. S. (1923) 'The beating of a drum', *Nation and Athenaeum*, 6 October.

—— (1975) 'The metaphysical poets', in F. Kermode (ed.) *Selected Prose of T. S. Eliot*, New York: Harcourt Brace Jovanovich.

Engle, Lars (1993) *Shakespearean Pragmatism: Market of his Time*, Chicago: University of Chicago Press.

Erickson, P. (1985) *Patriarchal Structures in Shakespeare's Drama*, Berkeley, CA: University of California Press.

Everitt, A. (1966) 'Social mobility in early modern England', *Past and Present* 33: 56–73.

Ferguson, W. (1948) *The Renaissance in Historical Thought: Five Centuries of Interpretation*, Cambridge, MA: Houghton Mifflin.

Fiedler, L. A. (1972) *The Stranger in Shakespeare*, New York: Stein and Day.

—— (1991) *Fiedler on the Roof: Essays on Literature and Jewish Identity*, Boston, MA: David R. Godine.

Findlay, A. (1999) *A Feminist Perspective on Renaissance Drama*, Oxford and Malden, MA: Blackwell.

Fiske, John (1987) *Television Culture*, London: Methuen.

Fitzgeffrey, H. (1617) *Satyres and Satyricall Epigrams: With Certain Observations of Blackfryers*.

Florio, J. (1598) *A Worlde of Wordes or Most copious and Exact Dictionarie in Italian and English*, STC 11098, London.

Forman, S. (1974a) *Autobiography*, in A. L. Rowse, *Sex and Society in Shakespeare's Age: Simon Forman the Astrologer*, New York: Scribner's.

—— (1974b) 'The Bocke of Plaies and Notes therof per formane for Common Pollicie' (Bodleian Ashm. MS. 208, fols. 200–207v), in *The Riverside Shakespeare*, ed. G. B. Evans, Boston, MA: Houghton Mifflin.

Foster, H. (ed.) (1983) *The Anti-Aesthetic: Essays on Postmodern Culture*, Port Townsend, WA: Bay Press.

Foucault, M. (1970) *The Order of Things: An Archaeology of the Human Sciences*, New York: Pantheon.

—— (1984) 'Nietzsche, genealogy, history', trans. D. Bouchard and S. Simon, in D. E. Bouchard (ed.) *Language, Counter-memory, Practice: Selected Essays and Interviews by Michel Foucault*, Ithaca, NY: Cornell University Press.

Freedman, B. (1991) *Staging the Gaze: Postmodernism, Psychoanalysis, and Shakespearean Comedy*, Ithaca, NY: Cornell University Press.

Freedman, J. (1998) 'Angels, monsters, and Jews: intersections of queer and Jewish identity in Kushner's *Angels in America*', *PMLA* 113: 90–102.

Frye, S. (1992) 'The myth of Elizabeth at Tilbury', *Sixteenth Century Journal* 23: 95–114.

Gabrielson, A. (1930) 'Early modern English . . .', *Studia Neophilologica* 3, 1–2: 1–10.

Garber, M. (1987) *Shakespeare's Ghost Writers: Literature and the Uncanny Causality*, New York: Methuen.

—— (1992) *Vested Interests*, New York: Routledge.

—— (1998) 'Roman numerals', in *Symptoms of Culture*, New York: Routledge.

Gellrich, M. (1988) *Tragedy and Theory: The Problem of Conflict Since Aristotle*, Princeton, NJ: Princeton University Press.

Gilman, S. (1991) *The Jew's Body*, London: Routledge.

—— (1996) *Smart Jews*, Lincoln, NB: University of Nebraska Press.

Girard, R. (1991) *A Theater of Envy: William Shakespeare*, New York: Oxford University Press.

Goddard, H. (1951) *The Meaning of Shakespeare*, volume 1 of 2, Chicago: Phoenix Books, University of Chicago Press.

Goldberg, J. (1986) *Voice Terminal Echo: Postmodernism and English Renaissance Texts*, New York: Methuen.

—— (1990) *Writing Matter from the Hands of the English Renaissance*, Stanford, CA: University of Stanford Press.

Goldhagen, D. (1997 rpt [1996]) *Hitler's Willing Executioners: Ordinary Germans and the Holocaust*, New York: Vintage.

Grady, H. (1991) *The Modernist Shakespeare: Critical Texts in a Material World*, Oxford: Clarendon.

—— (1996) *Shakespeare's Universal Wolf: Studies in Early Modern Reification*, Oxford: Clarendon.

—— (1999) 'Renewing modernity: changing contexts and contents of a nearly invisible concept', *Shakespeare Quarterly* 50, 3: 268–84.

—— (2000) 'On the need for a differentiated theory of (early) modern subjects', in J. Joughin (ed.) *Philosophical Shakespeares*, London: Routledge.

Graves, T. (1920) 'Notes on the Elizabethan theaters', *Studies in Philology* 17: 170–82.

—— (1922a) 'Recent literature of the English Renaissance', *Studies in Philology* 19: 249–91.

—— (1922b) 'Some references to Elizabethan theaters', *Studies in Philology* 19: 317–327.

Greenblatt, S. (1978) 'Marlowe, Marx, and anti-Semitism', *Critical Inquiry* 5: 291–307.

—— (1980) *Renaissance Self-Fashioning: From More to Shakespeare*, Chicago: University of Chicago Press.

—— (1988a) *Shakespearean Negotiations*, Berkeley, CA: University of California Press.

—— (1988b) *Representing the English Renaissance*, Berkeley, CA: University of California Press.

—— (1990) 'Marlowe, Marx and anti-Semitism', *Learning to Curse: Essays in Early Modern Culture*, London: Routledge.

—— (1996) 'An English obsession', *New York Times Book Review*, August 11: 12–13.

—— (gen. ed.) (1997) *The Norton Shakespeare: Based on the Oxford Edition*, New York: W. W. Norton.

Gross, J. (1992) *Shylock: Four Hundred Years in the Life of a Legend*, London: Chatto and Windus.

Gurr, A. (1993) 'The general and the caviar: learned audiences in the early theatre', *Studies in the Literary Imagination* 26: 7–20.

—— (1996) *Playgoing in Shakespeare's London*, 2nd edn, Cambridge: Cambridge University Press.

Habermas, J. (1987) *The Philosophical Discourse of Modernity*, trans. Frederick Lawrence, Cambridge, MA: MIT Press.

—— (1992) *The Structural Transformation of the Public Sphere: An Inquiry into a Category of Bourgeois Society*, trans. T. Burger with the assistance of F. Lawrence, Oxford: Polity Press.

Hackett, H. (1995) *Virgin Mother, Maiden Queen*, New York: St Martin's Press.

Hall, S. *et al.* (eds) (1996) *Modernity: An Introduction to Modern Societies*, Oxford: Blackwell.

Halpern, R. (1997) *Shakespeare among the Moderns*, Ithaca, NY: Cornell University Press.

Hanson, E. (1998) *Discovering the Subject in Renaissance England*, Cambridge: Cambridge University Press.

Harbage, A. (1941) *Shakespeare's Audience*, New York: Columbia University Press.

Harington, J. (1804) *Nugae Antiquae*, vol. I, London.

Hattaway, M. (1982) *Elizabethan Popular Theatre: Plays in Performance*, London: Routledge.

Hawkes, T. (1975) *Shakespeare's Talking Animals: Language and Drama in Society*, London: Edward Arnold.

—— (ed.) (1996a) *Alternative Shakespeares*, vol. 2, London and New York: Routledge.

—— (1996b) 'Introduction', in T. Hawkes (ed.) *Alternative Shakespeares*, vol. 2, London: Routledge.

Hebel, J. and Hudson, H. H. (eds) (1929) *Poetry of the English Renaissance 1509–1660*, New York: F. S. Crofts.

Heisch, A. (1975) 'Queen Elizabeth I: parliamentary rhetoric and the exercise of power', *Signs* 1, 1: 31–55.

Heywood, T. (1841) *An Apology for Actors*, London: Shakespeare Society.

Hibbard, G. R. (ed.) (1987) *The Oxford Shakespeare: Hamlet*, Oxford: Oxford University Press.

Honigmann, E. A. J. (1976) *Shakespeare: Seven Tragedies: the Dramatist's Manipulation of Response*, New York: Barnes and Noble.

Horkheimer, M. and Adorno, T. W. (1972) *Dialectic of Enlightenment*, trans. John Cumming, New York: Seabury. Reprinted (1997) New York: Continuum.

Howard, J. (1984) *Shakespeare's Art of Orchestration*, Urbana, IL: University of Illinois Press.

—— (1986) 'The new historicism in Renaissance studies', *English Literary Renaissance* 16: 13–43.

—— (1988) 'Crossdressing, the theatre, and gender struggle in early modern England', *Shakespeare Quarterly* 39: 418–40.

—— (1994) *The Stage and Social Struggle in Early Modern England*, London: Routledge.

Howard, J. and Rackin, P. (1997) *Engendering a Nation: A Feminist Account of Shakespeare's English Histories*, London: Routledge.

Hume, D. (1757) *Four Dissertations. I. The Natural History of Religion. II. Of the Passions. III. Of Tragedy. IV. Of the Standard of Taste*, London: A. Millar.

Hunter, G. K. (1964) 'The theology of Marlowe's *The Jew of Malta*', *Journal of the Warburg and Courtauld Institutes* 27: 211–40.

Jameson, F. (1984) Foreword to F. Lyotard, *The Postmodern Condition: A Report on Knowledge*, trans. G. Bennington and B. Massumi, Minneapolis, MN: University of Minnesota Press.

—— (1991) *Postmodernism; or, The Cultural Logic of Late Capitalism*, Durham, NC: Duke University Press.

Jardine, L. (1996) *Reading Shakespeare Historically*, London: Routledge.

Jenkins, H. (ed.) (1982) *The Arden Hamlet*, London: Methuen.

Jewell, J. (1611) *A Replie vnto M. Hardings Answer*, London: John Norton.

Jonson, B. (1925–63) *Ben Jonson*, ed. C. H. Hereford and Percy Simpson, 11 vols, Oxford: Clarendon.

Joughin, J. J. (1996) 'Shakespeare and de-traditionalisation: learning from L.A.', *Litteraria Pragensia: Studies in Literature and Culture* 6, 12: 57–75.

—— (ed.) (1997a) *Shakespeare and National Culture*, Manchester: Manchester University Press.

—— (1997b) 'Shakespeare, national culture and the lure of transnationalism', in J. J. Joughin (ed.) *Shakespeare and National Culture*, Manchester: Manchester University Press.

Jusserand, J. J. (1894, 1904) *Histoire littéraire du peuple anglais*, Paris.

Kaganoff, B. C. (1977) *A Dictionary of Jewish Names and their History*, New York: Schocken.

Kahn, V. (1985) *Rhetoric, Prudence, and Skepticism in the Renaissance*, Ithaca, NY: Cornell University Press.

Kant, I. (1965 [1790]) *First Introduction to the Critique of Judgment*, trans. J. Haden, Indianapolis, IN: Bobbs-Merrill.

Kantorowicz, E. (1957) *The King's Two Bodies*, Princeton, NJ: Princeton University Press.

Kastan, D. S. (1986) 'Proud majesty made a subject: Shakespeare and the spectacle of rule', *Shakespeare Quarterly* 37: 459–75.

Kelly, J. (1984) 'Did women have a Renaissance?', in *Women, History, and Theory*, Chicago: University of Chicago Press.

Kennedy, R. (1998) 'Speech prefixes in some Shakespearean quartos', *Papers of the Bibliographical Society of America*, Charlottesville, VA: University of Virginia Press, 92, 2: 191–202.

Kerrigan, W. and Braden, G. (1989) *The Idea of the Renaissance*, Baltimore, MD: Johns Hopkins University Press.

Kimbrough, R. (1982) 'Androgyny seen through Shakespeare's disguise', *Shakespeare Quarterly* 33: 17–33.

King, J. N. (1990) 'Queen Elizabeth I: representations of the Virgin Queen', *Renaissance Quarterly* 43: 30–74.

Kipnis, L. (1998) 'Adultery', *Critical Inquiry* 21, 2: 289–327.

Klein, D. (1910) *Literary Criticism from the Elizabethan Dramatists*, New York: Sturgis and Walton.

Knight, G. W. (1949) *The Wheel of Fire: Interpretation of Shakespeare's Tragedy*, rev. edn, London: Methuen.

Koselleck, R. (1985) *Futures Past: On the Semantics of Historical Time*, trans. Keith Tribe, Cambridge, MA: MIT Press.

Kott, J. (1966) *Shakespeare our Contemporary*, trans. Boleslaw Taborski, New York: Doubleday.

Kristeller, P. O. (1970) 'Paul Oskar Kristeller, "The modern system of the arts"', in M. Weitz (ed.) *Problems in Aesthetics*, 2nd edn, New York: Macmillan.

Kuhn, A. (ed.) (1990) *Alien Zone: Cultural Theory and Contemporary Science Fiction Cinema*, New York: Verso.

Lanyer, A. (1993) *Salve Deus Rex Judaeorum* in *The Poems of Aemilia Lanyer*, ed. S. Woods, Cambridge, MA: Harvard University Press.

Leavis, F. R. (1952) *The Common Pursuit*, London: Chatto and Windus.

Levin, C. (1994) *The Heart and Stomach of a King*, Philadelphia: University of Pennsylvania Press.

Levin, R. (1980) 'The relation of external evidence to the allegorical and thematic interpretation of Shakespeare', *Shakespeare Studies* 13: 1–29.

Levine, L. (1994) *Men in Women's Clothing*, Cambridge: Cambridge University Press.

Lévi-Strauss, C. (1966) *The Savage Mind*, Chicago: University of Chicago Press.

Lewalski, Barbara K. (1962) 'Biblical allusion and allegory in *The Merchant of Venice*', *Shakespeare Quarterly* 13: 327–43.

—— (1979) *Protestant Poetics and the Seventeenth-Century Lyric*, Princeton, NJ: Princeton University Press.

Lewis, W. (1927) *The Lion and the Fox: The Role of the Hero in the Plays of Shakespeare*, London: G. Richards.

Long, W. B. (1997) 'Perspectives on provenance: the context of varying speech-heads', in G. W. Williams (ed.) *Shakespeare's Speech Headings*, Newark, NJ: University of Delaware Press.

Luther, M. (1883–1919) *Kritische Gesamtausgabe*, Weimar: H. Böhlau.

—— (1955–76) *Luther's Works: American Edition*, ed. J. Pelikan and H. T. Lehman, Philadelphia, PA and St Louis, MO: Concordia and Fortress Press.

Lyotard, F. (1984) *The Postmodern Condition: A Report on Knowledge*, trans. G. Bennington and B. Massumi, Minneapolis, MN: University of Minnesota Press.

McCarthy, T. (1997) 'F/x-fueled "Starship" a rousing ride', *Variety* 368, 13: 98–100.

McKerrow, R. B. (1997) 'A suggestion regarding Shakespeare's manuscripts', in G. Walton Williams (ed.) *Shakespeare's Speech Headings*, Newark, DE: University of Delaware Press.

McPherson, D. C. (1990) *Shakespeare, Jonson, and the Myth of Venice*, Newark, DE: University of Delaware Press.

Mahood, M. (1987) *Shakespeare: The Merchant of Venice*, Cambridge: Cambridge University Press.

Malamud, B. (1950) *The Magic Barrel*, New York: Dell.

Mallin, E. (1996) *Inscribing the Time: Shakespeare and the End of Elizabethan England*, Berkeley, CA: University of California Press.

Marcus, L. (1988) *Puzzling Shakespeare*, Berkeley, CA: University of California Press.

—— (1992) 'Renaissance/early modern studies', in S. Greenblatt and G. Gunn (eds) *Redrawing the Boundaries: The Transformation of English and American Literary Studies*, New York: Modern Language Association.

Marsden, J. I. (ed.) (1991) *The Appropriation of Shakespeare: Post-Renaissance Reconstructions of the Works and the Myth*, Hemel Hempstead: Harvester Wheatsheaf.

Maslin, J. (1997) '"Starship Troopers": no bugs too large for this swat team', *New York Times on the Web*, 7 November.

Matthiessen, F. O. (1931) *Translation: An Elizabethan Art*, Cambridge, MA: Harvard University Press.

—— (1941) *American Renaissance: Art and Expression in the Age of Emerson and Whitman*, London: Oxford University Press.

Maus, K. E. (1995) *Inwardness and Theater in the English Renaissance*, Chicago: University of Chicago Press.

—— (1997a) 'Introduction to *Measure for Measure*', in S. Greenblatt (gen. ed.) *The Norton Shakespeare*, New York: W. W. Norton.

—— (1997b) 'Introduction to *The Merchant of Venice*', in S. Greenblatt (gen. ed.) *The Norton Shakespeare*, New York: W. W. Norton.

Michelet, J. (1852–67) *Histoire de France jusqu'au XVIe siècle*, 17 vols, Paris: L. Hachette.

Middleton, P. (1998) 'Does literary theory give you a sense of *déjà vu?*', *Textual Practice* 12, 1: 148–63.

Modleski, T. (ed.) (1986a) *Studies in Entertainment: Critical Approaches to Mass Culture*, Bloomington, IN: Indiana University Press.

—— (1986b) 'The terror of pleasure: the contemporary horror film and postmodern theory', in T. Modleski (ed.) *Studies in Entertainment: Critical Approaches to Mass Culture*, Bloomington, IN: Indiana University Press.

Montaigne, M. de (1987) 'An apology for Raymond Sebond', in M. Screech (ed. and trans.) *The Complete Essays of Montaigne*, New York: Penguin.

Montrose, L. (1980) '"Eliza, Queene of shepheardes", and the pastoral of power', *English Literary Renaissance* 10: 153–82.

—— (1989) 'Professing the Renaissance: the poetics and politics of culture', in H. A. Veeser (ed.) *The New Historicism*, New York: Routledge.

—— (1996) *The Purpose of Playing: Shakespeare and the Cultural Politics of the Elizabethan Theatre*, Chicago: University of Chicago Press.

Moody, A. D. (1991) 'The letter of the law', in T. Wheeler (ed.) *The Merchant of Venice: Critical Essays*, New York: Garland.

Mullaney, S. (1988) *The Place of the Stage: License, Play, and Power in Renaissance England*, Chicago: University of Chicago Press.

Munro, J. (ed.) (1932) *The Shakspere Allusion-Book: A Collection of Allusions to Shakspere from 1591 to 1700*, 2nd edn, 2 vols, London: Oxford University Press.

Nashe, T. (1966) *The Works of Thomas Nashe*, ed. R. B. McKerrow, rev. F. P. Wilson, 5 vols, New York: Barnes and Noble.

Norris, C. (1985) 'Post-structuralist Shakespeare: text and ideology', in J. Drakakis (ed.) *Alternative Shakespeares*, London: Methuen.

Norwood, R. (1945) *The Journal of Richard Norwood: Surveyor of Bermuda*, ed. W. F. Craven and W. B. Hayward, New York: Scholars' Facsimiles and Reprints.

Oberman, H. A. (1982) *Luther: Man between God and the Devil*, trans. Eilenn Walliser-Scwarzbart, New York: Doubleday.

—— (1984) *The Roots of Anti-Semitism in the Age of Renaissance and Reformation*, trans. J. I. Porter, Philadelphia, PA: Fortress Press.

Orgel, S. (1996) *Impersonations*, Cambridge: Cambridge University Press.

Osborne, P. (1995) *The Politics of Time: Modernity and Avant-Garde*, London: Verso.

Park, C. C. (1980) 'As we like it: how a girl can be smart and still popular', in C. R. S. Lenz, G. Greene and C. T. Neely (eds) *The Woman's Part*, Urbana, IL: University of Illinois Press.

Patterson, A. (1984) *Censorship and Interpretation: The Conditions of Writing and Reading in Early Modern England*, Madison, WI: University of Wisconsin Press.

Peterson, D. (1988) 'Lyly, Greene, Shakespeare, and the recreation of princes', *Shakespeare Studies* 20: 67–88.

Popkin, R. (1988) 'Theories of knowledge', in C. Schmitt and Q. Skinner (eds) *The Cambridge History of Renaissance Philosophy*, Cambridge: Cambridge University Press.

Pritchard, A. (1994) 'Puritans and the Blackfriars Theater: the cases of Mistresses Duck and Drake', *Shakespeare Quarterly* 45, 1: 93–5.

Prosser, S. (1992) '"Queen o'er myself:" a study of Portia as Queen Elizabeth', unpublished MA thesis, University of Texas at Austin.

Prynne, W. (1633) *Histrio-Mastix*, London.

Rabkin, N. (1967) *Shakespeare and the Common Understanding*, New York: Free Press.

Rackin, P. (1987) 'Androgyny, mimesis, and the marriage of the boy heroine on the English Renaissance stage', *PMLA* 102: 29–41.

Redwine, J. Jr (ed.) (1970) *Ben Jonson's Literary Criticism*, Lincoln, NB: University of Nebraska Press.

Rice, G. P. Jr (ed.) (1966) *The Public Speaking of Queen Elizabeth*, New York: AMS Press.

Roach, J. (1996) *Cities of the Dead: Circum-Atlantic Performance*, New York: Columbia University Press.

Rogin, M. (1987) *Ronald Reagan: The Movie and Other Episodes in Political Demonology*, Berkeley, CA: University of California Press.

—— (1998) *Independence Day, Or How I Learned to Stop Worrying and Love the Enola Gay*, London: British Film Institute.

Rollins, H. E. (ed.) (1920) *Old English Ballads, 1553–1625, Chiefly from Manuscripts*, Cambridge: Cambridge University Press.

Rorty, R. (1989) *Contingency, Irony and Solidarity*, Cambridge: Cambridge University Press.

Rose, G. (1992) *The Broken Middle: Out of our Ancient Society*, Oxford: Blackwell.

Rubin, J. S. (1992) *The Making of Middlebrow Culture*, Chapel Hill, NC: North Carolina University Press.

Salingar, L. (1991) 'Jacobean playwrights and "judicious" spectators', *Renaissance Drama* ns, 22: 209–34.

Scragg, L. (1973) 'Macbeth on horseback', *Shakespeare Survey* 26: 81–8.

Shackford, M. H. (1929) *Plutarch in Renaissance England*, np, Wellesley, MA.

Shakespeare, W. (1935) *Julius Caesar*, with Maxwell Anderson's *Elizabeth the Queen*, New York: Noble and Noble.

Shapiro, J. (1996) *Shakespeare and the Jews*, New York: Columbia University Press.

Sharpe, J. A. (1980) *Defamation and Sexual Slander in Early Modern England: The Church Courts at York*, York: Borthwick Institute of Historical Research, University of York.

Shell, M. (1982) *Money, Language and Thought*, Baltimore, MD: Johns Hopkins University Press.

Sheppard, Gerald T. (ed.) (1989) *The Geneva Bible: The Annotated New Testament, 1602 Edition*, New York: Pilgrim Press.

Sohmer, S. (1996) 'Certain speculations on Hamlet, the calendar, and Martin Luther', *Early Modern Literary Studies* 2, 1: 5.1–51.

Spevack, M. (1973) *The Harvard Concordance to Shakespeare*, Cambridge, MA: Harvard University Press.

Stallybrass, P. (1992) 'Transvestism and the "body beneath": speculating on the boy actor', in S. Zimmerman (ed.) *Erotic Politics*, New York: Routledge.

Stone, L. (1964) 'The educational revolution in England, 1560–1640', *Past and Present* 28: 41–80.

—— (1966) 'Social mobility in England, 1500–1700', *Past and Present* 33: 16–55.

Strong, R. (1977) *The Cult of Elizabeth*, Berkeley, CA: University of California Press.

Taine, H. (1863–4) *Histoire de la littérature anglaise*, 5 vols, Paris.

Taussig, M. (1993) *Mimesis and Alterity: A Particular History of the Senses*, London: Routledge.

Taylor, C. (1989) *Sources of the Self: The Making of the Modern Identity*, Cambridge, MA: Harvard University Press.

Taylor, G. (1991) *Reinventing Shakespeare: A Cultural History from the Restoration to the Present*, Oxford: Oxford University Press.

Teague, F. (1992) 'Queen Elizabeth in her speeches', S. P. Cerasano and M. Wynne-Davies (eds) *Gloriana's Face*, Detroit, MI: Wayne State University Press.

Thirsk, J. (1978) *Economic Policy and Projects: The Development of a Consumer Society in Early Modern England*, Oxford: Clarendon.

Thomas, K. (1976) *Rule and Misrule in the Schools of Early Modern England*, Reading: University of Reading Press.

Thorp, W. (1928) *The Triumph of Realism in Elizabethan Drama, 1558–1612*, Princeton, NJ: Princeton University Press.

—— (ed.) (1938) *Herman Melville: Representative Selections*, New York: American Book Co.

—— (ed.) (1947) *Moby-Dick; or, The Whale, by Herman Melville*, New York: Oxford University Press.

Tillyard, E. M. W. (1943) *The Elizabethan World Picture*, London: Macmillan.

Tofte, R. (1994) *The Poetry of Robert Tofte*, ed. J. N. Nelson, New York: Garland.

Tompkins, J. P. (1980) 'The reader in history', in J. P. Tompkins (ed.) *Reader-Response Criticism: From Formalism to Post-Structuralism*, Baltimore, MD: Johns Hopkins University Press.

Toulmin, S. (1990) *Cosmopolis: The Hidden Agenda of Modernity*, New York: Free Press.

Trousdale, M. (1982) *Shakespeare and the Rhetoricians*, Chapel Hill, NC: University of North Carolina Press.

Vattimo, G. (1988) *The End of Modernity*, Cambridge: Polity Press.

Vickers, B. (1995) *The Critical Heritage 1623–1801*, 6 vols, London: Routledge.

Weimann, R. (1989) 'Bifold authority in Shakespeare's theater', *Shakespeare Quarterly* 39: 403–17.

—— (1997) 'A divided heritage: conflicting appropriations of Shakespeare in (East) Germany', in J. J. Joughin (ed.) *Shakespeare and National Culture*, Manchester: Manchester University Press.

Wells, S. and Taylor, G. with J. Jowett and W. Montgomery (1987) *William Shakespeare: A Textual Companion*, Oxford: Clarendon.

Wheeler, R. (1981) *Shakespeare's Development and the Problem Comedies*, Berkeley, CA: University of California Press.

Whigham, F. (1979) 'Ideology and class consciousness in *The Merchant of Venice*', *Renaissance Drama* n.s. 10: 93–115.

White, H. O. (1935) *Plagiarism and Imitation during the English Renaissance*, Cambridge, MA. Reprinted (1965) New York: Octagon.

Williams, L. (1989) *Hard Core: Power, Pleasure and the 'Frenzy of the Visible'*, Berkeley, CA: University of California Press.

Williamson, J. (1986) 'Woman is an island: femininity and colonization', in T. Modleski (ed.) *Studies in Entertainment: Critical Approaches to Mass Culture*, Bloomington, IN: Indiana University Press.

Williamson, K. (1997) 'War path', *Box Office*, 133, 10: 18–20.

Wilson, R. (1993) *Will Power*, Detroit, MI: Wayne State Press.

Wilson, S. (1995) *Cultural Materialism: Theory and Practice*, Cambridge, MA: Blackwell.

Wood, D. (ed.) (1990) *Philosophers' Poets*, London and New York: Routledge.

Woodmansee, M. (1994) *The Author, Art, and the Market: Rereading the History of Aesthetics*, New York: Columbia University Press.

Wright, L. (1928) 'Variety-show clownery on the pre-restoration stage', *Anglia* 52: 51–68.

—— (1931a) 'Handbook learning of the Renaissance middle class', *Studies in Philology* 28: 58–86.

—— (1931b) 'The reading of Renaissance English women', *Studies in Philology* 28: 671–88.

—— (1935) *Middle-Class Culture in Elizabethan England*, Chapel Hill: University of North Carolina Press.

Yates, F. (1975) *Astraea*, London: Routledge and Kegan Paul.

Žižek, Slavoj (1989) *The Sublime Object of Ideology*, London and New York: Verso.

—— (1994) 'How did Marx invent the symptom?', in S. Žižek (ed.) *Mapping Ideology*, New York: Verso.

Zuidervaart, L. (1991) *Adorno's Aesthetic Theory: The Redemption of Illusion*, Cambridge, MA: MIT Press.

# Index